Interpretation for our time

THINK OF JUST ABOUT EVERYTHING IN TERMS OF COMMUNICATION.

S. I. Hayakawa

This book is about INTERPRETATION as it relates to COMMUNICATION.

Therefore—

Its language is clear,

Its arrangement is simple,

Its illustrations are carefully chosen.

Its purpose is to COMMUNICATE with as little confusion and misunderstanding as possible.

But—

You must do your part by approaching its contents with an open mind and sincere attention.

ALL COMMUNICATION IS TWO-WAY.

Are you criticizing the young professor in the picture for having his foot on the desk?

Or, are you trying to hear what he is saying?

IS HE COMMUNICATING?

We believe he at least has a *foothold* on the art of INTERPRETATION FOR OUR TIME.

Have you?

Interpretation for our time

BAXTER M. GEETING
Professor of Speech
Sacramento State College

Who goes forth
But pauses
To reflect on that
Just passed . . .

Think now of
The time of preparation,
And of
The time of action.

To fear Tomorrow
Is to fear oneself . . .
We are Tomorrow and
Tomorrow is now.

George Calder

Wm. C. Brown Company Publishers
Dubuque, Iowa

BROWN

SPEECH SERIES

Edited by

BAXTER M. GEETING, PH.D.
Sacramento State College
Sacramento, California

Manufactured by
WM. C. BROWN CO. INC., Dubuque, Iowa
Printed in U. S. A.

foreword

Having been closely identified with general semantics for many years, I am delighted to see how contemporary scholars and teachers are adapting its ideas to learning in the classroom. In this book, the author has created a close relationship between the student and the field of oral interpretation, emphasizing the importance of self-scrutiny and self-evaluation as steps toward improved communication.

In our time when many people are urging us to read faster (and I agree that rapid silent readers are generally better readers, quicker to grasp and retain what they read), there is a kind of thoughtful reading that tends to be neglected — and that is the art of reading aloud, reading for communication with others, reading for meaning in its fullest sense.

I say meaning in its fullest sense, because printed words stand for spoken words, which *are* the living language. Ultimately, what the writer hears in his mind's ear must be brought to life in sound. Not all writing needs such treatment, of course. Some writings, when read aloud, merely put people to sleep. But poetry, drama, stories, skillful exposition and argument, if successful, all carry over and above the message the evaluation that the writer places on that message. That evaluation is communicated not only by the connotative power of the words he uses, but also by their sound — the crispness or sonority or the folksiness or formality of his sentences, the music and the flow and the excitement or tranquillity of his words and rhythms.

Oral interpretation, then is a kind of role-playing, in which the reader enacts, with voice and face and hands and feet and body motion, the passage he is reading. As Professor Geeting emphasizes, all the reader's interpretative powers are called into play — his basic understanding, in the lexical sense, of the language; the flexibility and range of his voice; the expressiveness of his body movements; and, most important of all, the imagination and empathy by means of which he may utter, as if they were his own, the words of others.

If we are striving for empathy, we must obviously learn to become good listeners. In this book the art of listening is emphasized, and rightly so, since listening is essential to understanding both one's self and others.

v

In practicing oral interpretation the student needs an anthology of readings that provides both variety and vitality. This book provides such a selection, carefully arranged so as to give the student an orderly progression of materials with which the lessons of the text can be illustrated and realized in the student's own practice.

Oral interpretation as public performance, whether individually or in a group, whether on the platform or before a television camera, is an important art form, deserving of sound preparation. But, as the author also reminds us, oral interpretation is equally important in everyday life. "In almost every area of speech, from chanting nursery rhymes as you rock a baby to presenting a case before the Supreme Court, there are uses for the interpretative art," Dr. Geeting writes.

Students doing homework together understand their lessons better when they read passages to each other and discuss them. Husbands and wives are brought closer together in thought and feeling if they make it a practice for one to read while the other listens and does chores. Business contracts and political programs often become clear only after being read aloud and mulled over. And a baby's chance of growing up into a thoughtful and intelligent adult is enormously enhanced if he has been read to throughout his childhood.

I hope, therefore, that students using this book will not regard oral interpretation as merely something you take in school. Unless you spend your days in solitary confinement, you are going to need it all your life.

S. I. HAYAKAWA

Professor of English
San Francisco State College

Dear friend,

This class and this textbook are placed at your disposal for the purpose of giving you new understandings about, and involving you in, the art of oral interpretation. How unusual it would be if we could start together by eliminating preconceived notions of the subject and of ourselves—beginning, as it were, with a freshly cleaned blackboard ready to receive new ideas and new impressions!

But we can't.

We come to this class, being what we are. We bring to this study built-in appreciations, perceptions, and prejudices that place each one of us on a little different platform from which to start the journey of exploration.

This book is planned, however, to give each one as fair a start as possible. Its organization is built on what students of human behavior have found to be a productive approach to the learning process.

Thus, Part I concentrates on an examination and reshaping, if needed, of ATTITUDES toward the field of interpretation, toward ourselves, and toward listening. All learning is founded on receptive attitudes.

Part II surveys MATERIALS at our disposal for oral interpretation, discussing how we can judge and evaluate, prepare and creatively program, literary materials for use in various formal and informal audience situations.

Part III brings us to a study of specific SKILLS, particularly those relating to the use of the voice and body. At this point, more intensive practice in such skills becomes desirable, for now we have a foundation of attitudes and a knowledge of materials which give us a basis for seeing the need of better voice, meaningful movement, and communicative gestures.

Part IV, APPLICATIONS, discusses various situations in which oral interpretation is used by the individual and the group. Particular attention is given to specific applications in the mass media, radio and television.

While it is hoped this book is soundly planned, having four well-constructed sides—ATTITUDES, MATERIALS, SKILLS, and APPLICATIONS—we do hope, also, that it will not be accepted as a rigid framework for learning. The sides are interlocking. The wise teacher and student will use the book sensibly. Reference to various chapters should be made as needed.

Well organized authors usually preface their textbooks with statements of one, two, or three worthy-sounding purposes. This text is multipurposed. Among its several aims, however, are these: improved self-concepts and speech personality; improved listening ability; greater understanding and appreciation of literature; facility in the art of interpreting orally from the printed page, and humility for "the very considerable number of things" each of us, as student or teacher, still does not know.

Welcome to the study of oral interpretation for our time! Above all else, we hope it helps YOU become better acquainted with YOURSELF and better able to COMMUNICATE WITH OTHERS.

Most sincerely,

Baxter M. Geeting, Ph.D.

contents

attitudes

changing attitudes
toward interpretation

Ne'er look for birds of this year in the nests of the last.
Cervantes, *Don Quixote*

Much print and a lot of breath have been wasted on efforts to define oral interpretation. Some definitions run on to fifty words without a period! Most textbooks devote a chapter or two to "the meaning of interpretation." But we offer no definition.

In a way, this whole book is a definition. We hope, with its help in this class, you will arrive at an understanding of oral interpretation which has real meaning for you. Interpretation is like New Orlean jazz. When Louis Armstrong was asked to define it he said, "Man, when you got to ask what it is, you'll never get to know."

It is hard to define something like interpretation, which has changed greatly over the years and which even now means different things to different people. Even interpretation teachers don't agree. Some still call it "reading aloud." Others see it as the re-creation of an author's precise feelings and emotions. Some see it as a literary act. Others see it as a speech act. Why can't it be either . . . both . . . or perhaps something else of a more comprehensive nature? Do we all have to agree on a definition?

We are AFFECTED by what we read. We INTERPRET a selection to ourselves. When we read it to others, we try to tell them how it affected us. In other words, the material is undergoing a double interpretation — our interpretation of our interpretation. This is the process, not a definition. And that is about all we can say at the moment on which we may agree.

But let us not depreciate the study of interpretation because we can not define it precisely. It is a study with much meaning to each individual, whatever his background, interests, and ambitions. A proper definition for you will differ from that of your neighbor. Your definition will be influenced by the uses to which you put your new knowledges, attitudes, and skills developed in this class.

You may find interpretation helps you in becoming a skillful conversationalist or a professional platform reader. Between the two is a world of difference, of course, but one cannot say that ONE is more significant than the OTHER. Somewhere between the two will be your particular identification with the field of interpretation.

common understandings about interpretation

Although we will avoid defining oral interpretation, it is profitable to discuss some common understandings about it. When we say it is a widening art, we mean it is no longer the sole province of the professional reader as it once was, and it may not involve public performance at all. It no longer necessarily means entertaining others, as it once did, because its purpose may be to SELL, EDUCATE, PERSUADE, ENLIGHTEN, INSPIRE, OR INDOCTRINATE.

Interpretation today may be more aptly described by what it is NOT. It isn't acting in a play, although it may be reading from a play or participating in the reading of a play. It isn't making a formal speech, although within the formal speech one may use his knowledge of interpretation in quoting literary passages. It isn't debating, although here again one may interpret an author's opinion to prove a point. In almost every area of speech, from chanting nursery rhymes as you rock a baby to presenting a case before the Supreme Court, there are uses for the interpretative art.

communication and interpretation

Communication is the heart of interpretation. We can safely agree that its chief function is to get the ideas of one person across to another person (or groups of people). Such ideas may be, and most often are, quoted from a printed page. They may be, and most often are, the ideas of someone other than the interpreter, but they may be his alone. In any case, YOU, as interpreter, are responsible for getting them into the MINDS of others by a process we call communication.

Communication involves a great deal more than oral skill. There are several levels of communication, and your ability as an interpreter depends upon your understanding of these levels.

It is relatively easy to communicate the message of "FIRE!" if you have a loud voice and the smell of smoke is already descending on a crowded hall.

It is relatively difficult to communicate the message of Thomas Wolfe as he wrote:

Something has spoken to me in the night,
Burning the tapers of the waning year;
Something has spoken to me in the night.
And told me I shall die, I know not where.

In the case of the quotation from Thomas Wolfe, a significant part of successful communication depends upon the transferral of the feelings of the author to the listener. Don Geiger has explained this type of interpretation quite clearly by saying, ". . . the job of the oral interpreter is to communicate ATTITUDES . . . MOODS or SENTIMENTS . . . or in the language of psychology, SETS or DISPOSITIONS TO RESPOND."[1] He goes on to explain what every effective interpreter must learn — that to know the meaning of a word or phrase is important, but not enough to convey understanding.

"The oral reader is engaged in the great task of NAMING the world . . . not as science names the world [but] in terms of human interest. . . . He has learned the names of items . . . with the ultimate aim of taking ATTITUDES toward those items."[2]

The technical aspects of interpretation are related to the mechanical and physical controls and to voice, diction, bodily movement, and speaking patterns. The psychological and emotional aspects of communication involve higher and more sophisticated levels of understanding. Meaning and mood of much literary material cannot be interpreted without a full knowledge of those higher levels.

current uses of interpretation

Instead of being relegated to the useless and frivolous, as it has been in certain historical periods, oral interpretation is one of the most utilitarian of skills in our time. Few persons can function successfully without

---

[1]Don Geiger, "Oral Interpretation and the New Criticism," *Quarterly Journal of Speech,* Dec. 1950, Vol. 36, pages 508-513.
[2]*Ibid.*

the ability on occasion to interpret what they read to others in such a way as to communicate with them.

Executives who stumble over the printed page are suspected of being poorly educated or inefficient. Ministers who read from the Bible as if it were a dust-dry tome are, in the minds of some of their auditors, committing a sacrilege. English teachers who read from great literary works in such a way as to put their students to sleep or kill in them the appreciation of the literature being studied are criminally negligent of their greatest obligation in teaching: to inspire and awaken and motivate learning.

Opportunities for using interpretative skills are endless. In addition to the traditional areas of entertainment, such skills may be applied to social reform, homemaking, business, politics, education, and religion. Undoubtedly, you could extend this list with very little stretching of the imagination.

a backward glance at interpretation

Now that we have discussed the broadening aspects of the field of interpretation, it is interesting to review ever so briefly what has happened in the past in the name of "reading" or "interpretation" or "elocution." Much poor performance and emphasis on the artificial in teaching have plagued the development of the field, but it did survive largely through the efforts of sensible and courageous individuals who kept it in the mainstream of valuable learning.

Poetic competitions and reading aloud can be traced back to the days of Homer, who more than 3,000 years ago entertained the urbane Greeks with his elegant words given to the accompaniment of his four-stringed cithara. But it was not until the beginning of the nineteenth century that reading aloud found a place in the collegiate curriculum. Harvard put in a few courses in 1806 and other colleges followed with courses called "declamation" and "elocution."

A number of biased and narrow approaches to the field of interpretation characterized its development in the 1800's. One group championed the mechanical aspect, a second hailed the natural approach, and a third held more sanely to the middle road. But the field of interpretation gained very little academic respect until the twentieth century. It flourished in the private institution and under private teachers, some representing the worst in superficiality, some maintaining high standards throughout a difficult period and preserving interpretation as an ART.

One of the greatest flowerings of interpretation on the American platform occurred between 1840 and 1900. During this period Charles Dickens toured the country reading from his own works, and a number of fine actors and actresses gave programs of readings as they sat on the stage and interpreted from manuscript.

From 1900 to 1925 was another significant period in the development of American interpretative art. Such artists as Elias Day, Jessie Rae Taylor, Benjamin Chapin, William Battis, and Sidney Landon will be remembered by a good many living today. Their performances undoubtedly influenced our country to give genuine respect to the art of interpretation and encouraged colleges to start offering courses in their curriculums in this field from about 1925 on.

Just a few of the early teachers who influenced the curriculum in interpretation are Samuel S. Curry, Phidelah Rice, and Maxfield Parrish (the artist, too). Teachers of this calibre brought the art of interpretation to American campuses in academically sound courses representing a blending of the best which had come out of the past. As a result, through balancing technique and method with thought and expression, we now have what is called by most teachers today the "eclectic" approach — the best of many approaches brought together into one.

a forward look at interpretation

There is reason to believe, as we look toward the future of this field, that it is moving in the direction of skillful naturalism. What do we mean by that?

The current emphasis is on simplicity. Close-ups on television have influenced us to accept with greater appreciation than ever before the person who reads effortlessly, without noticeable gesture, and with complete understanding. Such performers as Eric Sevareid, with simple dignity, and Danny Kaye, with exuberant informality, have shown us the varying ways in which different personalities can COMMUNICATE naturally and effortlessly.

The general cultural level of this country may have been damaged by television programming (a most controversial point), but the fact remains that it has brought a vigorous demand for skill in oral interpretation. The American public has little patience with the pompous, insincere, affected, and hesitant person. It has no time for the person who can not communicate the thoughts of others (and his thoughts too) with both ease and style. We like a quiet, well modulated voice and easily understood diction (and if it be STANDARD diction, please not TOO "STANDAHD"! We like the person who develops his own particular brand of uniqueness. We are bored by cliché people.

We are not drifting away from the ART of interpretation. The present trend is toward that type of art which doesn't call attention to itself. It is an effortless-appearing art. It is an unobtrusive style by means of which the listener is brought into such intimacy with the material being presented that he may not even notice (pray that he won't) the gesture, voice, or manner of the interpreter.

This trend toward an effortless-appearing art is both encouraging and discouraging to the student newly come to the field of oral interpretation. If he looks upon it as assurance that he won't have to develop a dramatic style suitable to the interpretation of Shakespeare's great moments, it may seem encouraging. If he looks upon it as a demand for the development of such consummate skill (primarily as a demand for his growth as a person) that none of his artistry is showing, it may prove discouraging at first.

At this point, all earnest students should rest assured that attention to the known ingredients which go into the capable communication of ideas WILL result in vast improvement of interpretative power. There is now at our disposal a well organized and respectable body of learning relative to the art of interpretation which serves well in the improvement of native talent, whatever it may be.

summary

A definition of interpretation is a somewhat individual thing, influenced by your relation to the field and the use to which you hope to put your skill. Lacking a positive definition, however, we may agree that interpretation is a widening art, the uses of which reach out into most fields of endeavor, from homemaking to politics.

At the basis of all interpretation is communication, involving attitudes toward words which will convey meaning and mood. Communication also implies the transferral of intended attitudes from author to listener.

Although interpretation can be traced to the time of Homer, it has been a part of the college curriculum a relatively short time. Great actors, performers, and teachers brought the art to its present respected place, academically and professionally. The future indicates increasing emphasis on skillful naturalism because of the influence of mass media such as television.

applications: ───────────────────────────

1. Your first reading establishes you as A PERSON with certain interests, abilities, and attitudes. Select a short piece of prose or a poem which will represent YOU. Practice it carefully. Be prepared to read it with a familiarity that is almost akin to memorization (but use your manuscript). Introduce the selection in a memorable way —in a way which will establish YOU as someone the class wants to know better. You might use humor. It is effective in getting attention. Keep the selection short; cut it, if necessary, so that it is around three minutes in length. Try for a one-minute introduction.
2. Listen to some speaking records, noting the way professionals enunciate, inflect, pause, and vary volume to communicate. Don't mimic them, but experiment in your own way with similar techniques in reading your chosen selection.
3. If possible, when you think you are prepared, tape your reading and play it back. Are you satisfied with yourself? If not, try again. But don't be discouraged if you're still not happy with the sound. Dissatisfaction (not discouragement) is a healthy basis for improvement.
4. Throughout your total preparation keep in mind that successful interpretation IS communication. It IS NOT a display of oral skill.

preview of chapter 2:

CHANGING ATTITUDES TOWARD YOURSELF

Basic to the study of interpretation is the discovery of what we may possess in the way of potential talent. Even more important is a thoughtful consideration of those personal attitudes which will influence progress in the interpretative arts.

A wise teacher of interpretation, J. B. Kerfoot, once said, "We are populous with unrealized selves; with might-have-beens; with partially weres; with sometimes ares; with may-yet-bes. The terms of one's own equipment are the only terms in which anything can reach us."

Let us now turn to an analysis of our own equipment for this class, and to a consideration of that most fascinating of all subjects — OURSELVES!

changing attitudes
toward yourself

Know thyself.
Socrates

. . . our knowledge of . . . ourselves involves unavoidable factors of deception and self-deception.
Korzybski

The emotionally maladjusted person . . . is in difficulty first because communication within himself has broken down, and second because as a result of this his communication with others has been damaged.
Carl R. Rogers

In interpretation you have a unique instrument with which to perform — YOURSELF. Your performance will depend on an accurate appraisal of your personal equipment and on what you are able to do with it.

It is encouraging to realize now that there is almost always room for vast improvement in one's native endowment physically, mentally, spiritually, and esthetically. Your immediate task is to establish a reliable communication system within yourself, because if you can't talk to yourself on honest terms you will certainly not be able to communicate with others.

Fortunately, most of us find when we get to know ourselves that we are BETTER than we thought we were. The world has long taught us to regard ourselves as objects born in sin, condemned to begin with. Modern psychology has gone far in assuring us that we must accept ourselves for what we are before we can establish any warm relationships with others. Self-acceptance is the first law of this class. No one is going to condemn you for having a voice, appearance, or understanding of poetry that can stand improvement. If you were already perfect, you would probably be on coast-to-coast television today or, more likely, in an asylum for the insane.

Let us examine ourselves, then, keeping in mind that to know and accept ourselves is the most important step we can take toward maturity as individuals and success as oral interpreters.

the value of learning to interpret yourself

This is an age with great emphasis on personality. In terms of sheer physical numbers, we live in a frightening time, and the population explosion gives promise that things are going to get worse. It is imperative that we develop personality (or individuality) if we are going to be effective in our society. It is this struggle for personality that often is our undoing, and we take up odd styles, grow beards, and proclaim weird philosophies in order to establish ourselves as Somebody.

Probably the most important thing we should do now is stop and take a look at ourselves to see if we are relying on some affectation as a means of establishing a felt personality.

There are a certain number of highly privileged individuals who can afford to be without speech personality. A handful of writers, laboratory technicians and scientists, and creative artists who work behind closed doors in seclusion from the world can get along very well without knowing how to communicate orally. But the rest of us depend greatly on the force of the speech personality to make an impression on others and to bring us the desired response from them.

Few of us have been really encouraged to develop good speech personalities. Parents usually are against them. Teachers are too. Children who might be natural-born leaders often are discouraged by the vigorous denial of their compulsions to be heard.

We are taught from early grades to read silently. Early reading aloud is but a step in the process of eventual silent reading, and no thought is given to interpretation. We are taught to concentrate QUIETLY on the printed page, and oral enthusiasm in the grades is more apt to be punished than applauded.

But the fact is that speech personality will not only give us an effective means of communicating with others, but will provide us with altogether admirable qualities for distinguishing ourselves in a society composed of great masses of people. Interpreting ourselves to others by means of a good speech personality is also a most effective way of maintaining personal maturity and sanity in a complicated and confusing world.

examining your present cocoon[1]

You come to this class encased in a cocoon of belief about yourself. It may approximate the actual self, but rare indeed is the person whose convictions about himself match what the world knows him to be. (The world may have a false picture.)

Some individuals adopt extreme cocoons. One person may believe himself to be very handsome, intelligent, and talented when he is only egotistical. Another may see himself as unattractive, stupid, and without talent when he is only introverted. But each of these individuals is undoubtedly out of touch *with reality* and out of focus with life. They are in trouble and must take steps to pick away at their cocoons to find out who they really are. Most of us suffer *in some degree* from beliefs about ourselves which limit and warp personal progress.

It is not too difficult to determine a sizable body of facts about ourselves. Unless one really is psychologically unsound, he may start unraveling his own cocoon by adopting a determination to be objective in self-evaluation. He may look in the mirror objectively, listen to a recording of his voice dispassionately, and start in earnest to think about the IMAGE he is creating in the minds of those around him. Most people suffer from too little respect for themselves rather than from an overdose of confidence. Wendell Johnson points out that "various investigations made by psychologists have served to demonstrate beyond reasonable dispute that feelings of inferiority are the rule rather than the exception among people generally." He goes on to recall that Dr. Alfred Adler, the eminent Viennese psychologist, in building an elaborate theory of human behavior, endeavored to explain a widespread maladjustment by "negative self-evaluation" which he labeled the "inferiority complex," a term well known to us today.

There are those who admire the aloof person and look upon qualities of communication with suspicion. Emily Dickinson, speaking in her cool poetic voice, amusingly commented:

---

[1]Ideas in this section are suggested by a chapter on "Verbal Cocoons" in Wendell Johnson, *People in Quandaries,* New York: Harper and Brothers Publishers, 1946, Chapter 1.

I'm nobody! Who are you?
Are you nobody, too?
Then there's a pair of us — don't tell!
They'd banish us, you know.

How dreary to be somebody!
How public, like a frog
To tell your name the livelong day
To an admiring bog!

Not many of us, however, find comfort in being nobody. It is easy to subside into a drab and inexpressive personality, easier than it is to exert the effort to realize the potential of the verbal self. So much superficial nonsense has been written about "personality development" that it has brought a bad reputation to the whole field of speech improvement. For these and a number of other reasons, people fail to make of their verbal selves anything better than the thing they have fallen into the habit of being. Our society is marked by the number of individuals who appear to have "just given up."

The goal of becoming an interesting, adjusted, mature, and communicative person is an entirely realistic goal. It is basic to being a good interpreter of literary material, of course. It is well within the realm of possibility for those who will make the effort.

Let us examine immediate steps which may be taken.

viewing your image

In this class, the first thing you may do is to determine what type of an instrument you have at your command. You need to analyze physical characteristics and appearance and do what you can to improve them at once (if they need improving). The first thing you present in interpretation is your physical self, and before you open your mouth to speak, you have established some sort of image. Is it that of an attractive, poised, interesting individual? If so, good! If not, why not?

One of the most attractive persons I have ever had in class, and one of the finest interpreters, was a badly crippled girl. She was unable to stand alone, unable to walk to the front of the classroom unaided. She had, however, come to terms with herself. She had realized that she had a face and a voice to work with — and very little more. She hadn't even a beautiful face, but she had practiced the creation of an illusion of beauty through skillful make-up and faultless grooming. She looked into the faces of others with searching interest. Within moments after her appearance in front of the class, those in the room saw a poised, attractive person. Her rich and vibrant voice reinforced confidence in her resources. Given so little in comparison with those about her, she had fully developed the personal attributes she had in her favor and had made of herself an attractive image.

In this day of urgency in advertising, it is difficult to determine style as opposed to fashion, good taste as opposed to indoctrinated appeal. We may be persuaded that something is attractive when it is an esthetic monstrosity. It is not easy to select appropriate clothes and arrive at attractive hair styles, but it is essential to keep in mind basic principles of good taste and style if the ultimate image is to be one which will appeal to the majority.

As you start with the immediate problem of making yourself a person you respect and one whom others will want to listen to, keep the image foremost in your mind. Don't allow exaggerations in hair, make-up, clothes, or posture to interfere with the best-looking person you can be.

An attractive image, however, is one which may be remembered. For this you need a note of originality. Here is where artistry enters the picture, and here is where so many people go wrong. Originality in appearance is desirable, but it should not take over. It should represent the accent, not the total picture. Without it, you run the risk of falling into the stereotype of "the well-scrubbed American girl" or the "Ivy-league boy" or any one of a number of other neat, pleasing, but monotonous categories.

WHAT CAN YOU DO TO MAKE YOURSELF ATTRACTIVE, PLEASING, AND DIFFERENT?

listening to your voice

While we do not, at this point, wish to undertake a detailed examination of the voice, which will be dealt with later in Chapter 10, we must take it into immediate consideration because there are ways we can start improvement now.

It may be you have not listened to yourself as others hear you. If so, tape or record your natural speaking voice and your stage voice (if you have a stage voice and if it is different).

DOES YOUR VOICE PROPERLY DESCRIBE THE IMAGE YOU HAVE IN MIND AND WHICH YOU WANT TO PROJECT?

Without technical information about the voice, and without a scientific analysis of your personal problems, can you even now detect immediate improvements which could be made by conscious effort? Could you improve your tone quality by lowering it? Could you improve your diction by more careful attention to syllabication? Does your voice sound drab and monotonous, and could you make it more lively by merely thinking about it, getting off "dead center" now and then to relieve a tendency to vocal monotony?

Perhaps a conscious avoidance of an annoying lisp or a hissing "S" will make you immediately sound more pleasing to others. Perhaps a firmer attack, striving to eliminate an apologetic or muffled tone quality will make you sound better right now. Undoubtedly, there ARE improvements which can be made by you through your recognition of vocal shortcomings.

An earnest young man, sincerely interested in becoming a better interpreter of the Bible and desirous of entering the ministry, had been reared in the hills of Kentucky. Although highly intelligent, he came to a class in interpretation with a massive amount of regional accent.

When he started to read: "Oh Lord, ayer Lord, how excellent is thay nayme . . ." members of the class started to snicker, and the magic of the selection was all but lost. It took no more than five minutes of listening on his part to clear up the "ayer" to a richly rounded "our," and conscientious attention to a few of the more flagrant differences between his accent and accepted pronunciations soon sent him on the road to dramatic self-improvement in the ability to communicate the meaning and beauty of Biblical passages.

Another young man, highly skilled as an actor, discovered by listening to his own voice how theatrical and lacking in communicative warmth it had become. At first he found it almost impossible to read simply:

I'm going out to clean the pasture spring;
I'll only stop to rake the leaves away
(And wait to watch the water clear, I may);
I shan't be long. — You come too.

He had not realized the tremendous gap between Robert Frost and Shakespeare until he listened to himself reading Frost with Shakespearean overtones. His sensitive ear quickly detected the problem, and it was with much better understanding that he continued:

I'm going out to fetch the little calf
That's standing by the mother. It's so young,
It totters when she licks it with her tongue.
I shan't be gone long. — You come too.

Sometimes the highly trained voice is damaging to the image we want to create. The student who has spent his life acting on a stage, projecting in a dramatic way, might do well to practice reading such selections as "Little Boy Blue" by Eugene Field or some of Joan Walsh Anglund, striving to get "the human touch," working for personal contact between interpreter and audience. It is not easy to read with a voice long trained for stage work a simple, comfortable, kindly message like those contained in works of Joan Walsh Anglund.

A brook can be a friend in a special way.
It talks to you with splashy gurgles.
It cools your toes and lets you sit
quietly beside it when you don't feel
like speaking.

One thing you will learn in this class: IT TAKES MANY VOICES TO BE AN EFFECTIVE INTERPRETER.

reviewing your background

Of course you are a great deal more than what appears on the surface. Your image and your voice are your immediate connections with your listeners, but it doesn't take long for them to discover YOU as revealed in YOUR BACKGROUND.

Your background is an area where you are somewhat limited by family, home, experience, education, and influence. But even here, you may start improvement from where you are. Accept your background for what it is. Don't waste time condemning it. Just try to measure it realistically and see what steps may be taken to improve your opportunities for learning.

If your background has been such that you have never heard and learned to appreciate great poetry, music, and drama; if you have never traveled more than fifty miles from home; if you have never experienced the friendships of intelligent and creative people, you are limited. But accept this as fact. The best approach to handling this fact is to recognize it as such and stop allowing it to influence your thinking and judgment in areas to which your knowledge does not at present extend. Stop labeling things you do not understand as "bad," "stupid," or "unartistic"; stop laughing at people whose culture you do not understand; stop calling those with superior knowledge "eggheads" and start listening to what they have to give you in the way of personal help.

THE FIRST STEP TOWARD IMPROVING YOUR OWN BACK-GROUND IS TO EXPAND YOUR HORIZONS.

This you can do in a number of ways — through reading, through attending plays and musical events, through visiting museums, through taking advantage of EVERY OPPORTUNITY to learn more about people, places, cultures, and ideas.

YOUR PROGRESS AS AN INTERPRETER WILL IMPROVE IN DIRECT PROPORTION TO YOUR UNDERSTANDINGS ABOUT YOUR-SELF AND EVERYTHING AROUND YOU. Understandings can be built up systematically by a conscientious program of self-education. If you see you are suffering now from a somewhat limited background, start improving the foreground.

When you come to the interpretation of a work of literature, if your background (this is sometimes called a "frame of reference") has not met with the author or the theme of his writing, do not endeavor to interpret his material for the class until you have had time to familiarize yourself with him and his writing. In the beginning of this course, though your contribution be humble, let it be something you honestly understand and appreciate. To "read" something beyond your emotional and intellectual comprehension will serve only to make you feel awkward and appear ridiculous. But each time you read, show that you have matured in all aspects of the art of interpretation, the emotional and intellectual as well as the mechanical or technical.

YOU CAN INTERPRET ONLY WHAT YOU UNDERSTAND. To improve understanding you must enrich your background. To enrich your background, you must constantly study and seek experiences in all areas of living.

realizing your potential

Whether or not we realize it, we are strongly influenced by a pattern of thinking in our society which proclaims the two-sidedness of everything from marriage to politics. We look at *either* this side *or* that of an issue. Commonly, we ignore the great in-between.

This type of thinking stems from the great Greek scholar, Aristotle, who established three basic laws about the behavior of people: First, that "they act . . . talk . . . feel AS IF a thing is what it is . . . man is man, truth is truth, etc. This we may call . . . the law of identity."

Second, "they speak and . . . behave AS IF . . . anything must either be a particular thing or it must not be that particular thing. . . . We may call this the . . . law of the excluded middle."

And third, "they conduct themselves AS IF . . . something cannot both be a particular thing and also not be that particular thing. . . . We may refer to this as the . . . law of non-contradiction."[2]

Although Aristotle was a brilliant observer of mankind and stated three basic observations accurately, subsequent misinterpretation of these laws has led men to adopt attitudes toward behavior which are utterly damaging to life adjustment. From these laws men came to think in a way which has been called "logically." That is, if A is A, then everything must be either A or not A. Logic became what we refer to as "common sense." We hear, for example, "It's just common sense. You're either for a thing or you're against it."

Through no fault of Aristotle's, men have misinterpreted his laws to mean that a person is either a success or a failure, beautiful or ugly, talented or untalented. It follows, in the common-senseness of the so-called Aristotelian tradition, that you come to this class conceiving of yourself as a performer or nonperformer.

Many thoughtful scholars have detected the fallacy in such thinking. But it is hard to uproot a pattern of thought which has fastened itself on men over a period of 2,300 years. However, it is a fact that in nature there is NO SUCCESS OR FAILURE. Things are seldom "good" or "bad." Few people are born performers, few born nonperformers.

Applying this understanding to yourself, you should not AT THIS TIME endeavor to judge yourself ON PERFORMANCE ABILITY, because your potential for modification and change is great. Few performers come ready-made. Good performers are usually self-made, despite the earnest efforts of textbooks and teachers of interpretation.

Your progress in the art of performance is not limited by basic talent half so much as it is by your concept of yourself (do you know and accept yourself?) and your determination to realize your full potential.

summary

It is possible to free ourselves from the cocoon of built-in perceptions. The willingness to examine objectively the image, the voice, and the background is the first step. The determination to start immediate improvement in each area is the second. Performance potential can be approached through honest self-analysis and the setting up of a program of self-improvement. It is limited only by the degree of determination to make of oneself the finest possible instrument for interpretation.

---

[2]Johnson, *op. cit.*, Chapter 1, Section on "Either-Or."

applications: _____

1. The class may have made certain judgments about you and what they expect of you as a reader. Now is your opportunity to experiment with a change of pace. If your first reading was serious, try humor this time. If your first reading was humorous, be serious, inspirational, or perhaps merely factual. Before your image is set, try different approaches. Perhaps you wish to watch yourself in the mirror as you practice. If this makes you too self-conscious, don't — yet.
2. Pay attention to your appearance. Endeavor to dress appropriately.
3. Listen closely to your voice. Tape or record your selection again, if possible, and listen for possible improvements which can be made, now.
4. If you are fighting a problem of stage fright, try not to let it get you down. The majority of the class is feeling much as you do. With a few more opportunities to read, fear will become secondary to the exhilaration you feel at becoming somewhat skilled.
5. Read the following selections which tend to set one to thinking about himself, perhaps to changing attitudes toward himself. Then, search out other selections from your reading which can be used in this class to expand understandings about yourself.

preview of chapter 3:
CHANGING ATTITUDES TOWARD LISTENING

As most intelligent people know, all communication is a two-way process. Together with the problem of changing some attitudes toward yourself, it is necessary that you re-examine your attitudes toward those who will be listening to you.

What about them? Do they understand you? If they aren't getting your message or reacting as you wish to your interpretation, is it your fault or theirs? Or the fault of both of you? Or some other factor? Or, is there a variety of causes?

Let us turn next to an examination of our attitudes toward the person on the other end of the communication process (an end on which we frequently find ourselves). Let us observe the listener . . . the audience.

What does listening imply?

selections for study and interpretation

In an appealing bit of poetry, Georgia Douglas Johnson, a Negro poet of gentle sensitivity, says, "Your world is as big as you make it." In this little poem, THE POET SPEAKS, she asks each of us some very simple and very important questions.

THE POET SPEAKS

Georgia Douglas Johnson

How much living have you done?
From it the patterns that you weave
Are imaged:
Your own life is your totem pole,
Your yard of cloth,
Your living.

How much loving have you done?
How full and free your giving?
For living is but loving
And loving only giving.

Pulitzer Prize winning poet, Theodore Roethke, probed the mysteries of self, expressing in many of his poems (as he does in OPEN HOUSE) feelings that arose from intense personal experience. See if you can re-create his feelings as you read this poem.

OPEN HOUSE

Theodore Roethke
(1908-1963)

My secrets cry aloud.
I have no need for tongue.
My heart keeps open house,
My doors are widely swung.
An epic of the eyes
My love, with no disguise.

My truths are all foreknown,
This anguish self-revealed.
I'm naked to the bone,
With nakedness my shield.
Myself is what I wear:
I keep the spirit spare.

This anger will endure,
The deed will speak the truth
In language strict and pure.
I stop the lying mouth:
Rage warps my clearest cry
To witless agony.

Housman's poetry often expressed a melancholy sense of
the transient quality of youth. In reading the following
bit of verse, endeavor to capture the rueful spirit in which
it is written.

WHEN I WAS ONE-AND-TWENTY

A. E. Housman
(1859-1936)

When I was one-and-twenty
　I heard a wise man say,
"Give crowns and pounds and guineas
　But not your heart away;
Give pearls away and rubies
　But keep your fancy free."
But I was one-and-twenty,
　No use to talk to me.

When I was one-and-twenty
　I heard him say again,
"The heart out of the bosom
　Was never given in vain;
'Tis paid with sighs a-plenty
　And sold for endless rue."
And I am two-and-twenty,
　And oh, 'tis true, 'tis true.

pockets at night. But she married a neat man. After 10 years of utter misery, however, she divorced him, explaining:

"He was no fun to live with. Year after year I found exactly the same things in his pockets."

Later she married a thoroughly disorderly man whose pockets resembled a department store hit by a hurricane.

"I never knew life could be so exciting," she chortled, and they lived happily ever after.

Perhaps that is why neat men are so jealous of disorderly men. They know women never find them dull.

Some 400 years ago, the witty contemporary of Shakespeare, Ben Jonson, also noted certain alluring qualities about a lack of neatness.

STILL TO BE NEAT

Ben Jonson
(1537?-1637)

Still to be neat, still to be dressed,
As you were going to a feast;
Still to be powdered, still perfumed:
Lady, it is to be presumed,
Though art's hid causes are not found,
All is not sweet, all is not sound.

Give me a look, give me a face.
That makes simplicity a grace;
Robes loosely flowing, hair as free:
Such sweet neglect more taketh me
Than all the adulteries of art;
They strike mine eyes, but not my heart.

William Wordsworth was devoted to reforming poetic diction in his day. In the preface to his LYRICAL BALLADS he proposed "a selection of language really used by men." A humanitarian, he was interested in what common men really thought and felt. Are there not, at times, moments when you, too, feel the world is too much with you, laying waste your powers?

THE WORLD IS TOO MUCH WITH US

William Wadsworth
(1770-1850)

> The world is too much with us; late and soon,
> Getting and spending, we lay waste our powers:
> Little we see in Nature that is ours;
> We have given our hearts away, a sordid boon!
> The sea that bares her bosom to the moon;
> The winds that will be howling at all hours,
> And are up-gathered now like sleeping flowers;
> For this, for everything, we are out of tune;
> It moves us not. — Great God! I'd rather be
> A pagan suckled in a creed outworn.
> So might I, standing on this pleasant lea,
> Have glimpses that would make me less forlorn;
> Have sight of Proteus rising from the sea;
> Or hear old Triton blow his wreathed horn.

". . . WHEN WE TURN THE PAGES OF THE REALIST"
A Fable from THE LANTERN-BEARERS

Robert Louis Stevenson
(1850-1894)

There is one fable that touches very near the quick of life: the fable of the monk who passed into the woods, heard a bird break into song, hearkened for a trill or two, and found himself on his return a stranger at his convent gates; for he had been absent fifty years, and of all his comrades there survived but one to recognize him. It is not only in the woods that this enchanter carols, though perhaps he is native there. . . .

All life that is not merely mechanical is spun out of two strands: seeking for that bird and hearing him. And it is just this that makes life so hard to value, and the delight of each so incommunicable; and just a knowledge of this, and a remembrance of those fortunate hours in which the bird has sung to us, that fills us with such wonder when we turn the pages of the realist. There, to be sure, we find a picture of life in so far as it consists of mud and of old iron, cheap

changing attitudes toward yourself

desires and cheap fears, that which we are ashamed to remember and that which we are careless whether we forget; but of the note of that time-devouring nightingale we hear no news.

Practically all of his life Robert Louis Stevenson was a consumptive. His last voyage took him to the South Sea, where he died, and a tablet marked his grave on a Pacific peak, bearing this epitaph:

REQUIEM

Robert Louis Stevenson

Under the wide and starry sky,
Dig the grave and let me lie.
Glad did I live and gladly die,
    And I laid me down with a will.

This be the verse you grave for me:
Here he lives where he longed to be;
Home is the sailor, home from sea,
    And the hunter home from the hill.

W. E. Henley had one leg amputated at the age of 12 and when he was 24 tuberculosis of the bone threatened the other. The great Dr. Lister saved it from surgery. A close friend of Robert Louis Stevenson, Henley knew the fear and pain of suffering. *Invictus* shows his determination and defiance.

INVICTUS

W. E. Henley
(1849-1903)

Out of the night that covers me,
    Black as the Pit from pole to pole,
I thank whatever gods may be
    For my unconquerable soul.

In the fell clutch of circumstance
  I have not winced nor cried aloud.
Under the bludgeonings of chance
  My head is bloody, but unbowed.

Beyond this place of wrath and tears
  Looms but the horror of the shade,
And yet the menace of the years
  Finds, and shall find me, unafraid.

It matters not how strait the gate,
  How charged with punishments the scroll,
I am the master of my fate:
  I am the captain of my soul.

". . . Emily Brontë created a dream world, and made it more real than reality." Louis Untermeyer

FALL, LEAVES, FALL

Emily Brontë
(1818-1848)

Fall, leaves, fall; die, flowers, away;
Lengthen night and shorten day;
Every leaf speaks bliss to me
Fluttering from the autumn tree.

I shall smile when wreaths of snow
Blossom where the rose should grow;
I shall sing when night's decay
Ushers in a drearier day.

The Spanish-born poet, novelist, critic, and teacher, George Santayana, studied and taught at Harvard in the field of philosophy. He was a true cosmopolite, at home here and abroad, conversant with the ancient and the modern. "All times my present, everywhere my place," he says. Would that we all could live so richly and leave so fine a will!

WILL OF GEORGE SANTAYANA

George Santayana
(1863-1952)

I give back to the earth what the earth gave,
All to the furrow, nothing to the grave,
The candle's out, the spirit's vigil spent;
Sight may not follow where the vision went.

I leave you but the sound of many a word
In mocking echoes haply overheard,
I sang to heaven. My exile made me free.
From world to world, from all worlds carried me.

Spared by the furies, for the Fates were kind,
I paced the pillared cloisters of the mind;
All times my present, everywhere my place,
Nor fear, nor hope, nor envy saw my face.

Blow what winds would, the ancient truth was mine,
And friendship mellowed in the flush of wine,
And heavenly laughter, shaking from its wings
Atoms of light and tears for mortal things.

To trembling harmonies of field and cloud,
Of flesh and spirit was my worship vowed.
Let form, let music, let all-quickening air
Fulfil in beauty my imperfect prayer.

The great Indian poet and philosopher, Rabindranath Tagore, whom Mahatma Gandhi called "The Great Teacher," gave credit for his poetry and ideas to "experiential reality." He sought an understanding of the wonder of the world and mankind through creative experiences of the mind, the senses, through travel, and through constant alertness to all areas of art, science, and religion. He believed in what he called "the processes of self-creation." In 1916-1917, he lectured in the United States on *Personality*, expressing ideas such as the following:

"The world is what we perceive it to be"
THE WORLD OF PERSONALITY

Rabindranath Tagore[3]
(1861-1941)

. . . . It is almost a truism to say that the world is what we perceive it to be. We imagine that our mind is a mirror, that it is more or less accurately reflecting what is happening outside us. On the contrary our mind itself is the principal element of creation. The world, while I am perceiving it, is being incessantly created for myself in time and space. . . . .

If we could fully know what a piece of music was in Beethoven's mind, we could ourselves become so many Beethovens. But because we cannot grasp its mystery, we may altogether distrust the elements of Beethoven's personality in his sonata — though we are fully aware that its true value lies in its power of touching the depth of our own personality. But it is simpler to observe the facts when that sonata is played upon the piano. We can count the black and white keys of the keyboard, measure the relative lengths of the strings, the strength, velocity and order of sequence in the movements of fingers and triumphantly assert that this is Beethoven's sonata. . . we may forget that both in its origin and object dwell the personality of man, and however accurate and orderly may be the facts of the interactions of the fingers and strings they do not comprehend the ultimate reality of the music.

. . . .

Because of the mind instruments which we possess we also have found our place as creators. . . . Our freedom as a creator finds its highest joy in contributing its own voice in the concert of the world music.

PERSONAL SYMBOLS

(From a eulogy to Ed Murrow,
distributed, 1965, by the Hall Syndicate, Inc.)

Eric Sevareid
(1912-   )

We hold to bits and pieces from our lives, all of us. For me it happens to be a canoe paddle with mutilated blade, saved from a wildly improbable adventure that ended at Hudson's Bay. For John F. Kennedy it was that piece of cocoanut shell on which he had carved a message, taken by the island native

---

[3]As presented in A TAGORE READER, edited by Amiya Chakravarty, New York: The Macmillan Company, and Galt, Ontario: Brett-Macmillan Ltd., 1961, pages 264-69.

who helped to save his life in the PT boat adventure of the war. . . . All men have seen a glimpse of Camelot.

What is it in some human spirits that makes men remember them long after they are gone? It is not the sound and stable virtues; it is not their industriousness or their steady goodness. It is the intensity with which they lived. It is the magic in them that makes their presence a moment of magic, their simplest gestures somehow remarkable, their most casual words extraordinary and to be remembered. It is the incandescence within them that illuminates their way and gathers to them, like moths to the light, friends, strangers, the curious, the hangers on, all those who need the light and the magic in their lives. . . . God bless the artists, for without them we do not know where we have been, what we were doing, why we live.

Few poems have caused so many young people to stop and think about the significance of life choices as Robert Frost's THE ROAD NOT TAKEN. It is well to remember, as Frost said, a poem often is "a momentary stay against confusion."

THE ROAD NOT TAKEN

Robert Frost
(1874-1963)

Two roads diverged in a yellow wood,
And sorry I could not travel both
And be one traveler, long I stood
And looked down one as far as I could
To where it bent in the undergrowth;

Then took the other, as just as fair
And having perhaps the better claim,
Because it was grassy and wanted wear;
Though as for that the passing there
Had worn them really about the same,

And both that morning equally lay
In leaves no step had trodden black.
Oh, I kept the first for another day!
Yet knowing how way leads on to way,
I doubted if I should ever come back.

I shall be telling this with a sigh
Somewhere ages and ages hence:
Two roads diverged in a wood, and I —
I took the one less traveled by,
And that has made all the difference.

changing attitudes toward listening

What we attend to and what interests us are synonymous terms.
William James

There are two aspects to communication . . . output . . . and intake . . . how to listen well [is] a relatively neglected subject.
S. I. Hayakawa

Listening is the other half of talking.
Stuart Chase

As every effective interpreter instinctively knows, the most artistic performance can fail unless the audience has been taken into consideration in the planning and execution of program material. Communication, which is at the heart of oral interpretation, is — as we have said before and undoubtedly will repeat often —a two-way process. Yet much instruction in the art of interpretation has been given in the past and still is being given with little or no attention to the role of the listener and the art of listening.

the significance of listening in the communication cycle

The past ten years have seen improvement in awareness of listening as at least half of the communication cycle. Some of this awareness has come about as a result of shocking revelations concerning the inadequacy of listening practices among Americans. Several years ago Stuart Chase noted:

> Americans are not very good listeners in face-to-face groups, although hardy enough in front of microwaves. In general they talk more than they listen. Competition in our culture puts a premium on self-expression, even if the individual has nothing to express. What he lacks in knowledge he can make up for by pounding the table. He takes a course in personality development, hoping to learn to "sell himself." How many of us while ostensibly silent are inwardly preparing a statement to stun the company when we get the floor — and so are not listening at all? Yet it really is not difficult to learn to listen, *just unusual*[1] [Italics mine.]

A fairly recent survey demonstrated that college freshmen have, on the average, only a 68 per cent comprehension of lectures immediately after they are given. Unfortunately, the inference in this type of statistic is that the freshmen are at fault. Obviously, the blame can be shared by the professors who have failed to learn the art of communication (or interpretation of subject matter) despite the fact that many of them have impressive academic titles from respected universities and have written extensively in their respective fields.

A number of surveys have shown that adults spend from 45 to 65 per cent of their waking hours in LISTENING, that they are more influenced by what they HEAR than by what they READ, but that THEY UNDERSTAND ONLY 50 PER CENT of what they hear!

With increased awareness of the significance of listening, some effort has been made in elementary and secondary schools to improve listening skills. Instead of admonishing students to PAY ATTENTION some teachers are presenting listening as an area of study in the language arts. But the rate of incorporating listening in public school curriculums is distressingly slow. A recent survey in California, for example, showed that of the nine best and most used secondary school speech texts, three were of no value in relation to listening and of the ten most used and best recognized secondary school English texts, only four paid sufficient attention to listening as a subject.

Industry has been more alert to the values of developing listening skill, realizing the benefits that accrue from effective communication. In 1961, a survey of 100 business firms showed that vice-presidents understand about two-thirds of what they hear; supervisors get about 56 per cent; plant man-

---

[1] Stuart Chase, *Power of Words*, New York: Harcourt, Brace and Company, 1954, Chapter 15, "Learning to Listen," page 165.

agers, about 40 per cent; and foremen, about 30 per cent. On the production level, workers understand only about 20 per cent of what they hear! The conclusion, naturally, was that "the ability to understand . . . sets a man apart."

In 1960 one writer commented, "Only now are we beginning to realize that listening is a complex and vital process which cannot be taken for granted, any more than reading, writing, or arithmetic."

You, no doubt, have been the victim of apathetic regard for the value of listening skills in your previous school and home training. It may be you are no more than a half-time listener. If you are to become an effective interpreter, however, you must understand the significance of listening, how to improve your own listening habits, and how to influence those listening to you. This chapter is intended to give you some helpful clues to the problem of understanding new attitudes toward listening and to acquiring skill in this vital part of the communication process.

the role of the listener

Effective interpretation and listening are integrated processes.

Empathy is the adhesive which holds them together.

The successful interpreter fully appreciates these truths and can not only perform but can put himself in the role of listener.

What is that role?

The ideal listener, of course, is the person who constantly helps the performer. He is not merely "paying attention." He is evaluating, anticipating, and reacting emotionally as well as intellectually. A good listener opens his mind and heart to the performer. He is, as the French say, "an able assistant."

Some people are able to present a pretty good picture of The Listener without doing much actual listening. They act the part while planning future activities, musing on personal problems, or allowing their minds to drift at will.

Assuming the role of listener, as you will much of the time in this course, will give you an opportunity to discover valuable clues for detecting sincerity and superficiality in listeners. Subtle reactions (and some not so subtle!) of those around you will take on significance as you pursue your study of listening. Having participated as a listener will give you understanding in the ways of influencing an audience to be cooperative and properly empathic.

analysis of listening habits
(good, bad, and indifferent)

An important telephone executive, Charles S. Woodruff, listed what he believes are the four major reasons people have trouble understanding each other, and all four relate to how people listen. The four barriers to effective oral communication are these:

1. Listening only to a speaker's words. Frequently, in doing this, we fail to get his meaning.
2. Not being skilled in good listening habits. We are too interested in what we have to say to listen for information from the speaker.
3. Closing one's mind to information which does not fit into previously selected conclusions.
4. Being ready to "jump to conclusions" rather than listening for facts. This is sometimes called "inference proneness."[2]

As you observe those around you, look for the habits that distinguish the good and the bad listener and all of those persons in between who neither contribute to nor detract from the effectiveness of the person who is speaking (the indifferent listeners).

Let us endeavor to list some of the basic listening habits which separate the helpful from the unhelpful auditors. The list may be extended as you become more skilled in your role as listener. On the positive side, the helpful auditor:

1. Appears attentive, receptive, and cooperative.
2. Keeps his eyes on the speaker most of the time.
3. Maintains a poised and relatively quiet attitude physically. Avoids restlessness and unnecessary movement.
4. Shows by facial reactions such as a smile or lifting of the eyebrow that he is receiving the message.
5. Does not allow interruptions from outside, such as people entering or leaving, street noises, etc., to distract his attention from the performer.
6. Avoids coughing, clearing throat, raucous laughter, and other vocal or nasal noises which might damage empathy.
7. Expresses appreciation in appropriate manner by laughing at proper times, applauding when opportunity is right.

---

[2]Charles S. Woodruff, vice-president, Pacific Telephone and Telegraph Company, in a speech before the Sacramento Chapter, Society of Real Estate Appraisers, in 1963.

Although it may appear redundant, enough wretched listening has occurred in the past to make it seem helpful to reverse the above points and list some bad habits. The negative auditor:

1. Appears bored, inattentive, or even hostile.
2. Averts eyes from speaker; looks away almost purposefully, or looks down, or closes eyes as if asleep (the worst!).
3. Moves about restlessly in seat, drums fingers, crosses and uncrosses legs, etc.
4. Allows face to express contempt, inattention; yawns; maintains immobility of face, showing no reaction at all.
5. Shows signs of distraction by outside noises, movement in room, watches those entering or leaving.
6. Coughs, clears throat, laughs noisily and at wrong times, blows nose loudly, etc.
7. Sits in sullen silence when and if time comes to express enjoyment in laughter or show appreciation through applause.

The habits of the indifferent listener are harder to pin down. He is the one who is somewhere between the really helpful and the downright unhelpful, distracting people in the audience. It is a temptation to classify him with the bad listener, but one is not always justified in being so arbitrary.

essential elements of listening

While outward habits such as those listed usually give evidence of what is going on inside an auditor, there are times when they give a distorted picture.

We have all known individuals who practice closing their eyes, apparently withdrawing to the land of the unconscious, when attending a performance, but who later participate in a lively discussion of the performance indicating they had given it their undivided attention. Such listeners are PERFORMING badly as listeners, but they must be employing certain basic elements of good listening or they would not be able to appraise a performance later. Contrariwise, we have observed the smiling, nodding listener who gives surface indication of listening well but who later shows his empathy has been no more than skin deep (it did not penetrate his brain).

WHAT ARE THE ESSENTIAL ELEMENTS OF LISTENING?

They are varied and complex. They may be defined broadly as (1) physical, (2) psychological, and (3) semantical. While it is not our purpose here to undertake a technical discussion of these elements, it is imperative that we have some awareness of them, since we know that listening involves more than that which meets the eye.

Let us first consider the physical elements of listening. They are considerably more significant than the bodily and facial attitudes described under habits of listening, although these habits are closely connected with them. Habits are "outward evidences" of physical elements of listening. In addition, the human system reacts voluntarily and involuntarily to stimuli which we are not always able to control. The smooth functioning of interpreter-audience communication may be interrupted by problems of sight, hearing loss, and muscular tension beyond the control of either the speaker or the listener. Attention span in individuals varies, and we cannot always program material to compensate for this variation. But being aware of this factor, we can try.

Physical elements of listening sometimes beyond our control also include room arrangements. Microphones may be poorly adjusted and ruin a performance both for interpreter and for audience. Chairs may be placed so far apart that empathy is ruined. Most experienced interpreters will endeavor to have a compact seating arrangement with not too much space between performer and audience. It is much easier to stimulate and influence the compact group.

Finally, although the average speaker talks at the rate of about 125 words per minute, the average listener can receive words at the rate of from 400 to 700 words per minute. The interpreter will remember this fact when maintaining contact, realizing that a too slow speed (all the time) will encourage the wandering mind, bored face, and tired response.

Psychologically, the most important element of listening is attention. Unless the listener has given his attention to the speaker (and he won't unless the speaker motivates him to do so), no true listening will take place. A myriad of devices, ranging from humor to the long pause, may be used, but once the speaker has attention he must realize its fragile quality and work hard to keep it while he is speaking.

The second vital psychological element in listening is perception, and this is where individual differences among listeners will be evident. Perception will vary as much as individual backgrounds, intelligence, and interests. But the able interpreter will introduce stimuli to encourage all auditors to explore within themselves for perceptions, to listen with the "inner ear," to interpret what they hear.

Finally, the third element, psychologically speaking, is reaction. Reactions also will depend on individual differences, but here again the skilled interpreter will have some measure of control over this element of listening and will seek the desired reactions.

Semantically, factors which influence listening grow out of individual differences in the comprehension of words or symbols for ideas. One writer has clearly explained the problem by saying, "If you use symbols (words) that you know, but which I do not know, I cannot follow you." Carrying this idea further, of course, we reach the conclusion that probably no two people attach the same meanings to any given words. I, for example, might have had a perfect mother who made the term "motherhood" mean unselfishness, devotion, and nobility to me. You might have had one of the despicable kind condemned by a contemporary writer as "vipers" and, to you, ·the term "motherhood" implies control, pressure, and demagoguery. If I read a poem on motherhood, are we going to agree on its meaning?

Although an able interpreter may not be able to control all the elements of listening which influence his listeners, to understand what they are and to watch for evidences of them in operation through the surface reactions of members of an audience will be of great assistance in bringing about desired empathy. The intelligent interpreter will assess subconsciously his performance by observing signs of good contact in the physical, psychological, and semantical areas of listening

the interpreter's responsibility in listening

We are now ready to go back to our initial statement in this chapter, in which we commented that "the most artistic performance can fail unless the audience has been taken into consideration in the planning and execution of program material."

It is the interpreter's responsibility to go MORE THAN HALF WAY in assuring that the audience is listening effectively. He will, first of all, discover before he meets them WHO they are. He will PLAN FOR THEM. He will not plan for some nebulous group of unknowns. He will select material which they will find understandable and which they will appreciate if it is properly presented. HE WILL PROGRAM FOR THE AUDIENCE.

In the execution of his material, the interpreter will project himself INTO THE ROLE OF THE LISTENER as much as possible. He will be conscious of all the elements of listening which have been discussed and endeavor to execute his reading in such a way as to make it effective in accordance with these elements.

What concrete steps may the interpreter take in realizing these goals of intelligent performance?

He will do the following:

1. Capture interest, thus creating voluntary listeners.
2. Say something important, thus creating purposeful listeners.
3. Motivate listening continually, thus creating self-disciplined listeners.
4. Present his material clearly, thus creating attentive listeners.
5. Present his material artfully, thus creating appreciative listeners.
6. Encourage friendly attention, thus creating cooperative listeners.

In fulfilling his obligations to the audience, the interpreter finally will NOT lose patience with his audience if they assume attitudes of poor listening. Often the performer is inclined to blame failure of communication on listeners. "They were a terrible audience!" he will reflect. It may be he is justified in condemning them, but he should never show the faintest suggestion that he is dissatisfied with them while performing, unless they are actually discourteous. Only then should he remind them of their responsibility in concrete terms. Barring discourtesy, the interpreter should, by manipulation of the foregoing outlined controls, persuade his audience to be helpful, cooperative, and creative in listening to him.

Probably no one has better expressed the interpreter's responsibility than the teacher who once said, "He should listen to himself as closely as he asks others to receive him."

The effective interpreter must know by experience what it means TO BE a good listener, and then do all in his power to provide the conditions for his auditors to fulfill THEIR roles successfully.

the listener's responsibility in listening

By now it must be obvious to all students of interpretation that the successful listener may not always be a successful interpreter, but THE SUCCESSFUL INTERPRETER MUST KNOW WHAT IT MEANS TO BE A GOOD LISTENER.

Since 90 per cent of your time in this class probably will be taken up in listening, and at least 50 per cent of it outside will be spent in the same manner, it is probably even MORE IMPORTANT that you master the art of listening than that you master the art of interpretation.

Someone has commented, "A good speaker deserves a good audience." An interpreter will soon discover that unless he HAS a good audience, he will fall far short of his best performance.

changing attitudes toward listening

summary

In this chapter we have discussed various elements of listening and have noted surface appearances or habits of both good and bad listening. We have outlined the physical, psychological, and semantical elements of listening which go beyond surface indications of attention or inattention and have stressed the importance of understanding the many factors which influence those to whom we speak to listen to us attentively, passively, or indifferently.

With these understandings in mind, it should now be possible for you to improve your own listening techniques not only for the sake of those who will be helped by you, as listener, but for your own enjoyment of participation in the audience situation.

It is the listener's responsibility to give attention, to adjust to physical conditions, to show appreciation. Anything less than this marks him as a selfish, discourteous, and apathetic listener. The rewards for good listening are as great for the listener as they are for the performer — greater! A wise person observed, "Good listening is an asset . . . the man who listens well earns dividends in information, in understanding, and in esteem."

applications: _____

1. First of all, observe yourself as a listener. Make an honest analysis of your "listenability." Write down at least five ways in which you can improve attitudes toward listening from now on:

   a.

   b.

   c.

   d.

   e.

2. Explain what is meant by this statement: As performer or listener you are deeply involved in a learning situation.
3. Select several pieces of prose and poetry related to listening to add to the following selections. Take at least one of these and prepare it for presentation to the class, noting particular ways in which you motivate attention and hold it.

preview of chapter 4:

DEVELOPING TASTE IN LITERATURE
FOR ORAL INTERPRETATION

Having worked on the problem of receptive ATTITUDES in the first three chapters, we now approach the second part of this book, which deals with MATERIALS. Our first investigation will concern the development of taste in ferreting out suitable selections for oral interpretation. We will see how attitudes of inquiry and open-mindedness help us in this area. We will also examine some criteria for judging good literature.

selections for study and interpretation

LISTENING

an excerpt from an article by
Brenda Ueland which appeared in
THE LADIES HOME JOURNAL, November, 1941.

Listening is a magnetic and strange thing, a creative force. . . . The friends that listen to us are the ones we move toward, and we want to sit in their radius as though it did us good, like ultraviolet rays. . . . When we are listened to, it creates us, makes us unfold and expand. Ideas actually begin to grow within us and come to life. It makes people happy and free when they are listened to. . . . When we listen to people there is an alternating current, and this recharges us so that we never get tired of each other. We are constantly re-created.

Now there are brilliant people who cannot listen much. They have no ingoing wires on their apparatus. They are entertaining but exhausting too. I think it is because these lecturers, these brilliant performers, by not giving us a chance to talk, do not let us express our thoughts and expand; and it is this expressing and expanding that makes the little creative fountain inside us begin to spring and cast up new thoughts and unexpected laughter and wisdom.

I discovered all this about three years ago, and truly it made a revolutionary change in my life. Before that, when I went to a party I would think anxiously: "Now try hard. Be lively. Say bright things. Talk. Don't let down." And when tired, I would have to drink a lot of coffee to keep this up. But now before going to a party, I just tell myself to listen with affection to anyone who talks to me, TO BE IN THEIR SHOES WHEN THEY TALK; to try to know them without my mind pressing against theirs, or arguing, or changing the subject. No. My attitude is: "Tell me more. This person is showing me his soul. It is a little dry and meager and full of grinding talk just now, but presently he will begin to think, not just automatically to talk. He will show his true self. Then he will be wonderfully alive." . . . .

A masterful description of listening in communication is found in Chapter 13 of LORD JIM:

From
LORD JIM

Joseph Conrad
(1857-1924)

". . . It's extraordinary how we go through life with eyes half shut, with dull ears, with dormant thoughts. Perhaps it's just as well; and it may be that it is this very dullness that makes life to the incalculable majority so supportable and so welcome. Nevertheless, there can be but few of us who had never known one of these rare moments of awakening when we see, hear, understand ever so much — everything — in a flash — before we fall back again into our agreeable somnolence. I raised my eyes when he spoke, and I saw him as though I had never seen him before. I saw his chin sunk on his breast, the clumsy folds of his coat, his clasped hands, his motionless pose, so curiously suggestive of his having been simply left there. Time had passed indeed: it had overtaken him and gone ahead. It had left him hopelessly behind with a few poor gifts: the iron-grey hair, the heavy fatigue of the tanned face, two scars, a pair of tarnished shoulder-straps; one of those steady, reliable men who are the raw material of great reputations, one of those uncounted lives that are buried without drums and trumpets under the foundations of monumental successes. 'I am now third lieutenant of the *Victorieuse*' (she was the flagship of the French Pacific squadron at the time), he said, detaching his shoulders from the wall a couple of inches to introduce himself. I bowed slightly on my side of the table, and told him I commanded a merchant vessel at present anchored in Rushcutters' Bay. He had 'remarked' her — a pretty little craft. He was very civil about it in his impassive way. I even fancy he went the length of tilting his head in compliment as he repeated, breathing visibly the while, 'Ah, yes. A little craft painted black — very pretty — very pretty (*très coquet*).' After a time he twisted his body slowly to face the glass door on our right. 'A dull town (*triste ville*),' he observed, staring into the street. It was a brilliant day; a southerly buster was raging, and we could see the passers-by, men and women, buffeted by the wind on the sidewalks, the sunlit fronts of the houses across the road blurred by the tall whirls of dust. 'I descended on shore,' he said, 'to stretch my legs a little, but . . .' He didn't finish, and sank into the depths of his repose. 'Pray — tell me,' he began, coming up ponderously, 'what was there at the bottom of this affair — precisely (*au juste*)? It is curious. That dead man, for instance — and so on.'

" 'There were living men, too.' I said; 'much more curious.'

" 'No doubt, no doubt,' he agreed half audibly, then, as if after mature consideration, murmured, 'Evidently.' I made no difficulty in communicating to him what had interested me most in this affair. It seemed as though he had a right to know: hadn't he spent thirty hours on board the *Patna* — had he not taken the succession, so to speak, had he not done 'his possible'? He listened to me, looking more priest-like than ever, and with what — probably on account of his downcast eyes — had the appearance of devout concentration. Once or twice he elevated his eyebrows (but without raising his lids), as one would say 'The devil!' Once he calmly exclaimed, 'Ah, bah!' under his breath, and when I had finished he pursed his lips in a deliberate way and emitted a sort of sorrowful whistle.

"In any one else it might have been an evidence of boredom, a sign of indifference; but he, in his occult way, managed to make his immobility appear profoundly responsive, and as full of valuable thoughts as an egg is of meat. What he said at last was nothing more than a 'very interesting,' pronounced politely, and not much above a whisper. Before I got over my disappointment he added, but as if speaking to himself, 'That's it. That *is* it.' His chin seemed to sink lower on his breast, his body to weigh heavier on his seat. I was about to ask him what he meant when a sort of preparatory tremor passed over his whole person, as a faint ripple may be seen upon stagnant water even before the wind is felt. 'And so that poor young man ran away along with the others,' he said, with grave tranquillity.

"I don't know what made me smile: it is the only genuine smile of mine I can remember in connection with Jim's affair. But somehow this simple statement of the matter sounded funny in French. . . . '*S'est enfui avec les autres,*' had said the lieutenant. And suddenly I began to admire the discrimination of the man. He had made out the point at once: he did get hold of the only thing I cared about. I felt as though I were taking professional opinion on the case. His imperturbable and mature calmness was that of an expert in possession of the facts, and to whom one's perplexities are mere child's-play. 'Ah! The young, the young,' he said, indulgently. 'And after all, one does not die of it.' 'Die of what?' I asked, swiftly. 'Of being afraid.'"

In this famous selection of Walt Whitman, we are invited to participate in many forms of listening and to experience many empathic sensations. Interpretation of these lines calls for careful study first to determine the poet's meanings, and then for a wide range of voice and emotional expression.

From
SONG OF MYSELF

Walt Whitman
(1819-1892)

Now I will do nothing but listen,
To accrue what I hear into this song, to let sounds contribute
toward it.

I hear bravuras of birds, bustle of growing wheat, gossip of
flames, clack of sticks cooking my meals.
I hear the sound I love, the sound of the human voice,
I hear all sounds running together, combined, fused or following,
Sounds of the city and sounds out of the city, sounds of the day
and night,
Talkative young ones to those that like them, the loud laugh
of work-people at their meals,

The angry base of disjointed friendship, the faint tones of the
 sick,
The judge with hands tight to the desk, his pallid lips pronounc-
 ing a death-sentence,
The heave'e'yo of stevedores unlading ships by the wharves, the
 refrain of the anchor-lifters,
The ring of alarm-bells, the cry of fire, the whirr of swift-
 streaking engines and hose-carts with premonitory tinkles
 and color'd lights,
The steam-whistle, the solid roll of the train of approaching cars,
The slow march play'd at the head of the association marching
 two and two,
(They go to guard some corpse, the flag-tops are draped with
 black muslin.)

I hear the violoncello, ('tis the young man's heart's complaint,)
I hear the key'd cornet, it glides quickly in through my ears,
It shakes mad-sweet pangs through my belly and breast.

I hear the chorus, it is a grand opera,
Ah, this indeed is music — this suits me.

A tenor large and fresh as the creation fills me,
The orbic flex of his mouth is pouring and filling me full.

I hear the train'd soprano (what work with hers is this?)
The orchestra whirls me wider than Uranus flies,
It wrenches such ardors from me I did not know I possess'd
 them,
It sails me, I dab with bare feet, they are lick'd by the indolent
 waves,
I am cut by bitter and angry hail, I lose my breath,
Steep'd amid honey'd morphine, my windpipe throttled in fakes
 of death,
At length let up again to feel the puzzle of puzzles,
And that we call Being.

De la Mare defies our best efforts to state precise meaning,
yet his poetry is full of significance and open to many in-
terpretations. "The Listeners" could be read as a story, as
a sermon of courage in the face of fear, or as a symbolic
quest for truth. How do you feel it might be interpreted?

THE LISTENERS

Walter de la Mare
(1873-1956)

"Is there anybody there?" said the Traveler,
    Knocking on the moonlit door;
And his horse in the silence champed the grasses
    Of the forest's ferny floor:
And a bird flew up out of the turret,
    Above the Traveler's head:
And he smote upon the door again a second time;
    "Is there anybody there?" he said.
But no one descended to the Traveler;
    No head from the leaf-fringed sill
Leaned over and looked into his gray eyes,
    Where he stood perplexed and still.
But only a host of phantom listeners
    That dwelt in the lone house then
Stood listening in the quiet of the moonlight
    To that voice from the world of men:
Stood thronging the faint moonbeams on the dark stair
    That goes down to the empty hall,
Hearkening in an air stirred and shaken
    By the lonely Traveler's call.
And he felt in his heart their strangeness,
    Their stillness answering his cry,
While his horse moved, cropping the dark turf,
    'Neath the starred and leafy sky;
For he suddenly smote on the door, even
    Louder, and lifted his head: —
"Tell them I came, and no one answered,
    That I kept my word," he said.
Never the least stir made the listeners,
    Though every word he spake
Fell echoing through the shadowiness of the still house
    From the one man left awake:
Aye, they heard his foot upon the stirrup,
    And the sound of iron on stone,
And how the silence surged softly backward,
    When the plunging hoofs were gone.

materials

developing taste
in literature
for oral interpretation

An appreciation and understanding of literature cannot be easily achieved by a reliance upon faith, hope, and charity . . . in making his evaluation of literature, the student must keep a balance of the emotional and the intellectual.[1]

Chloe Armstrong and Paul D. Brandes

How much easier it is for the student merely to express himself than to undergo the hard discipline of study necessary to understand a great poem.

Wayland Maxfield Parrish

There is an unfortunate emphasis placed by some educators on the accumulation of factual knowledge. The educated person is thought of as one who can display encyclopedic knowledge at a moment's notice on any given subject. Such a person, however, may be completely lacking in taste, in the ability to make value judgments, and in the general understandings necessary to distinguish the artistic from the monstrous.

It requires not only a storehouse of knowledge, but a creative handling of such knowledge, to develop taste in any area. A cook may be able to identify all types of seasonings. Unless she also knows how to combine them

---

[1]Chloe Armstrong and Paul D. Brandes, *The Oral Interpretation of Literature,* New York: McGraw-Hill Book Company, Inc., 1963, pages 8-9.

creatively in a palatable way, her factual knowledge actually may be a hazard to the preparation of a tasty meal.

One of the valuable benefits to be derived from a class in oral interpretation is the development of literary taste in general and taste in literature for oral interpretation in particular. There IS a difference, as you will come to realize or may already know. Through the analysis, preparation, and performance of literary material, you will develop understanding of the basic ingredients of literature WORTHY of critical praise.

While it is not the aim of this textbook or of your instructor to make of you a literary snob, undoubtedly it is our mutual hope that this class will give you sensitivity to, and empathy for, selections of greater literary merit than those which you may now appreciate. However high you may be on the totem pole of literary appreciation, there is probably room for progression upward.

How, then, does one develop literary taste, particularly in relation to oral interpretation?

starting with an attitude of inquiry and objectivity

As we have learned in earlier chapters, nothing can exert much influence on understanding unless the student is in a receptive attitude, which is an attitude of inquiry and objectivity. In other words, a first task is to place oneself in the attitude of the good listener — opening mind and heart to what an author has to say and to how he says it — giving his work COMPLETE ATTENTION.

As you read or listen to a selection for the first time, continually question, both intellectually and emotionally: Is the author describing real or imaginary experiences? Is he reporting vicarious experience or motivated by it? Does he use words and phrases with attention to their SOUND, to their REAL or INFERRED meaning, to their EMOTIONAL impact? Is the author's basic intention to entertain, to inform, or to impress dramatically? Is this initial reading or hearing of the selection motivating me to reread or listen to it again? Is the selection challenging? These and similar questions should be prodding you as you approach a piece of literature for the first time.

Also, you should be earnestly seeking to rid yourself on this first reading (or hearing), of subjective preferences, prejudices, and preconceived conclusions. "Objectivity is a rare talent and always has been," someone wisely commented.

Perhaps you have always preferred the poem with defined rhythm and perfect rhyme. When you encounter Masefield's *Sea Fever,* it is most agreeable and completely satisfying to you to read:

I must go down to the seas again, to the lonely sea and the sky;
And all I ask is a tall ship, and a star to steer her by.

Your toe starts to swing and your blood to pound as you feel the beat of this graceful poem. You love the force and the strength of it. You love the way each esthetically pleasing line is linked to its predecessor with a rhyming word.

What a difference to encounter, for the first time, something like this:

April is the cruellest month, breeding
Lilacs out of the dead land, mixing
Memory and desire, stirring
Dull roots with spring rain.

T. S. Eliot in *The Waste Land* seems to be telling us that spring, which poets have taught us to love as the time of birth and hope, is, rather, a time of agony for some. If you are a tired soul impatient for death, April can be cruel, Eliot says, with its insistence on the continuation of life. The idea of the poem may be mildly shocking, the rhythm elusive, the rhyme disappointing. Eliot may seem to be striving for something completely opposite to literature we have felt sure was true and beautiful, therefore in good taste. Yet, his works undoubtedly will become classics of twentieth century literature, and it is not wise to reject them until you have given them a chance to be understood. If Eliot's poetry and that of other poets, past and contemporary, with whom you may not now be well acquainted, does not please you as does Masefield's, at least reserve judgment until you have studied further.

Interestingly enough, Eliot himself gave a token of his understanding of the amazement of some who encountered him:

How unpleasant to meet Mr. Eliot!
With his features of clerical cut
And his brow so grim
And his mouth so prim
And his conversations, so nicely
Restricted to What Precisely

And If and Perhaps and But.
How unpleasant to meet Mr. Eliot!

Eliot is said to have been a mystic. But he was in touch with reality too, don't you think? Isn't there a note of human sympathy and wry humor in his remark, "How unpleasant to meet Mr. Eliot!"?

pursuing with an attitude of the open mind

An open mind, like a little learning, can be a dangerous thing unless it is equipped with some sort of sifting device, generally referred to as DISCRIMINATION. This term, however, is NOT a good one because it implies opposition or exclusion. As we are using it, we mean by discrimination some thoughtful process for arriving at literary judgments.

Although the taste makers in literature seldom agree on measurements of quality in literary works, there are certain areas of almost unanimous agreement in the literary world. Obviously, we are in better shape if we can find a little island of well-being in the vast sea of literature, knowing that when we are on it we are relatively "safe" and "right."

Certain selections, by certain authors, generally are thought of as praiseworthy by the reasonably well educated. Certain other selections, by certain other authors, generally are considered of dubious quality. We could, for example, cite Shakespeare as an author who pleases most educated people. On the dubious side, we could suggest Edgar Guest. Of this much, we can be fairly certain. From this point, resting in the midst of a body of generally approved literature (and avoiding the generally disapproved), we may proceed.

In addition to specific selections and authors we feel sure are "good," we should have reliable criteria for judging other things which may come to our attention, particularly in current literature where we don't have prepackaged judgments. From our little island, equipped with these criteria for judging (or sifting the better from the poorer material) we can pursue our search for literature for oral interpretation with an open, not empty, mind. Although in literary judgments one may be safe in staying with known works of quality, it is more rewarding to try to learn HOW TO RECOGNIZE what is worth liking, rather than to continue liking only what you know — or what it seems safe to know.

What criteria for judging will prevent open-mindedness from being merely empty-headedness?

criteria for judging literature
for oral interpretation

By now you have been reminded of something you un-
doubtedly know: by far the most popular criterion for judging literature is:

1. Select Material Which Has Withstood the Tests of Time.

This is also the dullest of the criteria and the one most certain to rob
you of the creative experience of judging for yourself. Using this method
of selection, you don't need to develop discrimination. Get a good,
standard anthology and stand pat on your little island of classics. The
classic test is a safe one, saves time, saves energy, saves controversy, is
most frequently used, destroys initiative, and stunts personal growth. In
classes in oral interpretation, where emphasis frequently is on problems
of voice, gesture,. and stage presence, the quicker a vehicle in the way
of a classic bit of prose or poetry is discovered, the better. Then one can
get on to the "serious" business of interpretation!

We urge you, however, to free yourself from depending on this criterion. Part of your time here should be spent in selecting material from
the constant flow of contemporary work and also from less famous works
of many fine writers of the past. Discover some good literature for yourself and include it in your personal anthology (discussed in Chapter 8).

A second criterion for judging material is:

2. Select Material Which Has Recognized Qualities of Good Writing Style.

Since the publication of *Literature as a Fine Art*[2] in 1941 by the
eminent Professor C. C. Cunningham of Northwestern University's Department of Interpretation, many teachers of interpretation have continued to analyze and judge literary works by certain intrinsic and
extrinsic qualities he enunciated. Cunningham, postulating that all arts
"spring from the same rootstock," found that a good poem or narrative
or other literary work, like a good picture or musical composition, will
have as intrinsic qualities: unity, harmony, variety, contrast, balance and
proportion, and rhythm. These elements, he said, lie within the circum-
ference of the work of art.

In addition, he said, there are certain extrinsic qualities which "spill-
over" and which are found to be a part of any true work of art. These
are four: universality ("the degree . . . to which the work of art pos-
sesses an aesthetic, emotional or thought content that gives it significance
as a commentary on life"), individuality (how it differs from other con-

---

[2]Cornelius Carman Cunningham, *Literature as a Fine Art*, New York:
The Ronald Press Company, 1941.

cepts and treatments), suggestiveness (the way it asks the observer or hearer to translate it into his own experience), and aesthetic distance (a sense of unreality setting it apart from "mere nature.")

By applying these criteria for judging, say the followers of Cunningham, not without certain justification, we may feel confidence in discovering whether a piece of writing has literary worth.

It is interesting to note, however, that in his very commendable book, Cunningham singled out, by way of illustration of "Fromentin's pronouncement regarding very small works as exemplars of great principles of art," REQUIEM FOR A MODERN CROESUS by Lew Sarett. For three pages he extolled this selection and this poet. This poem met all the criteria with distinction. And yet today Sarett and his poems are seldom, if ever, found in anthologies of distinguished literature.

The primary difficulty with all well-defined yardsticks of judgment is that they can be applied in such a way as to prove or disprove almost anything. Like statistics, they need to be used with a sense of their *relative* rather than their *certain* value.

At times specific selections may not seem to conform graciously and easily to the principles of intrinsic and extrinsic artistic worth laid down by Cunningham, but we know intuitively that we have found something which will be challenging to interpret. We *know* it is good material. Should we throw it out if it isn't a classic and if it doesn't have the prescribed qualities of intrinsic and extrinsic merit?

Definitely not!

One thing oral interpreters should do is free themselves from restrictions imposed by critics, writers, and academicians on criteria for judging the printed page. NOT ALL FINE WRITING IS FINE FOR ORAL PERFORMANCE. Some excellent expository writing can be read silently with delight, but when read orally may sound dull, involved, and complex. Contrariwise, a very simple statement may move a multitude.

By all means give heed to the elements of good writing style and endeavor to select literature which measures up. But remember that a danger in judging all literature by carefully prescribed evaluative yardsticks is that YOU may apply the yardstick in such a way as to judge something great which is merely mediocre, or rule out entirely some interesting experimental material which just doesn't conform to the rules.

We now present a third criterion for judging literature for oral interpretation.

3. Select Material Which Holds Up When Read Aloud Repeatedly.

We have said that not all fine writing makes for fine oral reading. Much has been written exclusively for silent reading. It was never intended for reading aloud. That is not to say it can not be read with clarity. It is simply to say that, having choice in the matter, we should make selections which lend themselves to oral interpretation. It is here that criteria for judging literature have been ignored by most members of the literati.

All material for oral interpretation should be judged on its hearability. This cannot always be discovered on a first reading aloud.

Often we are intrigued by something when we first discover it. Upon a second reading aloud our enthusiasm begins to fade. By the fourth reading of it, we find the material shallow and trivial, monotonous, motivated by emotions or ideas we didn't understand or want to present, or disappointing for other reasons.

Only by at least two or three oral readings can we judge the HEAR-ABILITY and durability of a selection and discover whether it is really suitable for oral interpretation technically, thematically, emotionally, intellectually, and semantically.

When we have read it aloud at least three times and have found it to our liking, when we know and like the SOUND of it, know we like to express its MEANING (not all poems have to mean something, though), know we are capable of interpreting it technically speaking (have sufficient voice, for example), and feel we won't tire of it, then we can feel pretty sure we have discovered a selection worth considering for oral interpretation.

A fourth criterion, and one which again relates more specifically to judgments of material for oral work, is:

4. Select Material Which Will Stimulate The Audience Beneficially.

Cicero recognized that three ends of discourse were to delight, to move, and to teach. These ends may, very practically, be applied to interpretation. We might ask ourselves, in hearing a selection, will this material entertain, inspire or move, or enlighten (perhaps all three) some audience? If a piece reads well aloud, it will almost certainly be able to answer this question in the affirmative.

With limited time, the wise student will rule out material of little or very limited use no matter how praiseworthy it may be in literary circles.

summary

It takes creative handling of knowledge to develop taste in any area. Through analysis, preparation, and performance you can better understand the basic ingredients of literature worthy of critical praise.

An attitude of inquiry and objectivity is essential in approaching literary judgments, as in an open (but not empty) mind.

Criteria for judging may be summarized under four headings: (1) Select classic material (safe but dull). (2) Select material which has recognized qualities of good writing style (restrictive, eliminating newer and experimental material). (3) Select material which holds up when read aloud repeatedly. (4) Select material beneficially stimulating to the audience.

applications: _____

1. Choose a selection with utmost care, keeping in mind the criteria for judging good material for oral interpretation given in Chapter 4. Keep notes of material considered and rejected and reasons for rejection.
2. Prepare your selection by gathering background material about the author, critical writings concerning his work, and judgments of other critics of the selection you have chosen. Make your own evaluation of the selection, noting personal agreements or disagreements with what others have said.
3. Read the selection aloud at least six times before coming to class. Have it almost memorized, if possible, but use your manuscript.
4. If possible, enlist the help of a classmate to listen to you in preparing this selection. Note his criticisms and strive to correct problems before your class presentation.
5. Read the following selections, which have been included because **THEY READ ALOUD WELL**. Select at least five additional examples from contemporary literature which, in your opinion, bear up well under all the tests given in this chapter for oral interpretative qualities.

preview of chapter 5:
DEVELOPING AN UNDERSTANDING OF
PROSE AND POETRY OF THE PAST (to 1900)

From a literary heritage of acknowledged masters of spoken and written words who have lived in previous centuries, we can find excellent material for interpretation. We need not fear that everything before this century will sound dull and out of date. On the contrary, much prose, poetry, and drama of the Greeks, literature of the Bible, and work of other generations of novelists, essayists, and dramatists is as fresh and exciting to the ear as on the day it was conceived. One of our richest sources of poetry for oral interpretation is the work of eminent lyricists of periods preceding this century. Let us see what ore we can mine out of the rich resources of world literature!

selections for study and interpretation

ENDYMION by John Keats was written when he was scarcely 23. In it he is searching for ideal beauty. It is built on a Greek myth of the shepherd Endymion. Keats was to die of tuberculosis only three years later, but in that time he wrote a great amount of mature poetry which reads aloud easily and beautifully.

A Thing of Beauty
From ENDYMION

John Keats
(1795-1821)

A thing of beauty is a joy for ever:
Its loveliness increases; it will never
Pass into nothingness; but still will keep
A bower quiet for us, and a sleep
Full of sweet dreams, and health, and quiet breathing.
Therefore, on every morrow, are we wreathing
A flowery band to bind us to the earth,
Spite of despondence, of the inhuman dearth
Of noble natures, of the gloomy days,
Of all the unhealthy and o'er-darkened ways
Made for our searching: yes, in spite of all,
Some shape of beauty moves away the pall
From our dark spirits. Such the sun, the moon,
Trees old and young, sprouting a shady boon
For simple sheep; and such are daffodils
With the green world they live in; and clear rills
That for themselves a cooling covert make
'Gainst the hot season; the mid-forest brake,
Rich with a sprinkling of fair musk-rose blooms:
And such too is the grandeur of the dooms
We have imagined for the mighty dead;
All lovely tales that we have heard or read:
An endless fountain of immortal drink,
Pouring into us from the heaven's brink.

Hopkins loved colorful words, extravagant phrases, and grand ideas.

PIED BEAUTY

Gerard Manley Hopkins
(1844-1889)

>Glory be to God for dappled things —
>>For skies of couple-color as a brinded cow;
>>>For rose-moles all in stipple upon trout that swim;
>Fresh-firecoal chestnut-falls; finches' wings;
>>Landscape plotted and pieced — fold, fallow, and plow;
>>And all trades, their gear and tackle and trim.
>
>All things counter, original, spare, strange;
>>Whatever is fickle, freckled (who knows how?)
>>With swift, slow; sweet, sour; adazzle, dim;
>He fathers-forth whose beauty is past change:
>>>Praise Him.

It is a challenge to read the rushing language of Hopkins, with its piling on of image — textures — feelings — all the auditory, sensory, perceptual experiences of man.

GOD'S GRANDEUR

Gerard Manley Hopkins

>The world is charged with the grandeur of God.
>>It will flame out, like shining from shook foil;
>>It gathers to a greatness, like the ooze of oil
>Crushed. Why do men then now not reck his rod?
>
>Generations have trod, have trod, have trod;
>>And all is seared with trade; bleared, smeared with toil;
>>And wears man's smudge and shares man's smell; the soil
>Is bare now, nor can foot feel, being shod.
>
>And for all this, nature is never spent;
>>There lives the dearest freshness deep down things;
>And though the last lights off the black West went
>>Oh, morning, at the brown brink eastward, springs —
>Because the Holy Ghost over the bent
>>World broods with warm breast and with ah! bright wings.

In contrast to Hopkins and his extravagant phrases, Emily Dickinson wrote in a concise, aphoristic manner. Nearly all of her almost 2,000 poems are short. Only two of them were published in her lifetime.

THERE IS NO FRIGATE LIKE A BOOK

Emily Dickinson
(1830-1886)

There is no frigate like a book
　　To take us lands away,
Nor any coursers like a page
　　Of prancing poetry.

This traverse may the poorest take
　　Without oppress of toll;
How frugal is the chariot
　　That bears a human soul!

THE HEART ASKS PLEASURE FIRST

Emily Dickinson

The heart asks pleasure first,
And then, excuse from pain;
And then, those little anodynes
That deaden suffering;

And then, to go to sleep;
And then, if it should be
The will of its Inquisitor,
The liberty to die.

Emily Dickinson

To make a prairie it takes a clover and one bee, —
One clover, and a bee,
And revery.

The revery alone will do
If bees are few.

Long favorites with oral readers, the lyrical poems of Christina Rossetti fall somewhere between Hopkins and Dickinson. They are full of terse statements but they have an emotional and moving intensity of feeling.

WHEN I AM DEAD, MY DEAREST

Christina Rossetti
(1830-1894)

When I am dead, my dearest,
Sing no sad songs for me;
Plant thou no roses at my head,
Nor shady cypress-tree:
Be the green grass above me
With showers and dewdrops wet;
And if thou wilt, remember,
And if thou wilt, forget.

I shall not see the shadows,
I shall not feel the rain;
I shall not hear the nightingale
Sing on, as if in pain:
And dreaming through the twilight
That doth not rise nor set,
Haply I may remember,
And haply may forget.

REMEMBER

Christina Rossetti

Remember me when I am gone away,
Gone far away into the silent land;
When you can no more hold me by the hand,
Nor I half turn to go, yet turning stay.
Remember me when no more, day by day,

You tell me of our future that you planned;
Only remember me; you understand
It will be late to counsel then or pray.

Yet if you should forget me for a while
And afterwards remember, do not grieve;
For if the darkness and corruption leave
A vestige of the thoughts that once I had,
Better by far you should forget and smile
Than that you should remember and be sad.

A BIRTHDAY

Christina Rossetti

My heart is like a singing bird
  Whose nest is in a watered shoot;
My heart is like an apple-tree
  Whose boughs are bent with thick-set fruit;
My heart is like a rainbow shell
  That paddles in a halcyon sea;
My heart is gladder than all these
  Because my love is come to me.

Raise me a dais of silk and down;
  Hang it with vair and purple dyes;
Carve it in doves and pomegranates,
  And peacocks with a hundred eyes;
Work it in gold and silver grapes,
  In leaves and silver fleur-de-lys;
Because the birthday of my life
  Is come, my love is come to me.

In Japan the term "shibui" is used to describe things which
are satisfying to the spirit and fulfill the demands of good
taste. There is no word in English which quite explains
the scope of *shibui*, however, and it is therefore an interesting symbol to study as we endeavor to understand efforts of a Japanese to explain it to us:

SHIBUI

"Shibui Konomi"
WE JAPANESE, Book I
Fujiya Hotel, Ltd.
Miyanoshita, Hakone, Japan

. . . Japanese speak of *shibui* in relation to customs, houses, rooms, decorations and ornaments, persons, dress, as well as to the tone of voice. It marks the character of the old order of things, and sometimes of the new.

. . . .

A certain color scheme is essential in producing a *shibui* effect. A sculptured piece of white marble, for instance, cannot be *shibui* because it is devoid of color, but the prevalence of brilliant or bright color is antagonistic to *shibui*. The color of bran, the outer coat of kernels of rice, wheat, etc. is commonly called *shibui-kawa* (meaning astringent skin), and this color, or that of various shades of chestnut or russet in an art object is usually essential in securing a *shibui* effect. The color of ashes, unpolished silver and gold, and other colors constitute factors for producing a subdued and tranquil effect in an art object and it is the artistic employment of such colors or combinations of colors that imparts to Japanese art an indescribable *shibui* effect. . . .

A Japanese, in commenting upon a woman's kimono, might say: "Look at her *shibui konomi*" — meaning that the woman was dressed with discrimination in silk material of the traditional color, not showy, but rich in quality. In speaking of a voice as *shibui*, reference is made to its quality through the cultivation and training it has received.

developing an understanding of prose and poetry of the past (to 1900)

O friend unseen, unborn, unknown,
  Student of our sweet English tongue,
Read out my words at night, alone:
  I was a poet, I was young.

Since I can never see your face,
  And never shake you by the hand,
I send my soul through time and space
  To greet you. You will understand.

From "To a Poet a Thousand Years Hence"
by James Elroy Flecker

Literature, of course, was born of the spoken word. Long, long before men had thought of hacking in stone the words of their leaders, they had been celebrating, worshipping, entertaining each other, and communicating by means of speech.

Interestingly enough, poetry is said to be older than prose. That is, men probably were communicating by means of a rhythmically oriented system of sound even before they developed sounds into symbols for words. Also, most historians believe that primitive peoples relied on the poets among them (those with a certain "way with words") to carry on the myths, the legends, the chants, and the beliefs that contributed to the cultural heritage.

These weavers of words were at work ages before men knew how to record speech.

From the time when humans first thought of preserving spoken words, we have been building up a heritage of literature. Ancient Egypt left its record in the hieroglyphics on the walls of tombs. The Greeks left records of the tremendous part rhetoric, poetry, and drama played in their lives. The Middle Ages gave us the beautifully crafted manuscripts of the monks. The invention of printing in the mid-1400's accelerated the production of manuscript, and it was from this time on that a large share of what appeared in print was first WRITTEN, not SPOKEN, as in the past.

our debt to the Greeks

It is with the Greeks that the spoken word developed an eloquence and facility which probably never has been surpassed. Homer's heroes were fluent orators "able and ready to debate intelligently on any argument . . . with a natural facility of speech and readiness of invective." Herodotus first read his famous history aloud to friends and later to an audience in Athens. He was so appreciated that he was voted a sum equal to several thousand dollars. It is reported his reading moved listeners to tears.

It was not unusual in the Ecclesia, or assembly, of ancient Athens to have 6,000 citizens in attendance. This assembly met about 40 times a year and anyone was privileged to speak on any issue by securing the attention of the herald, placing the laurel wreath on his head, and starting to speak. Oral facility was a practical art. The ability to read aloud was prized as much as valor in war.

For those citizens who were not gifted, professional speechmakers were available. Corax, a busy ghost writer, drew up a set of rules to guide others on the art of rhetoric. Aristotle based his teachings on this rhetoric 120 years later. Between these two great teachers, the Golden Age of Rhetoric was bringing to a peak the art of persuasion, the craft of influencing others.

Ancient Greeks set a standard of oral performance which later civilizations have seldom attained. They established the importance and value of mastering the art of communication through speech, the art of interpreting what had been prepared in advance as well as the art of extemporaneous persuasion. To be an able speaker and interpreter was the first requirement of the educated man in Athens, and his leadership and influence rested on that ability. Through oral persuasion, Pericles brought into being a city of such beauty and perfection that no civilization since has quite equaled its refinement. Cicero remarked that Pericles had such "graces of persuasion" that even when he rose to contradict the people's favorites his words "became popular and agreeable to all men."

In addition to their stress on the importance of skill in the arts of oral interpretation, we are indebted to the Greeks for their insistence on PROPORTION in oral delivery as in all things. By proportion they meant freedom from extremes, or good taste. Aristotle called it the "mean." In his words, the mean "is neither too much nor too little. . . . Thus, then, every person who has knowledge shuns the excess and the defect, but seeks for the mean, and chooses it; not the absolute mean, but the relative one."

Even today, we can read with benefit from the three short books on rhetoric given us by Aristotle and take from them ideas on the art of speech which are readily adaptable to the field of interpretation.

We are grateful to the Greeks for an attitude of profound respect for the arts of speech and for a rich heritage of lyric poetry (the word *lyric* comes from the Greek *lyriko*, meaning *with the lyre* or *belonging to the lyre*), drama, and prose.

distinguishing prose from poetry

At this point we will digress for a little while to consider a question which has long concerned literary people, and that question is, what differentiates prose from poetry? Experts disagree, of course, and therefore dogmatic definitions of either prose or poetry are of dubious value. But it is helpful to note what some of them have had to say on the matter.

George Santayana, for example, said: "Poetry is something secret and pure, some magical perception lighting up the mind for a moment, like reflections in the water, playful and fugitive. Your true poet catches the charm of something . . . dropping the thing itself." This is not the type of comment which sheds much light on differences between prose and poetry. Many writers convey magical perceptions in prose.

Josephine Miles, in *The Ways of the Poem*, says:

Talking becomes poetry as walking becomes dancing. It takes on a form to give shape to a mood or idea. As the steps in dance do not merely follow one after another but are grouped, accented, and repeated, so the words in poetry are grouped by stresses, the stresses by lines. . . .

74

When you measure so closely what you are saying . . . you are probably not setting out on the long progress of the novel . . . not under-
taking the conflict of drama . . . rather you are focussing on the structure of sound, as in song. . . .[1]

To take our analysis of poetry as opposed to prose one step further, listen
to John Ciardi, eminent contemporary poet and critic, as he combines the
elements of emotion and structure in a statement which reads: "The poet's
way round is by way of rhythm, diction, image, and form. It is the right,
the duty, and the joy of his trade to be passionate about these things."[2]
Ciardi refers constantly to poetry as "an act of language" and reminds us
that although poetry may seem on the surface to be simple it is always
"compounded of many things at once."

The clue to a usable definition of poetry perhaps rests in that thought,
that poetry is made up of "many things at once." Poetry combines elements
of emotion, rhythm, and imagination in one artistic product.

There is another factor which should be considered. Prose is usually
more concerned with subject matter. Poetry is more often based on direct
experience. What happens happens TO the person reading or hearing the
poem. No one has summed up this observation more concisely than Archibald MacLeish, whose famous words on this subject declare "A poem should
not mean/ But be."

When we face the task of interpreting poetry, it is well for us to remember some of the differences we have suggested. A great poem often defies
our best efforts to distill its meaning. We may suspect, and rightly, that the
poet himself was not concerned with MEANING. He may have been very
concerned about rhythm, words, or emotion. "If the reader wishes to engage
in poetry," says Ciardi, "let him forget meaning." This statement may stretch
reason too far, but it does help an interpreter realize that poets often intend
for a poem just to be, and the sympathetic interpreter is the one who can
bring a poem into being, who can breathe life into it.

basic classifications of poetry

Traditionally, poetry has been classified as narrative, dramatic, and lyric. The first tells a story, the second presents a play, and the
third is song poetry and is usually emotional or expressive of human feelings.

[1]Josephine Miles, *The Ways of the Poem*, Englewood Cliffs, New
Jersey: Prentice-Hall, Inc., 1961, pages 1-2.
[2]John Ciardi, *Dialogue With An Audience*, Philadelphia: J. B. Lippin-
cott, Co. 1963.

Narrative Poetry

Homer was the greatest of the Greek narrative poets. His *Iliad* and *Odyssey* formed a standard upon which all later epic or narrative poetry was based. While the *Iliad* and the *Odyssey* do not lend themselves well to citation of brief passages, an excerpted selection is offered at the end of this chapter.

Other examples of outstanding narrative poetry from the past can be found in works of Dante, Chaucer, and Robert Browning, to mention only a few of the greatest.

Also classified under narrative or story-telling poetry, we have a wide variety of delightful ballads, some of popular origin, which have been handed down from generation to generation by word of mouth, and others which have been deliberately written by such poets as John Keats and Dante Gabriel Rossetti. (Stephen Vincent Benét has used this form in our century.)

Dramatic Poetry

Immediately, at mention of dramatic poetry, the Greek tragedies of such dramatists as Aeschylus, Sophocles, Euripides, and Aristophanes come to mind. Shakespeare's plays and those of Molière also may be classified as poetic in structure.

Lyric Poetry

The lyric poem gets its name from its ability to fit into a musical setting. It includes the sonnet, the ode, the hymn, and the elegy, examples of some of which will be given at the end of this chapter. Also there is the lyrical ballad written by such poets as Wordsworth (*Tintern Abbey*) and Coleridge (*The Rime of the Ancient Mariner*).

In connection with this type of poetry, we make special mention of the Bible, in which we can find some of the finest examples of Hebrew poetry. In general, Biblical poetry belongs in a class of the lyric because it either gives us rules of life in the form of proverbs or describes the poet's emotions in the presence of great joy or suffering. We shall be reading examples of Biblical poetry at the end of the chapter.

Many of our most popular poets of the past fall into this final classification, lyric. From 1750 to 1850 the lyric was in full flower, the age being one of great hope, inspiration, and romanticism. Lyrics of Goethe, Wordsworth, Shelley, Keats, and many others extolled the beautiful in life. The attachment to the lyric extends forcefully into our time. Although many modern poets give us free verse and blank verse based on realism and existentialism

— verse which challenges the intellectual literati — such efforts serve often to subvert the love of poetry among laymen. The decline of lyric poetry in the twentieth century makes it even more valuable for us to familiarize ourselves with great poetry of the past in order that we can have at our command good material for programs of a more popular nature.

basic classifications of prose

Traditionally, prose is divided into fiction and nonfiction. Fiction covers material which emphasizes plot or story, including the novel, short story, and even the play (some plays are primarily poetry, however, and it is difficult to categorize them). Nonfiction is difficult to categorize because there are so many types. We find essays, factual material, great orations, editorials, and such in this area.

From the ancient Greeks certain prose of Plato and Aristotle may be quoted quite appropriately in modern times. The speeches of Cicero and Caesar contain memorable passages.

Among the greatest sources of history for outstanding selections of prose is, again, the Bible. Writings of the ancient Hebrews in the Old Testament and later writings of the New Testament are rich in interpretative material.

A period of literary decline during the Middle Ages accompanied the interruption of communication between Rome and its outlying empire. Latin ceased to be a universal language and the crude forms of French, Italian, and Spanish that arose to take its place did not lend themselves to literary production.

Again, during the Renaissance, when men rediscovered the Greek and Roman classics, there was an upsurge in literary production. From this and later times we have a long, noble line of great writers including Dante, Montaigne, Shakespeare, Milton, Dryden, Pope, Addison, Swift, and Voltaire. Much of their work fits comfortably at times into programs if we are aware of it and give it an interesting introduction.

After 1850 the emphasis in prose shifted to realism, to a search for solutions to some of man's social and ethical problems. Answers to man's questions about himself were given in the novel and in the play. Among the best dramatists of the latter part of the nineteenth century are Ibsen, Shaw, and Chekhov. Novelists who have had tremendous influence on our literary heritage include Dickens, Hardy, and Galsworthy.

summary

Long before men thought of recording ideas in some manner, they were communicating by forms of speech, laying the foundations for our written heritage of literature. We have considerable literary material from all ages, but the ancient Greeks had a respect for the spoken word which has never been surpassed. From them we acquired an appreciation for proportion or good taste and to them we are indebted for much fine poetry, prose, and drama. From the time of the invention of printing, the production of manuscript has greatly accelerated the amount of material first *written,* not *spoken.*

Differences between prose and poetry are difficult to delineate but, in general, poetry is direct experience, less concerned with subject matter than prose, and is characterized by many elements including emotional magic, rhythm, and imagery.

Basic types of poetry traditionally have included the narrative, dramatic, and lyric. History gives us unlimited material of merit. Basic classifications of prose include fiction and numerous types of nonfiction including the essay, factual articles, orations, and other expository material.

Prose seems to have become more popular than poetry since the mid-1800's, due somewhat to the decline of lyric poetry, the rise of free verse, and the increase of subject matter which is not tasteful to the average man. We may well look to the past to find poetry which appeals and communicates to the layman.

applications: _____

1. Search anthologies available in the library to discover some outstanding examples of prose and poetry from various eras of the past. Select at least three of each (prose and poetry) which you feel could be used successfully today.
2. Give a paragraph or two of background material for each of your selections.
3. From these, select your favorite and prepare it for oral performance in class. Be prepared to supply enough background material to interest the class in hearing the selection. Proceed with its preparation in the manner you have been practicing, enlisting the help of a good listener if you can.
4. Read the following selections, which are good examples of some outstanding periods we have discussed in this chapter. Be prepared to give an honest reaction to each if called upon in class.

preview of chapter 6:

DEVELOPING AN UNDERSTANDING OF
PROSE AND POETRY OF OUR TIME

While it is valuable to appreciate and enjoy the great classics, all students of interpretation should be aware of the distinguished writing which has been taking place in our century. Readable prose can be found in the tremendous output of fiction and nonfiction since the turn of the century, but it takes a spirit of adventure to find it and courage to use it at times. We will be exploring this era of literature to see what nuggets we may upturn.

selections for study and interpretation

Somewhere in the ninth century B.C. the Homeric Poems, the earliest literary product of the world, were conceived. They lie "at the fountainhead" of all later literature in Europe. To the ancient Greek, the Iliad and the Odyssey of Homer were almost like a Bible. Both have to do with the Trojan War; the siege of Troy by the Greeks and the eventual sack of the city. In this excerpt from the Iliad, we may taste some of the dramatic quality of Homer's epic poetry.

Father and Son
THE ILIAD

(Pope's Translation)

Thus having spoke, the illustrious chief of Troy
    Stretched his fond arms to clasp the lovely boy.
    The babe clung crying to his nurse's breast,
Scared at the dazzling helm and nodding crest.
With sacred pleasure each fond parent smiled,
And Hector hasted to relieve his child;
The glittering terrors from his brows unbound,
And placed the beaming helmet on the ground;
Then kissed the child, and lifting high in air,
Thus to the gods preferred a father's prayer: —
    "O thou whose glory fills the ethereal throne,
And all ye deathless powers, protect my son!
Grant him, like me, to purchase just renown,
To guard the Trojans, to defend the crown,
Against his country's foes the war to wage,
And rise the Hector of the future age!
So when, triumphant from successful toils,
Of heroes slain he bears the reeking spoils,
Whole hosts may hail him with deserved acclaim,
And say, 'This chief transcends his father's fame;'
While pleased amidst the general shouts of Troy,
His mother's conscious heart o'erflows with joy."
    He spoke, and fondly gazing on her charms,
Restored the pleasing burden to her arms;
Soft on her fragrant breast the babe she laid,
Hushed to repose, and with a smile surveyed.

The troubled pleasure soon chastised by fear,
She mingled with the smile a tender tear.
The softened chief with kind compassion viewed,
And dried the falling drops, and thus pursued: —
"Andromache! my soul's far better part!
Why with untimely sorrows heaves thy heart?
No hostile hand can antedate my doom,
Till fate condemns me to the silent tomb.
Fixed is the term to all the race of earth;
And such the hard condition of our birth,
No force can then resist, no flight can save,
All sink alike, the fearful and the brave.
No more — but hasten to thy tasks at home,
There guide the spindle and direct the loom:
Me glory summons to the martial scene, —
The field of combat is the sphere for men;
Where heroes war, the foremost place I claim,
The first in danger as the first in fame."
　　Thus having said, the glorious chief resumes
His towery helmet, black with shading plumes,
His princess parts with a prophetic sigh;
Unwilling parts, and oft reverts her eye,
That streamed at every look; then moving slow,
Sought her own palace and indulged her woe.

The literary quality of many sections of the Bible can not
be surpassed. Oral interpreters may attempt to read from
various modern versions, but it seems difficult to find any
adaptations of the ancient words that equal in poetic quality
the King James version. In the following selections, lines
have been arranged for reading aloud in such a way as to
contribute to meaning, emphasis, and clarity.

WHAT IS MAN, THAT THOU ART MINDFUL OF HIM?
Psalm 8

O Lord our Lord,

how excellent is thy name in all the earth!
who hast set thy glory above the heavens.

Out of the mouth of babes and sucklings
hast thou ordained strength because of thine enemies,
that thou mightest still the enemy and the avenger.

When I consider thy heavens,
the work of thy fingers,
the moon and the stars, which thou hast ordained;
What is man, that thou art mindful of him?
and the son of man, that thou visitest him?

For thou hast made him a little lower than the angels,
and hast crowned him with glory and honour.
Thou madest him to have dominion over the works of thy hands;
thou hast put all things under his feet:
All sheep and oxen,
yea, and the beasts of the field;
The fowl of the air, and the fish of the sea,
and whatsoever passeth through the paths of the seas.

O Lord, our Lord,

how excellent is thy name in all the earth!

THE HEAVENS DECLARE THE GLORY OF GOD

Psalm 19

The heavens declare the glory of God;
and the firmament sheweth his handywork.

Day unto day uttereth speech,
and night unto night sheweth knowledge.
There is no speech nor language,
where their voice is not heard.
Their line is gone out through all the earth,
and their words to the end of the world.

In them hath he set a tabernacle for the sun,
Which is as a bridegroom coming out of his chamber,
and rejoiceth as a strong man to run a race.
His going forth is from the end of the heaven,
and his circuit unto the ends of it:
and there is nothing hid from the heat thereof.

The law of the LORD is perfect,
converting the soul:
the testimony of the LORD is sure,
making wise the simple.
The statutes of the LORD are right,
rejoicing the heart:
the commandment of the LORD is pure,
enlightening the eyes.
The fear of the LORD is clean,
enduring for ever:
the judgments of the LORD are true
and righteous altogether.

More to be desired are they than gold,
yea, than much fine gold:
sweeter also than honey and the honeycomb.

Moreover by them is thy servant warned:
and in keeping of them there is great reward.
Who can understand his errors?
cleanse thou me from secret faults.

.   .   .   .

Let the words of my mouth, and the meditation of my heart,
be acceptable in thy sight,
O LORD, my strength, and my redeemer.

THE LORD IS MY SHEPHERD

Psalm 23

The LORD is my shepherd;
I shall not want.

He maketh me to lie down in green pastures;
he leadeth me beside the still waters.
He restoreth my soul:
He leadeth me in the paths of righteousness
for his name's sake.

Yea, though I walk through the valley
of the shadow of death,
I will fear no evil:
for thou art with me:
thy rod and thy staff they comfort me.

Thou preparest a table before me
in the presence of mine enemies:
thou anointest my head with oil;
my cup runneth over.

Surely goodness and mercy
shall follow me all the days of my life:
and I will dwell
in the house of the LORD
forever.

TO EVERY THING THERE IS A SEASON
Ecclesiastes 3

To every thing there is a season,
and a time to every purpose under the heaven:
    A time to be born,
      and a time to die;
    A time to plant,
      and a time to pluck up that which is planted;
    A time to kill,
      and a time to heal;
    A time to break down,
      and a time to build up;
    A time to weep,
      and a time to laugh;
    A time to mourn,
      and a time to dance;
    A time to cast away stones,
      and a time to gather stones together;
    A time to embrace,
      and a time to refrain from embracing;
    A time to get,
      and a time to lose;
    A time to keep,
      and a time to cast away;
    A time to rend,
      and a time to sew;
    A time to keep silence,
      and a time to speak;
    A time to love,
      and a time to hate;
    A time of war,
      and a time of peace.

. . . .

I said in mine heart, God shall judge
the righteous and the wicked:
for there is a time there
for every purpose and for every work. . . .

CONSIDER THE LILIES HOW THEY GROW

Luke 12 (13-32, excerpted)

And one of the company said unto him,
Master, speak to my brother,
that he divide the inheritance with me.
And he said unto him,
Man, who made me a judge or a divider over you?

And he said unto them,
Take heed, and beware of covetousness:
for a man's life consisteth not
in the abundance of the things which he possesseth.

And he spake a parable unto them, saying,
The ground of a certain rich man
brought forth plentifully:
And he thought within himself, saying,
What shall I do,
because I have no room where to bestow my fruits?

And he said, This will I do:
I will pull down my barns, and build greater;
and there will I bestow all my fruits and my goods.
And I will say to my soul,
Soul, thou hast much goods laid up for many years;
take thine ease,
eat, drink, and be merry.

But God said unto him,
Thou fool,
this night thy soul shall be required of thee:
then whose shall those things be,
which thou hast provided?
So is he that layeth up treasure for himself,
and is not rich toward God.

And he said unto his disciples,
Therefore I say unto you,
Take no thought for your life,
what ye shall eat;
neither for the body,
what ye shall put on.
The life is more than meat,
and the body is more than raiment.

Consider the ravens:
for they neither sow nor reap;
which neither have storehouse nor barn;
and God feedeth them:
how much more are ye better than the fowls?
And which of you with taking thought
can add to his stature one cubit?

If ye then be not able
to do that thing which is least,
why take ye thought for the rest?

Consider the lilies
how they grow:
they toil not, they spin not;
and yet I say unto you,
that Solomon in all his glory
was not arrayed
like one of these.

If then God so clothe the grass,
which is to day in the field,
and to morrow is cast into the oven;
how much more will he clothe you,
O ye of little faith?

. . . .

Fear not, little flock;
for it is your Father's good pleasure
to give you the kingdom.

The following is considered one of the best short stories
ever told. In it Jesus is explaining the forgiving love of God

for his wayward children. He does it in less than 500 words, clearly, compactly, and beautifully.

THE PRODIGAL SON

(Arranged for reading from the King James Version)
Luke 15; 11-32.

A certain man had two sons: And the younger of them said to his father, "Father, give me the portion of goods that falleth to me." And he divided unto them his living.

And not many days after, the younger son gathered all together, and took his journey into a far country, and there wasted his substance with riotous living.

And when he had spent all, there arose a mighty famine in that land; and he began to be in want. And he went and joined himself to a citizen of that country; and he sent him into his fields to feed swine. And he would fain have filled his belly with the husks that the swine did eat: and no man gave unto him.

And when he came to himself, he said, "How many hired servants of my father's have bread enough and to spare, and I perish with hunger! I will arise and go to my father, and will say unto him, 'Father, I have sinned against heaven, and before thee, and am no more worthy to be called thy son: make me as one of thy hired servants.'"

And he arose, and came to his father. But when he was yet a great way off, his father saw him, and had compassion, and ran, and fell on his neck, and kissed him. And the son said unto him, "Father, I have sinned against heaven and in thy sight, and am no more worthy to be called thy son."

But the father said to his servants, "Bring forth the best robe, and put it on him; and put a ring on his hand, and shoes on his feet: And bring hither the fatted calf, and kill it; and let us eat, and be merry: For this my son was dead, and is alive again; he was lost, and is found." And they began to be merry.

Now his elder son was in the field: and as he came and drew nigh to the house, he heard music and dancing. And he called one of the servants, and asked what these things meant. And he said unto him, "Thy brother is come; and thy father hath killed the fatted calf, because he hath received him safe and sound."

And he was angry, and would not go in: therefore came his father out, and entreated him. And he, answering, said to his father, "Lo, these many years do I serve thee, neither transgressed I at any time thy commandment; and yet thou never gavest me a kid, that I might make merry with my friends: But as soon as this thy son was come, which hath devoured thy living with harlots, thou hast killed for him the fatted calf."

And he said unto him, "Son, thou art ever with me, and all that I have is thine. It was meet that we should make merry, and glad: for this thy brother was dead, and is alive again; and was lost, and is found."

THE GREATEST OF THESE IS CHARITY

1 Corinthians 13

Though I speak with the tongues of men and of angels,
and have not charity,
I am become as sounding brass,
or a tinkling cymbal.

And though I have the gift of prophecy,
and understand all mysteries, and all knowledge;
and though I have all faith,
so that I could remove mountains,
and have not charity,
I am nothing.

And though I bestow all my goods to feed the poor,
and though I give my body to be burned,
and have not charity,
it profiteth me nothing.

Charity suffereth long, and is kind;
charity envieth not;
charity vaunteth not itself,
is not puffed up,
Doth not behave itself unseemly,
seeketh not her own,
is not easily provoked,
thinketh no evil;
Rejoiceth not in iniquity,
but rejoiceth in the truth;
Beareth all things,
believeth all things,
hopeth all things,
endureth all things.

Charity never faileth:
but whether there be prophecies, they shall fail;
whether there be tongues, they shall cease;
whether there be knowledge, it shall vanish away.

. . . .

When I was a child, I spake as a child,
I understood as a child,
I thought as a child:
but when I became a man, I put away childish things.

For now we see through a glass, darkly;
but then face to face:
now I know in part;
but then shall I know even as also I am known.

And now abideth faith, hope, charity,
these three;
but the greatest of these is charity.

Geoffrey Chaucer, living around 600 years ago, would have appealed to you as a person. He was a vigorous, witty, active, exciting fellow — not at all the dull poet we have come to think of when reading his work in its original dialect of the time. Translate it into modern English, as Louis Untermeyer has so charmingly in the following selections, and you feel the vibrancy of a man who lived in a world of reality. These two character portraits from THE CANTERBURY TALES are drawn from persons Chaucer met on a Canterbury pilgrimage in April of 1388, when he was in his late forties. Of the seven pilgrims he describes, we give two: one, a young man; one, a young woman.

A SQUIRE
Geoffrey Chaucer
(1340?-1400)
(modern version by Louis Untermeyer)

With him there was his son, a youthful Squire,
A merry blade, a lover full of fire;
With locks as curled as though laid in a press —
Scarce twenty years of age was he, I guess.
In stature he was of an average length,
Wondrously active, bright, and great in strength.
He proved himself a soldier handsomely
In Flanders, in Artois and Picardy,
Bearing himself so well, in so short space,
Hoping to stand high in his lady's grace.
Embroidered was his clothing, like a mead
Full of fresh flowers, shining white and red.
Singing he was, or fluting, all the day —
He was as fresh as is the month of May.

Short was his gown; his sleeves were long and wide;
Well did he sit his horse, and nimbly ride,
He could make songs, intune them or indite,
Joust, play and dance, and also draw and write.
So well could he repeat love's endless tale,
He slept no more than does the nightingale.
Yet he was humble, courteous and able,
And carved before his father when at table.

A PRIORESS

Geoffrey Chaucer
(modern version by Louis Untermeyer)

There also was a nun, a Prioress
Whose smile was simple. Quiet, even coy,
The worst oath that she swore was, "By Saint Loy!"
And she was known as Sister Eglantine.
Sweetly she sang the services divine,
Intoning through her nose the melody.
Fairly she spoke her French, and skillfully,
After the school of Stratford-at-the-Bow —
Parisian French was not for her to know.
Precise at table and well-bred withal
Her lips would never let a morsel fall;
She never wet her fingers in her sauce,
But carried every tidbit without loss
Of even the smallest drop upon her breast.
Manners and good behavior pleased her best.
She always wiped her upper lip so clean
That not a speck of grease was ever seen
Upon the cup from which she drank. Her food
was reached for neatly; she was never rude.
Though her demeanor was the very best,
Her mood was amiable, she loved a jest;
She always tried to copy each report
Of how the latest fashion ran at court,
And yet to hold herself with dignity.
But, speaking of her inner nature, she
Was so devout, so full of sympathy,
She would lament if she would have to see
A mouse caught in a trap, or it had bled.
A few small dogs she had, and these she fed
With roasted meat, or milk and sweetened bread,

And wept aloud if one of them were dead,
Or if a person struck and made them smart —
She was all goodness and a tender heart.
Her wimple draped itself a modest way;
Her nose was straight, her eyes transparent grey,
Her mouth was small, but very soft and red,
Hers was a noble and a fair forehead,
Almost a span in breadth, one realized;
For she was small but scarcely undersized.
Her cloak was well designed, I was aware;
Her arm was graced with corals, and she bare
A string in which the green glass beads were bold,
And from it hung a brilliant brooch of gold
On which there was engraved a large, crowned A,
Followed by *Amor vincit omnia.*

Shakespeare composed a series of 154 sonnets, probably between 1593 and 1601. They are written in three quatrains (four-line rhymed stanzas) and a couplet (two rhymed lines). Sonnets 1-126 were addressed to a beloved friend, a handsome young man, and 127-152 to a mysterious "Dark Lady." Some critics have made much of these sonnets as confessionals, but others agree with Browning that Shakespeare's relationships were platonic. In any case, they present the poet at his best in some of the finest lines ever written.

SONNET XXIX

William Shakespeare
(1564-1616)

When, in disgrace with fortune and men's eyes,
I all alone beweep my outcast state,
And trouble deaf heaven with my bootless cries,
And look upon myself, and curse my fate,
Wishing me like to one more rich in hope,
Featured like him, like him with friends possess'd,
Desiring this man's art and that man's scope,
With what I most enjoy contented least;
Yet in these thoughts myself almost despising,
Haply I think on thee, and then my state,
Like to the larke at break of day arising

From sullen earth, sings hymns at heaven's gate;
  For thy sweet love remember'd such wealth brings
  That then I scorn to change my state with kings.

SONNET CXVI

William Shakespeare

Let me not to the marriage of true minds
Admit impediments. Love is not love
Which alters when it alteration finds,
Or bends with the remover to remove:
O, no! it is an ever-fixèd mark,
That looks on tempests and is never shaken;
It is the star to every wandering bark,
Whose worth's unknown, although his height be taken.
Love's not Time's fool, though rosy lips and cheeks
Within his bending sickle's compass come;
Love alters not with his brief hours and weeks,
But bears it out even to the edge of doom.
  If this be error and upon me proved,
  I never writ, nor no man ever loved.

The life of the sixteenth century Spanish genius, Cervantes, was one of vexation and disappointment, but he was avidly interested in books on chivalry. This combination of circumstances led him to write the marvelous story of the mad genius, Don Quixote (mad only north-northwest), a man of great learning, wit, generosity, courage, and virtue, but a victim of constant disappointment, who wanders the country with his esquire, Sancho Panza, exemplifying the matter-of-fact. Sancho is at times a glutton and a coward, but he is ever the devoted servant to his master.

George Santayana once wrote: "If we could have asked Cervantes what the moral of Don Quixote was to his own mind, he would have told us perhaps that it was this: that the force of idealism is wasted when it does not recognize the reality of things. . . . What is needed is not, of course, that idealism should be surrendered, either in literature or in life; but that in both it should be made efficacious by a better adjustment to the reality it would transform."

Don Quixote is one of the most diverting and delightful books ever written, and the following episode of the windmills, one of the most memorable stories in the book.

The Adventure of the Windmills
DON QUIXOTE

Cervantes
(1547-1616)
(Cut for public performance by Baxter Geeting)

He remained at home fifteen days very quietly, without showing any signs of a desire to take up with his former delusions; and during this time he held lively discussions with his two gossips, the curate and the barber, on the point he maintained, that knights-errant were what the world stood most in need of, and that in him was to be accomplished the revival of knight-errantry. . . .

Meanwhile Don Quixote worked upon a farm-laborer, a neighbor of his, an honest man (if indeed that title can be given to him who is poor), but with very little wit in his pate. In a word, he so talked him over, and with such persuasions and promises, that the poor clown made up his mind to sally forth with him and serve him as esquire. Don Quixote, among other things, told him he ought to be ready to go with him gladly, because at any moment an adventure might occur, that might win an island in the twinkling of an eye and leave him governor of it. . . . all which being settled and done, without taking leave, Sancho Panza of his wife and children, or Don Quixote of his housekeeper and niece, they sallied forth unseen by anybody from the village one night, and made such good way in the course of it that by daylight they held themselves safe from discovery, even should search be made for them.

Sancho rode on his ass like a patriarch, with his *alforjas* and *bota,* and longing to see himself soon governor of the island his master had promised him. . . .

And now said Sancho Panza to his master, "Your Worship will take care, Señor Knight-Errant, not to forget about the island you have promised me, for be it ever so big I'll be equal to governing it."

To which Don Quixote replied: — "Thou must know, friend Sancho Panza, that it was a practice very much in vogue with the knights-errant of old to make their squires governors of the islands or kingdoms they won, and I am determined that there shall be no failure on my part in so liberal a custom. . . .

"In that case," said Sancho Panza, "if I should become a king by one of those miracles your Worship speaks of, even Juana Gutierrez, my old woman, would come to be queen and my children infantes."

"Well, who doubts it?" said Don Quixote.

"I doubt it," replied Sancho Panza; "because for my part I am persuaded that though God should shower down kingdoms upon earth, not one of them would fit the head of Mari Gutierrez. Let me tell you, señor, she is not worth two maravedis for a queen; countess will fit her better, and that only with God's help."

"Leave it to God, Sancho," returned Don Quixote, "for he will give her what suits her best; but do not undervalue thyself so much as to come to be content with anything less than being governor of a province."

"I will not, señor, answered Sancho: "especially as I have a man of such quality for master in your Worship, who will be able to give me all that will be suitable for me and that I can bear."

At this point they came in sight of thirty or forty windmills that there are on that plain, and as soon as Don Quixote saw them he said to his squire, "Fortune is arranging matters for us better than we could have shaped our desires ourselves; for look there, friend Sancho Panza, where thirty or more monstrous giants present themselves, all of whom I mean to engage in battle and slay, and with whose spoils we shall begin to make our fortunes; for this is righteous warfare, and it is God's good service to sweep so evil a breed from off the face of the earth."

"What giants?" said Sancho Panza.

"Those thou seest there," answered his master, "with the long arms; and some have them nearly two leagues long."

"Look, your Worship," said Sancho; "what we see there are not giants but windmills, and what seem to be their arms are the sails that turned by the wind make the millstones go."

"It is easy to see," replied Don Quixote, "that thou art not used to this business of adventures; those are giants; and if thou art afraid, away with thee out of this and betake thyself to prayer, while I engage them in fierce and unequal combat."

So saying, he gave the spur to his steed Rosinante, heedless of the cries his squire Sancho sent after him, warning him that most certainly they were windmills and not giants he was going to attack. He however was so positive they were giants that he neither heard the cries of Sancho, nor perceived, near as he was, what they were; but made at them, shouting, "Fly not, cowards and vile beings, for it is a single knight that attacks you!"

A slight breeze at this moment sprang up, and the great sails began to move; seeing which, Don Quixote exclaimed, "Though ye flourish more arms than the giant Briareus, ye have to reckon with me."

So saying, and commending himself with all his heart to his lady Dulcinea, imploring her to support him in such a peril, with lance in rest and covered by his buckler, he charged at Rosinante's fullest gallop and fell upon the first mill that stood in front of him; but as he drove his lance-point into the sail the wind whirled it round with such force that it shivered the lance to pieces, sweeping with it horse and rider, who went rolling over the plain in a sorry condition. Sancho hastened to his assistance as fast as his ass could go, and when he came up found him unable to move, with such a shock had Rosinante fallen with him.

"God bless me!" said Sancho, "did I not tell your Worship to mind what you were about, for they were only windmills? and no one could have made any mistake about it but one who had something of the same kind in his head."

"Hush, friend Sancho," replied Don Quixote; "the fortunes of war more than any other are liable to frequent fluctuations; and moreover I think, and it is the truth, that that same sage Feiston who carried off my study and books has turned these giants into mills in order to rob me of the glory of vanquishing them, — such is the enmity he bears me; but in the end his wicked arts will avail but little against my good sword."

"God order it as he may," said Sancho Panza; and helping him to rise, got him up again on Rosinante, whose shoulder was half out; and then, discussing the late adventure, they followed the road to Puerto Lapice, for there, said Don Quixote, they could not fail to find adventures in abundance and variety, as it was a great thoroughfare.

In 1798, Samuel Taylor Coleridge and William Wordsworth published a volume of LYRICAL BALLADS in which Wordsworth's aim was to give "the charm of novelty to things of every day . . . to the loveliness and the wonders of the world before us." The following poem was one of the most successful and has charmed generations of readers with its artistic blending of perception and imagination.

THE DAFFODILS

William Wordsworth
(1770-1850)

> I wandered lonely as a cloud
> That floats on high o'er vales and hills,
> When all at once I saw a crowd,
> A host of golden daffodils,
> Beside the lake, beneath the trees
> Fluttering and dancing in the breeze.
>
> Continuous as the stars that shine
> And twinkle on the milky way,
> They stretched in never-ending line
> Along the margin of a bay:
> Ten thousand saw I at a glance
> Tossing their heads in sprightly dance.

The waves beside them danced, but they
Out-did the sparkling waves in glee:
A poet could not but be gay
In such a jocund company!
I gazed — and gazed — but little thought
What wealth the show to me had brought:

For oft, when on my couch I lie
In vacant or in pensive mood,
They flash upon that inward eye
Which is the bliss of solitude;
And then my heart with pleasure fills,
And dances with the daffodils.

George Gordon Byron (called Lord Byron) was a rebellious, melancholy cripple whose rakish and bizarre life has rather overshadowed his poetry; but reading it, we find a dynamic, rhythmic quality that lends itself to oral interpretation. The following sonnet is particularly fine. It refers to a political patriot, Bonnivard, who was imprisoned in the Castle of Chillon for his opinions; but, as anyone knows who has visited Chillon, Byron took liberties with fact both in this and his poem, THE PRISONER OF CHILLON.

SONNET ON CHILLON

George Gordon, Lord Byron
(1788-1824)

Eternal Spirit of the chainless Mind!
    Brightest in dungeons, Liberty! thou art,
    For there thy habitation is the heart —
The heart which love of thee alone can bind;
And when thy sons to fetters are consigned —
    To fetters, and the damp vault's dayless gloom,
    Their country conquers with their martyrdom,
And Freedom's fame finds wings on every wind.
Chillon! thy prison is a holy place,
    And thy sad floor an altar — for 'twas trod,
Until his very steps have left a trace
    Worn, as if thy cold pavement were a sod,
By Bonnivard! May none those marks efface!
    For they appeal from tyranny to God.

Shelley's lyrics such as ODE TO THE WEST WIND have become so popular that they tend to obscure his importance as a philosophical poet. A close friend of Byron, Shelley was also a poet passionately concerned with "reforming the world." Yet we remember and love his lyrical poetry such as the following. This was written, Shelley says, "in a wood that skirts the Arno, near Florence [Italy]." The wind, rising and falling in its tempestuousness, is suggested in the phrasing. See if you can catch the sweep of the wind in your interpretation.

ODE TO THE WEST WIND

Percy Bysshe Shelley
(1792-1822)

I

O wild West Wind, thou breath of Autumn's being,
Thou, from whose unseen presence the leaves dead
Are driven, like ghosts from an enchanter fleeing,

Yellow, and black, and pale, and hectic red,
Pestilence-stricken multitudes: O thou,
Who chariotest to their dark wintry bed

The winged seeds, where they lie cold and low,
Each like a corpse within its grave, until
Thine azure sister of the Spring shall blow

Her clarion o'er the dreaming earth, and fill
(Driving sweet buds like flocks to feed in air)
With living hues and odors plain and hill:

Wild Spirit, which are moving everyhere;
Destroyer and preserver; hear, oh, hear!

II

Thou on whose stream, 'mid the steep sky's commotion,
Loose clouds like earth's decaying leaves are shed,
Shook from the tangled boughs of Heaven and Ocean,

Angels of rain and lightning: there are spread
On the blue surface of thine aery surge,
Like the bright hair uplifted from the head

Of some fierce Maenad, even from the dim verge
Of the horizon to the zenith's height,
The locks of the approaching storm. Thou dirge

Of the dying year, to which this closing night
Will be the dome of a vast sepulchre,
Vaulted with all thy congregated might

Of vapors, from whose solid atmosphere
Black rain, and fire, and hail will burst: oh, hear!

V

Make me thy lyre, even as the forest is:
What if my leaves are falling like its own
The tumult of thy mighty harmonies

Will take from both a deep, autumnal tone,
Sweet though in sadness. Be thou, Spirit fierce,
My spirit! Be thou me, impetuous one!

Drive my dead thoughts over the universe
Like withered leaves to quicken a new birth!
And, by the incantation of this verse,

Scatter, as from an unextinguished hearth
Ashes and sparks, my words among mankind!
Be through my lips to unawakened earth

The trumpet of a prophecy! O Wind,
If Winter comes, can Spring be far behind?

During his early years, William Cullen Bryant was a Calvinist and wrote his best poetry, including THANATOPSIS. Later, he changed views entirely in religion and politics, becoming more liberal in both. But later work never equaled his earlier poetry, inspired by the convictions of youth.

"So live, that when thy summons comes. . . ."
from THANATOPSIS

William Cullen Bryant
(1794-1878)

> So live, that when thy summons comes to join
> The innumerable caravan, which moves
> To that mysterious realm, where each shall take
> His chamber in the silent halls of death,
> Thou go not, like the quarry-slave at night,
> Scourged to his dungeon, but, sustained and soothed
> By an unfaltering trust, approach thy grave
> Like one who wraps the drapery of his couch
> About him, and lies down to pleasant dreams.

Many poets have been influenced by the glory of Greece.
Keats loved to roam in the great London British Museum
where travelers today still see the delights of Grecian artistry
extolled in the following sonnet.

ON SEEING THE ELGIN MARBLES

John Keats
(1795-1821)

> My spirit is too weak — mortality
>   Weighs heavily on me like unwilling sleep,
>   And each imagined pinnacle and steep
> Of godlike hardship tells me I must die
> Like a sick eagle looking at the sky.
>   Yet 'tis a gentle luxury to weep
>   That I have not the cloudy winds to keep,
> Fresh for the opening of the morning's eye.
> Such dim-conceived glories of the brain,
>   Bring round the heart an indescribable feud;
> So do these wonders a most dizzy pain,
>   That mingles Grecian grandeur with the rude
> Wasting of old Time — with a billowy main —
>   A sun — a shadow of a magnitude.

ON FIRST LOOKING INTO CHAPMAN'S HOMER

John Keats

> Much have I travell'd in the realms of gold,
>   And many goodly states and kingdoms seen,
>   Round many western islands have I been
> Which bards in fealty to Apollo hold.
> Oft of one wide expanse had I been told
>   That deep-brow'd Homer ruled as his demesne:
>   Yet did I never breathe its pure serene
> Till I heard Chapman speak out loud and bold.
>
> Then felt I like some watcher of the skies
>   When a new planet swims into his ken;
> Or like stout Cortez when with eagle eyes
>   He stared at the Pacific — and all his men
> Look'd at each other with a wild surmise —
>   Silent, upon a peak in Darien.

An intellectual poet, essayist, and philosopher, who was also at times a teacher and minister, Emerson conceived of life as "spiritual vision" and felt the only way to understand reality was through intuition. His poetry was often harsh and sometimes preachy as in FORBEARANCE.

FORBEARANCE

Ralph Waldo Emerson
(1803-1882)

> Hast thou named all the birds without a gun?
> Loved the wood-rose, and left it on its stalk?
> At rich men's tables eaten bread and pulse?
> Unarmed, faced danger with a heart of trust?
> And loved so well a high behavior
> In man or maid, that thou from speech refrained,
> Nobility more nobly to repay? —
> O, be my friend, and teach me to be thine!

"I love your verses with all my heart," Robert Browning wrote to the 39-year-old invalid spinster, Elizabeth Barrett, adding, "And I love you too." His love was returned and they were secretly married and lived in Italy until her death. Elizabeth wrote her SONNETS FROM THE PORTU-GUESE for her husband with no thought of having them published. Critics have called her too emotional, but no one can deny the eloquence of her beautiful sonnet, HOW DO I LOVE THEE?

How Do I Love Thee?
SONNETS FROM THE PORTUGUESE

Elizabeth Barrett Browning
(1806-1861)

How do I love thee? Let me count the ways.
I love thee to the depth and breadth and height
My soul can reach, when feeling out of sight
For the ends of Being and ideal Grace.
I love thee to the level of every day's
Most quiet need, by sun and candle-light.
I love thee freely, as men strive for right;
I love thee purely, as they turn from praise.
I love thee with the passion put to use
In my old griefs, and with my childhood's faith.
I love thee with a love I seemed to lose
With my lost saints — I love thee with the breath,
Smiles, tears, of all my life! — and, if God choose,
I shall but love thee better after death.

Longfellow's poetry has been criticized for having been drawn from literature, rather than from life. He was a scholarly poet, a college professor. But his popularity did much to bring poetry to the attention of American audiences. His narrative poems such as EVANGELINE, HIA-WATHA, and THE COURTSHIP OF MILES STANDISH established a sort of native mythology. The simplicity and naturalness of poems like NATURE please us when we hear them.

NATURE

Henry Wadsworth Longfellow
(1807-1882)

As a fond mother, when the day is o'er
   Leads by the hand her little child to bed,
   Half willing, half reluctant to be led,
   And leave his broken playthings on the floor,
Still gazing at them through the open door,
   Nor wholly reassured and comforted
   By promises of others in their stead,
   Which, though more splendid, may not please him more;
So Nature deals with us, and takes away
   Our playthings one by one, and by the hand
   Leads us to rest so gently, that we go
Scarce knowing if we wish to go or stay,
   Being too full of sleep to understand
   How far the unknown transcends the what we know.

Whittier had slight formal education, but devoted himself
in essays, articles, and poems to the cause of abolition. After
the Civil War, he wrote his best poetry, including SNOW-
BOUND, which reflects his understanding of common New
England life and country folk.

Winter Night
From SNOW-BOUND

John Greenleaf Whittier
(1807-1892)

As night drew on, and, from the crest
Of wooded knolls that ridged the west,
The sun, a snow-blown traveller, sank
From sight beneath the smothering bank,
We piled, with care, our nightly stack
Of wood against the chimney-back, —
The oaken log, green, huge, and thick,
And on its top the stout back-stick;
The knotty forestick laid apart,
And filled between with curious art

The ragged brush; then, hovering near,
We watched the first red blaze appear,
Heard the sharp crackle, caught the gleam
On whitewashed wall and sagging beam,
Until the old, rude-furnished room
Burst, flower-like, into rosy bloom;
While radiant with a mimic flame
Outside the sparkling drift became,
And through the bare-boughed lilac-tree
Our own warm hearth seemed blazing free.
The crane and pendent trammels showed.
The Turks' heads on the andirons glowed;
While childish fancy, prompt to tell
The meaning of the miracle,
Whispered the old rhyme: *"Under the tree,*
When fire outdoors burns merrily,
There the witches are making tea."

Tennyson, popular and successful during his lifetime, fell
under the attack of critics at the turn of the century. Later
critics found much to praise in his metrical skill and imagery. One of his most successful poems, ULYSSES, pictures
the hero in old age speaking of his longing for adventure.
Tennyson was a Victorian poet (Queen Victoria appointed
him poet laureate) and this poem, like most of his, is influenced by his persistent urge to moralize.

ULYSSES

Alfred, Lord Tennyson
(1809-1892)

It little profits that an idle king
By this still hearth, among these barren crags,
Matched with an aged wife, I mete and dole
Unequal laws unto a savage race,
That hoard, and sleep, and feed, and know not me.
I cannot rest from travel; I will drink
Life to the lees. All times I have enjoyed
Greatly, have suffered greatly, both with those
That loved me, and alone; on shore, and when

Through scudding drifts the rainy Hyades
Vexed the dim sea. I am become a name;
For always roaming with a hungry heart
Much have I seen and known — cities of men
And manners, climates, councils, governments,
Myself not least, but honoured of them all —
And drunk delight of battle with my peers,
Far on the ringing plains of windy Troy.
I am a part of all that I have met;
Yet all experience is an arch wherethrough
Gleams that untraveled world whose margin fades
Forever and forever when I move.
How dull it is to pause, to make an end,
To rust unburnished, not to shine in use!
As though to breathe were life! Life piled on life
Were all too little, and of one to me
Little remains; but every hour is saved
From that eternal silence, something more,
A bringer of new things; and vile it were
For some three suns to store and hoard myself,
And this gray spirit yearning in desire
To follow knowledge like a sinking star,
Beyond the utmost bound of human thought.
    This is my son, mine own Telemachus,
To whom I leave the scepter and the isle —
Well-loved of me, discerning to fulfill
This labor, by slow prudence to make mild
A rugged people, and through soft degrees
Subdue them to the useful and the good.
Most blameless is he, centered in the sphere
Of common duties, decent not to fail
In offices of tenderness, and pay
Meet adoration to my household gods
When I am gone. He works his work, I mine.
    There lies the port; the vessel puffs her sail;
There gloom the dark, broad seas. My mariners,
Souls that have toiled, and wrought, and thought with me —
That ever with a frolic welcome took
The thunder and the sunshine, and opposed
Free hearts, free foreheads — you and I are old;
Old age hath yet his honor and his toil.
Death closes all; but something ere the end,
Some work of noble note, may yet be done,
Not unbecoming men that strove with gods.
The lights begin to twinkle from the rocks;

The long day wanes; the slow moon climbs; the deep
Moans round with many voices. Come, my friends.
'Tis not too late to seek a newer world.
Push off, and sitting well in order smite
The sounding furrows; for my purpose holds
To sail beyond the sunset, and the baths
Of all the western stars, until I die.
It may be that the gulfs will wash us down;
It may be we shall touch the Happy Isles,
And see the great Achilles, whom we knew.
Though much is taken, much abides; and though
We are not now that strength which in old days
Moved earth and heaven, that which we are, we are —
One equal temper of heroic hearts,
Made weak by time and fate, but strong in will
To strive, to seek, to find, and not to yield.

FLOWER IN THE CRANNIED WALL

Alfred, Lord Tennyson

Flower in the crannied wall,
I pluck you out of the crannies,
I hold you here, root and all, in my hand,
Little flower — but *if* I could understand
What you are, root and all, and all in all,
I should know what God and man is.

Browning and Tennyson lived across the nineteenth century.
Tennyson reflected the Victorian influences. Browning was
more liberal. He traveled widely, and when he married
Elizabeth Barrett, enjoyed a full and happy life in Italy
where some of his most expressive poetry was written.

DAY

Robert Browning
(1812-1889)

DAY!
Faster and more fast,
O'er night's brim, day boils at last:

Boils, pure gold, o'er the cloud-cup's brim
Where spurting and suppressed it lay,
For not a froth-flake touched the rim
Of yonder gap in the solid gray
Of the eastern cloud, an hour away;
But forth one wavelet, then another, curled,
Till the whole sunrise, not to be suppressed,
Rose, reddened, and its seething breast
Flickered in bounds, grew gold, then overflowed the world.

PROSPICE

Robert Browning

Fear death? — to feel the fog in my throat,
    The mist in my face,
When the snows begin, and the blasts denote
    I am nearing the place,
The power of the night, the press of the storm,
    The post of the foe;
Where he stands, the Arch Fear in a visible form,
    Yet the strong man must go:
For the journey is done and the summit attained,
    And the barriers fall,
Though a battle's to fight ere the guerdon be gained,
    The reward of it all.
I was ever a fighter, so — one fight more,
    The best and the last!
I would hate that death bandaged my eyes, and forbore,
    And made me creep past.
No! let me taste the whole of it, fare like my peers
    The heroes of old,
Bear the brunt, in a minute pay glad life's arrears
    Of pain, darkness and cold.
For sudden the worse turns the best to the brave,
    The black minute's at end,
And the elements' rage, the fiend-voices that rave,
    Shall dwindle, shall blend,
Shall change, shall become first a peace out of pain,
    Then a light, then thy breast,
O thou soul of my soul! I shall clasp thee again,
    And with God be the rest!

HOME-THOUGHTS, FROM ABROAD

Robert Browning

Oh, to be in England
Now that April's there,
And whoever wakes in England
Sees, some morning, unaware,
That the lowest boughs and the brush-wood sheaf
Round the elm-tree bole are in tiny leaf,
While the chaffinch sings on the orchard bough
In England — now!

And after April, when May follows,
And the whitethroat builds, and all the swallows!
Hark, where my blossomed pear-tree in the hedge
Leans to the field and scatters on the clover
Blossoms and dewdrops — at the bent-spray's edge —
That's the wise thrush; he sings each song twice over,
Lest you should think he never could recapture
The first fine careless rapture!
And though the fields look rough with hoary dew,
All will be gay when noontide wakes anew
The buttercups, the little children's dower,
— Far brighter than this gaudy melon-flower!

. . . "one of the most musical and most imaginative poems about poetry ever written." Louis Untermeyer

ODE

Arthur O'Shaughnessy
(1844-1881)

We are the music-makers,
    And we are the dreamers of dreams,
Wandering by lone sea-breakers,
    And sitting by desolate streams;
World-losers and world-forsakers,
    On whom the pale moon gleams:
Yet we are the movers and shakers
    Of the world for ever, it seems.

> With wonderful deathless ditties
> We build up the world's great cities,
>   And out of a fabulous story
>   We fashion an empire's glory:
> One man with a dream, at pleasure,
>   Shall go forth and conquer a crown;
> And three with a new song's measure
>   Can trample an empire down.
>
> We, in the ages lying
>   In the buried past of the earth,
> Built Nineveh with our sighing,
>   And Babel itself with our mirth;
> And o'erthrew them with prophesying
>   To the old of the new world's worth;
> For each age is a dream that is dying,
>   Or one that is coming to birth.

In the third chapter of MOBY DICK, OR THE WHITE WHALE, the narrator tells of a night at the "Spouter Inn," which has a "dark-looking den — the bar" attended by a "withered old man, who, for their money, dearly sells the sailors delirium and death." The narrator-stranger has asked for a place to sleep the night and has been promised only a share of a harpooner's bed, that being all the space left in the entire establishment. It being a bitter night, our narrator consents to this arrangement, but as a noisy set of mariners enter, "their beards stiff with icicles," he begins to distrust his prospective roommate.

The Spouter Inn
MOBY DICK

Herman Melville
(1819-1891)
(Cut for public performance by Baxter Geeting)

"Landlord," said I, going up to him, "Landlord, stop whittling. I come to your Inn and want a bed; you tell me you can only give me half a one; that the other half belongs to a harpooneer. . . . I now demand of you to speak out and tell me . . . whether I shall be in all respects safe to spend the night with him."

"Wall," said the landlord, fetching a long breath, "this harpooneer has just arrived from the South Seas, where he bought up a lot of 'balmed New Zealand heads, (great curios, ye know) and he's sold all on 'em but one, and that one he's trying to sell tonight, cause tomorrow's Sunday, and it would not do to be sellin' human heads about the streets when folks is goin' to churches. He wanted to, last Sunday, but I stopped him just as he was goin' out of the door with four heads hung on a string, for all the airth like a string of inions."

. . . "Depend upon it, landlord, that harpooneer is a dangerous man."

"He pays reg'lar," was the rejoinder. "But come, it's getting dreadful late, you had better be turning flukes . . . Come along here, I'll give ye a glim in a jiffy;" and so saying, he lighted a candle and held it toward me, offering to lead the way. But I stood irresolute; when looking at a clock in the corner, he exclaimed, "I vum it's Sunday — you won't see that harpooneer tonight; he's come to harbor somewhere — come along then; *do* come; *won't ye* come?"

I considered the matter a moment, and then upstairs we went, and I was ushered into a small room, cold as a clam, and furnished, sure enough, with a prodigious bed, almost big enough indeed for any four harpooneers to sleep abreast.

"There," said the landlord, placing the candle on a crazy old sea-chest, that did double duty as a wash-stand and centre table; "There, make yourself comfortable now, and good night to ye."

. . . I sat down on the side of the bed, and commenced thinking about this head-peddling harpooneer. . . . I got up and took off my monkey jacket, and then stood in the middle of the room thinking. . . . But beginning to feel very cold, I made no more ado, but jumped out of my pantaloons and boots, and then blowing out the light, tumbled into bed. . . . At last I slid off into a light doze, and had pretty nearly made a good offing toward the land of Nod, when I heard a heavy footfall in the passage, and saw a glimmer of light come into the room from under the door.

Lord save me, thinks I, that must be the harpooneer, the infernal head-peddler. But I lay perfectly still, and resolved not to say a word till spoken to. Holding a light in one hand, and that identical New Zealand head in the other, the stranger entered the room, and without looking toward the bed, placed his candle a good way off from me on the floor in one corner . . . and after some difficulty having opened his bag, he commenced fumbling in it, and presently pulled out a sort of tomahawk, and a sealskin wallet with the hair on. . . . I thought something of slipping out of the window, but it was the second floor back. . . . There was no time for shuddering, for now the savage went about something that completely fascinated my attention. Going to his heavy grego, or wrapall, which he had previously hung on a chair, he fumbled in the pockets, and produced at length a curious little deformed image with a hunch on its back . . . and removing the papered fire-board, sets up this little hump-backed image, like a ten-pin, between the andirons.

I now screwed my eyes hard toward the half-hidden image, feeling but ill at ease meanwhile, to see what was to happen next. First he takes about a double handful of shavings out of his grego pocket, and places them carefully before the idol; then laying a bit of ship's biscuit on top and applying the flame from the lamp, he kindles the shavings into a sacrificial blaze. Presently, after many hasty snatches into the fire, and still hastier withdrawals of his fingers, he at last succeeded in drawing out the biscuit; then blowing off the heat and ashes a little, he made a polite offer of it to the little Negro. . . . At last, extinguishing the fire, he took the idol up very unceremoniously and bagged it again in his grego pocket. . . .

All these queer proceedings increased my uncomfortableness, and seeing him now exhibiting strong symptoms of . . . jumping into bed with me, I thought it was high time, now or never, to . . . break the spell. . . .

But the interval I spent in deliberating what to say was a fatal one. Taking up his tomahawk from the table, he examined the head of it for an instant, and then holding it to the light, with his mouth at the handle, he puffed out great clouds of tobacco smoke. The next moment the light was extinguished, and this wild cannibal, tomahawk between his teeth, sprang into bed with me. I sang out, I could not help it now; and giving a sudden grunt of astonishment, he began feeling me.

"Who-ee debel you?" — he at last said — "you no speak-ee, dam-me, I kill-ee." And so saying, the lighted tomahawk began flourishing about me in the dark.

"Landlord, for God's sake, Peter Coffin!" shouted I. "Landlord! Watch! Coffin! Angels! Save me!"

"Speak-ee! tell-ee me who-ee be! or dam-me, I kill-ee!" again growled the cannibal, while his horrid flourishings of the tomahawk scattered the hot tobacco ashes about me. . . . But thank heaven, at that moment the landlord came into the room, light in hand, and leaping from the bed I ran up to him.

"Don't be afraid now," said he, grinning again. "Queequeg here wouldn't harm a hair of your head."

"Stop your grinning," shouted I, "and why didn't you tell me that that infernal harpooneer was a cannibal?"

"I thought ye know'd it; — didn't I tell ye, he was a peddlin' heads around town? — but turn flukes again and go to sleep. Queequeg, look here — you sabbee me, I sabbee you — this man sleepee you — you sabbee?"

"Me sabbee plenty," grunted Queequeg, puffing way at his pipe. . . .

"You gettee in," he added, motioning to me with his tomahawk, and throwing the clothes to one side. He really did this in not only a civil, but a really kind and charitable way. I stood looking at him a moment. For all his tattooings he was on the whole a clean, comely-looking cannibal. What's all this fuss I have been making about, thought I to myself — this man's a human being just as I am: he has just as much reason to fear me as I have to be afraid of him. Better sleep with a sober cannibal than a drunken Christian.

"Goodnight, landlord," said I, "you may go."

I turned in, and never slept better in my life.

Since his death in 1881, Dostoévsky's reputation has grown until now he is recognized as one of the greatest novelists of history. His work is distinguished by its psychological perceptiveness, philosophical understandings, and masterful craftsmanship. All of his finest skill is realized in this scene from CRIME AND PUNISHMENT, in which a poor student, Raskolnikov, who had murdered for money to help his family, meets Sonya, a young girl forced into prostitution to support a drunken father, his wife, and three small children.

The Bible Reading
CRIME AND PUNISHMENT

Fedor Mikhailovitch Dostoévsky
(1821-1881)
(Cut for public performance by Baxter Geeting)

Raskolnikov went straight to the water-side, where Sonya was living. The three-storied house was an old building, painted green. The young man had some difficulty in finding the dvornik, and got from him vague information about the quarters of the tailor Kapernasumov. After having discovered in a corner of the yard the foot of a steep and gloomy staircase, he ascended to the second floor, and followed the gallery facing the court-yard. Whilst groping in the dark, and asking himself how Kapernasumov's lodgings could be reached, a door opened close to him; he seized it mechanically.

"Who is there?" asked a timid female voice.

"It is I. I am coming to see you," replied Raskolnikov, on entering a small ante-room. There on a wretched table stood a candle, fixed in a candlestick of twisted metal.

"Is that you? Good heavens!" feebly replied Sonya, who seemed not to have strength enough to move from the spot.

"Where do you live? Is it here?" And Raskolnikov passed quickly into the room, trying not to look the girl in the face.

A moment afterwards Sonya rejoined him with the candle, and remained stock still before him, a prey to an indescribable agitation. This unexpected visit had upset her — nay, even frightened her. All of a sudden her pale face colored up, and tears came into her eyes. She experienced extreme confusion, united with a certain gentle feeling. Raskolnikov turned aside with a rapid movement and sat down on a chair, close to the table. In the twinkling of an eye he took stock of everything in the room.

This room was large, with a very low ceiling, and was only one let out by the Kapernasumovs; in the wall, on the left-hand side, was a door giving access to theirs. . . . Sonya's room was more like an out-house, of irregular rectangular shape. . . . contained scarcely any furniture. In the right-hand corner was the bed; between the bed and the door, a chair; on the same side, facing the door . . . stood a deal table, covered with a blue cloth; close to the table were two rush chairs. Against the opposite wall . . . was placed a small chest of drawers of unvarnished wood, which seemed out of place in this vacant spot. This was the whole of the furniture. The yellowish and worn paper had everywhere assumed a darkish color, probably the effect of the damp and coal smoke. Everything in the place denoted poverty. . . .

.   .   .   .

"Her lot is fixed," thought he, — "a watery grave, the madhouse, or a brutish existence! . . . . Is it possible that this creature, who still retains a pure mind, should end by becoming deliberately mire-like? . . . ."

.   .   .   .

. . . he examined the girl attentively. "And you — you often pray to God, Sonya?" he asked her.

No answer. Standing by her side, he waited for a reply. "What could I be, what should I be without God?" cried she in a low-toned but energetic voice, and whilst casting on Raskolnikov a rapid glance of her brilliant eyes, she gripped his hand.

"Come, I was not mistaken!" he muttered to himself. — "And what does God do for you?" asked he, anxious to clear his doubts yet more.

For a long time the girl remained silent, as if incapable of reply. Emotion made her bosom heave. "Stay! Do not question me! You have no such right!" exclaimed she, all of a sudden, with looks of anger.

"I expected as much!" was the man's thought.

"God does everything for me!" murmured the girl rapidly, and her eyes sank.

"At last I have the explanation!" he finished mentally, whilst eagerly looking at her.

He experienced a new, strange, almost unhealthy feeling on watching this pale, thin, hard-featured face, these blue and soft eyes which could yet dart such lights and give utterance to such passion; in a word, this feeble frame, yet trembling with indignation and anger, struck him as weird, — nay, almost fantastic. "Mad! she must be mad!" he muttered once more. A book was lying on the chest of drawers. Raskolnikov had noticed it more than once whilst moving about the room. He took it and examined it. It was a Russian translation of the Gospels, a well-thumbed leather-bound book.

"Where does that come from?" asked he of Sonya, from the other end of the room.

The girl still held the same position, a pace or two from the table. "It was lent me," replied Sonya, somewhat loth, without looking at Raskolnikov.

.   .   .   .

He took the book to the light, and turned it over. "Where is mention made of Lazarus?" asked he abruptly.

Sonya, looking hard on the ground, preserved silence, whilst moving somewhat from the table.

"Where is mention made of the resurrection of Lazarus? Find me the passage, Sonya."

The latter looked askance at her interlocutor. "That is not the place — it is the Fourth Gospel," said she dryly, without moving from the spot.

"Find me the passage and read it out!" he repeated, and sitting down again rested his elbow on the table, his head on his hand, and glancing sideways with gloomy look, prepared to listen.

Sonya at first hesitated to draw nearer to the table. The singular wish uttered by Raskolnikov scarcely seemed sincere. Nevertheless she took the book. "Have you ever read the passage?" she asked him, looking at him from out of the corners of her eyes. Her voice was getting harder and harder.

"Once upon a time. In my childhood. Read!"

"Have you never heard it in church?"

"I — I never go there. Do you go often yourself?"

"No," stammered Sonya.

.   .   .   .

"Read! I insist upon it! . . . ."

Sonya opened the book and looked for the passage. Her hands trembled. The words stuck in her throat. Twice did she try to read without being able to utter the first syllable.

"Now a certain man was sick, named Lazarus, of Bethany," she read, at last, with an effort; but suddenly, at the third word, her voice grew wheezy, and gave way like an over-stretched chord. Breath was deficient in her oppressed bosom. Raskolnikov partly explained to himself Sonya's hesitation to obey him; and in proportion as he understood her better, he insisted still more imperiously on her reading. He felt what it must cost the girl to lay bare to him, to some extent, her heart of hearts. She evidently could not, without difficulty, make up her mind to confide to a stranger the sentiments which probably since her teens had been her support. . . . when, what with a sottish father and a stepmother demented by misfortune, to say nothing of starving children, she heard nothing but reproach and offensive clamor. He saw all this, but he likewise saw that notwithstanding this repugnance, she was most anxious to read, — to read to him, and that now, — let the consequences be what they may! The girl's look, the agitation to which she was prey, told him as much, and by a violent effort over herself Sonya conquered the spasm which parched her throat, and continued to read the eleventh chapter of the Gospel according to St. John. She thus reached the nineteenth verse: —

"And many of the Jews came to Martha and Mary, to comfort them concerning their brother. Then Martha, as soon as she heard that Jesus was coming, went and met him; but Mary sat still in the house. Then said Martha unto Jesus, Lord, if thou hadst been here, my brother had not died. But I know that even now, whatsoever thou wilt ask of God, God will give it to thee."

Here she paused, to overcome the emotion which once more caused her voice to tremble.

"Jesus saith unto her, Thy brother shall rise again. Martha saith unto him, I know that he shall rise again in the resurrection at the last day. Jesus said unto her, I am the Resurrection and the Life; he that believeth in me, though he were dead, yet shall he live; and whosoever liveth and believeth in me shall never die. Believest thou this? She saith unto him," —

and although she had difficulty in breathing, Sonya raised her voice, as if in reading the words of Martha she was making her own confession of faith: —

"Yes, Lord: I believe that thou art the Christ, the Son of God, which should come into the world."

She stopped, raised her eyes rapidly on him, but cast them down on her book, and continued to read. Raskolnikov listened without stirring, without turning toward her, his elbows resting on the table, looking aside. Thus the reading continued till the thirty-second verse.

"Then when Mary was come where Jesus was, and saw him, she fell down at his feet, saying unto him, Lord, if thou hadst been here, my brother had not died. When Jesus therefore saw her weeping, and the Jews also weeping which came with her, he groaned in the spirit and was troubled, and said, Where have ye laid him? They said unto him, Lord, come and see. Jesus wept. Then said the Jews, Behold how he loved him. And some of them said, Could not this man, which opened the eyes of the blind, have caused that even this man should not have died?"

Raskolnikov turned towards her and looked at her with agitation. His suspicion was a correct one. She was trembling in all her limbs, a prey to fever. He had expected this. She was getting to the miraculous story, and a feeling of triumph was taking possession of her. Her voice, strengthened by joy, had a metallic ring. The lines became misty to her troubled eyes, but fortunately she knew the passage by heart. At the last line, "Could not this man, which opened the eyes of the blind —" she lowered her voice, emphasizing passionately the doubt, the blame, the reproach of these unbelieving and blind Jews, who a moment after fell as if struck by lightning on their knees, to sob and to believe. "Yes," thought she, deeply affected by this joyful hope, "yes, he — he who is blind, who dares not believe — he also will hear — will believe in an instant, immediately, now, this very moment!"

"Jesus therefore, again groaning in himself, cometh to the grave. It was a cave, and a stone lay upon it. Jesus said, Take ye away the stone. Martha, the sister of him that was dead, saith unto him, Lord, by this time he stinketh: for he hath been dead four days."

She strongly emphasized the word *four*.

"Jesus saith unto her, Said I not unto thee, that if thou wouldst believe, thou shouldst see the glory of God? Then they took away the stone from the place where the dead was laid. And Jesus lifted up his eyes, and said, Father, I thank thee that thou hast heard me. And I know that thou hearest me always; but because of the people which stand by I said it, that they may believe that thou hast sent me. And when he thus had spoken, he cried with a loud voice, Lazarus, come forth. *And he that was dead came forth,"* —

(on reading these words Sonya shuddered, as if she herself had been witness to the miracle)

"bound hand and foot with grave-clothes; and his face was bound about with a napkin. Jesus saith unto them, Loose him, and let him go. *Then many of the Jews which came to Mary, and had seen the things which Jesus did, believed on him."*

She read no more, — such a thing would have been impossible to her, — closed the book, and briskly rising, said in a low-toned and choking voice, without turning toward the man she was talking to, "So much for the resurrection of Lazarus." She seemed afraid to raise her eyes on Raskolnikov, whilst her feverish trembling continued. The dying piece of candle dimly lit up this low-ceiled room, in which an assassin and a harlot had just read the Book of books.

Variously interpreted as surrealism in print, as Freudian-inspired commentary, as symbolism of marvelous inventiveness, the famous ALICE'S ADVENTURES IN WONDERLAND and THROUGH THE LOOKING GLASS are alive with highly readable passages. Fantasy and nonsense, satire and parody run through them as does the delightful inverted logic for which they are renowned.

The Mock-Turtle's Education
ALICE'S ADVENTURES IN WONDERLAND

Lewis Carroll (Charles Lutwidge Dodgson)
(1832-1898)
(Cut for public performance by Baxter Geeting)

"When we were little," the Mock-Turtle went on at last more calmly, though still sobbing a little now and then, "we went to school in the sea. The master was an old Turtle — we used to call him Tortoise—"

"Why did you call him Tortoise, if he wasn't one?" Alice asked.

"We called him Tortoise because he taught us," said the Mock-Turtle angrily; "really you are very dull!"

"You ought to be ashamed of yourself for asking such a simple question," added the Gryphon; and then they both sat silent and looked at poor Alice, who felt ready to sink into the earth. At last the Gryphon said to the Mock-Turtle, "Drive on, old fellow! Don't be all day about it!" and he went on in these words: —

"Yes, we went to school in the sea, though you mayn't believe it —"

"I never said I didn't!" interrupted Alice.

"You did," said the Mock-Turtle.

"Hold your tongue!" added the Gryphon, before Alice could speak. again. The Mock-Turtle went on.

"We had the best of educations — in fact, we went to school every day —"

"*I've* been to a day-school too," said Alice; "you needn't be so proud as all that."

"With extras?" asked the Mock-Turtle a little anxiously.

"Yes," said Alice, "we learned French and music."

"And washing?" said the Mock-Turtle.

"Certainly not!" said Alice indignantly.

"Ah! then yours wasn't a really good school," said the Mock-Turtle in a tone of great relief. "Now at *ours* they had at the end of the bill, 'French, music *and washing* — extra.'"

"You couldn't have wanted it much," said Alice; "living at the bottom of the sea."

"I couldn't afford to learn it," said the Mock-Turtle with a sigh. "I only took the regular course."

"What was that?" inquired Alice.

"Reeling and Writhing, of course, to begin with," the Mock-Turtle replied; "and then the different branches of Arithmetic — Ambition, Distraction, Uglification, and Derision."

"I never head of 'Uglification,'" Alice ventured to say. "What is it?"

The Gryphon lifted up both its paws in surprise. "Never heard of uglifying!" it exclaimed. "You know what to beautify is, I suppose?"

"Yes," said Alice, doubtfully; "it means — to — make — anything prettier."

"Well then," the Gryphon went on, "if you don't know what to uglify is, you *are* a simpleton."

Alice did not feel encouraged to ask any more questions about it, so she turned to the Mock-Turtle and said, "What else had you to learn?"

"Well, there was Mystery," the Mock-Turtle replied, counting off the subjects on his flappers, — "Mystery, ancient and modern, with Seaography; then Drawling — the Drawling-master was an old conger-eel, that used to come once a week: *he* taught us Drawling, Stretching, and Fainting in Coils."

"What was *that* like?" said Alice.

"Well, I can't show it you, myself," the Mock-Turtle said: "I'm too stiff. And the Gryphon never learnt it."

"Hadn't time," said the Gryphon: "I went to the Classical master, though. He was an old crab, *he* was."

"I never went to him," the Mock-Turtle said with a sigh: "he taught Laughing and Grief, they used to say."

"So he did, so he did," said the Gryphon, sighing in his turn, and both creatures hid their faces in their paws.

"And how many hours a day did you do lessons?" said Alice, in a hurry to change the subject.

"Ten hours the first day," said the Mock-Turtle: "nine the next, and so on."

"What a curious plan!" exclaimed Alice.

"That's the reason they're called lessons," the Gryphon remarked: "because they lessen from day to day."

This was quite a new idea to Alice, and she thought it over a little before she made her next remark. "Then the eleventh day must have been a holiday?"

"Of course it was," said the Mock-Turtle.

"And how did you manage on the twelfth?" Alice went on eagerly.

"That's enough about lessons," the Gryphon interrupted in a very decided tone.

Best known for THE RED BADGE OF COURAGE, Stephen Crane, in his short life of 29 years, produced considerable writing that has won him a unique place in American literature. His odd type of poetic construction has been both condemned and admired, but it is dramatic when interpreted with a sense of the symbolism it represents.

THE HEART

Stephen Crane
(1871-1900)

In the desert
I saw a creature, naked, bestial,
Who, squatting upon the ground,
Held his heart in his hands,
And ate of it.
I said, "Is it good, friend?"
"It is bitter — bitter," he answered;
"But I like it
Because it is bitter,
And because it is my heart."

Phyllis McGinley has expressed so well the fickle quality of literary criticism. In this chapter we have presented some of the best authors of past prose and poetry. We turn now to areas of writing in our current century, approaching even some of the "avant-garde." But we do so with a certain timidity arising from the knowledge that much of what we may say in defense of choices in this text may be demolished by critics when they "foregather."

NOTES ON LITERARY REVIVALS

Phyllis McGinley
(1905-   )

It's hard
Keeping up with the *avant-garde*.
There was the time that Donne
Had a place in the sun.
His *lettres* were *belles* of pure gold
And they tolled and they tolled and they tolled,
Until critics in suitable haunts
Took up Kafka (Franz).
Then everyone wanted to herald
The genius of Scott Fitzgerald.
After that, among Prominent Names,
It was utterly Henry James.

In between, of course, there was room
For a Melville boom,
For a peek at Poe, for a dollop
Of Trollope,
And currently people report on
A scrambling aboard
The elegant wagons of Wharton
And Ford Madox Ford.

Oh, it's perfectly clear
That there's change when the critics forgather.
Last year was a Hawthorne year.
Coming up — Willa Cather?

And I'm happy the great ones are thriving,
But what puzzles my head
Is the thought that they needed reviving.
I had never been told they were dead.

developing an understanding
of prose and poetry
of our time (20th century)

> *We cannot read an author for the first time in the same way we read the latest book by an established author. In a new author, we tend to see either only his virtues or only his defects, and even if we do see both, we cannot see the relationship between them.*
> W. H. Auden

> *The universe is so vast, the universe is so various, that we owe it to ourselves to try to understand every kind of experience. . . . Not all the truth about the world, or about our lives, can be set down in straightforward prose, or even in straightforward poetry.*
> Gilbert Highet

It has been said repeatedly that the stumbling block to evaluating twentieth century literature is that we are too close to it. It is difficult to see it *in perspective,* which seems to be the only way we may view anything if we are to eliminate errors in judgment. But, by allowing only time to be the judge, much good, exciting, stimulating, and valuable writing is overlooked. Students and teachers of oral interpretation often fall within the category of the supercautious and much of the same literature has been dominating English and interpretation classes since it first found its way into textbooks. You will find in this text many of the old classics. But we encourage you to broaden your horizons and include in your own collection of readings some of the excellent things which are being written every day.

Not many twentieth century writers equal or surpass the skill of many of the classic authors we have referred to in the previous chapter, but the thrill of discovery is challenging and the search for new, untested material will enlarge your powers of appreciation and discrimination.

The separation of literature into "past" and "present" is questionable practice, of course. Already, much that has been written in the twentieth century has become classic. It is purely for convenience that we do this, since it does seem that a number of changes in attitudes and styles have developed among writers of the twentieth century. We still have authors writing in the Victorian mode, of course, and there are some of historical periods who wrote in such a way that their work will never seem out of style.

twentieth century fiction

If we could characterize fiction of this period, we would say it is concerned primarily with realism, with looking at the common man instead of some idealistic man, with searching for the unvarnished truth about life.

What has influenced fiction in the present century? Mainly, two world wars; a strong heritage of Freudian psychology which revealed a lot about human conduct (not much of it flattering); and the mass movement of men from the land to the city, where they seem to disintegrate and deteriorate more rapidly upon closer contact. All of these influences have focussed attention on the ugliness and sordidness of humanity. Writers have been motivated to write about what they saw, and much fiction has been dominated by oppression, injustice, and degeneracy.

So, in this century we have witnessed an increase in novels of social commentary, a field highlighted by such authors as Theodore Dreiser, Ernest Hemingway, Sinclair Lewis, William Faulkner, Erskine Caldwell, and John Steinbeck. We have seen a rise in novels dealing with the deviations of humanity from what has been considered ethical (such books are constantly battling the censors). We have had many novels dealing with the horrors of war by such eminent writers as Erich Maria Remarque (*All Quiet on the Western Front*), Hemingway (*A Farewell to Arms*), Norman Mailer (*The Naked and the Dead*), James Jones (*From Here to Eternity*), and Herman Wouk (*The Caine Mutiny*).

Within the last ten years or so, a couple of new themes, which have obsessed novelists, are the problems of integration and the possibility of extinction by nuclear war.

Our concern, as interpreters, is to find among these more recent types of material selections which can be quoted and read aloud. There is undoubtedly much excellent writing here, but the bulk of it does not readily adapt to entertainment or to emotional uplift (readers are expected to stimulate, not depress, their listeners).

There is mounting evidence that the American public is not happy with the situation in fiction. Of the more than 25,000 books published yearly, only 12 per cent are novels. Some critics have predicted the end of the 200-year-old literary form known as the novel. James Michener, one of the most successful writers of our time, has said only 80 novelists in the United States are able to make a living with their writing.

Out of the novels which are published each year, however, there are always a few which furnish us excellent, readable prose.

The short story has seen quite a change in status in the twentieth century. It has been altered almost entirely as a literary form and now seems to be on a real decline. This is a problem to the interpreter who has always enjoyed reading aloud a good short story. But we still have a number of magazines, anthologies, and newspapers which offer a variety of shorter narrative selections ranging from the "short-short" story of less than a thousand words to the "novella," which is really a short novel.

The trend in the short story now seems to be away from traditional plot, characterization, and theme. What now passes as a short story may more aptly be described as an episode or a candid-camera shot of some aspect of life (frequently sordid).

twentieth century nonfiction

By far the bulk of current writing, as we have said, is taking place in the area of nonfiction. Many of our outstanding novelists and short story writers have turned to the world of commentary, essay, research, and fact-finding to make a living. Some of them are writing for the movies and television. Their names appear quite frequently in our better magazines and quite often as scenarists of motion pictures. Some excellent sources for contemporary readings are the quality magazines such as *Harper's, Atlantic, Saturday Review,* and *Horizon,* to mention a few only.

Quite a few books are being published each year which include excellent essays, memoirs, humorous writings, and speeches adaptable for oral interpretation.

twentieth century poetry

In poetry, the twentieth century has been a time of revolt against old standards, styles, and forms of expression. Poets, like other creative artists, tend to align themselves with avant-garde movements, so a number of contemporary poets write in unrhymed free verse and blank verse.[1] Much of what is being written in the name of poetry is shallow, meaningless non-poetry. Some new poetry is excellent for imagery, word color, and symbolism, but does not read aloud well.

The major problem that we, as interpreters, battle in contemporary poetry is the problem of obscurity. We have explored the attitude, of course, that a poem should *be*, not necessarily mean anything. But there is a tendency of some modern poets to carry this privilege of being vague to the point of having their work lack all communication with the public. If a poem or work of prose cannot be made to arouse empathy in the persons who listen to it, then we may reasonably assume the fault is with the author, not the interpreter or the listener. Marya Mannes, whose essays are remarkable for their clarity and perception, comments on this condition among modern writers which leads them to write in a language nobody can understand. She says, wryly, "In a misguided attempt . . . to perfect the skill of communicating clearly to others, I have sacrificed the priceless ingredient of true talent: obscurity."

summary

By waiting for time to make judgments, we miss the challenge of discovering new works of merit for oral interpretation from among the vast output of contemporary writers. Our problems in finding "readings" are brought about by the tendency in many writers of the twentieth century to focus attention on the ugly, the sordid, the depressing. Another problem is the practice of many modern poets and writers to obscure meaning. Despite these problems, a great deal of excellent and challenging material for oral interpretation appears every year in new works of fiction, nonfiction, periodicals, and even newspapers. The search for it is worth the effort.

---

[1]Free verse generally is free of rules of versification; lines depend on meaningful stress rather than mechanical beat. Blank verse usually means unrhymed iambic pentameter, or, loosely, five accents, or beats, to the line. (Shakespeare used iambic pentameter frequently.)

applications: _____

1. Search magazines or anthologies of good collections of prose and poetry of the twentieth century for examples of readings you feel merit association with the classics. Select at least three of each (prose and poetry) which you would particularly like to use in class.
2. Prepare a paragraph or two of background material for each of your chosen selections.
3. Of these, take the one selection which most appeals to you and which you think might be surprising to the group. Proceed as before in preparing it for oral performance. Don't forget the help of a good listener.
4. Read carefully the following selections of poetry which give you in somewhat chronological order (according to date of poet's birth) the highlights of Twentieth Century Poetry. Be ready to give in class an honest and informed appraisal of each. For selections of Twentieth Century Prose you are referred to other chapters in this text which present outstanding selections in the field of essay, short story, novel, and nonfiction.

preview of chapter 7:
DEVELOPING AN UNDERSTANDING OF THE USES OF DRAMA IN ORAL INTERPRETATION

Oral interpreters have always made use of the valuable resources of material to be found in dramatic literature. Since plays are written primarily for oral performance, cuttings from such give interpreters ideal vehicles for many audience situations.

In giving readings from plays, however, many of us face a problem of breaking down mythological attitudes about our adequacies or inadequacies as interpreters. We will be exploring these as well as some of the types of drama suitable for oral interpretation.

selections for study and interpretation

(Twentieth Century Poetry)

> Housman was an English poet and Latin scholar, and his best known collection of poems, called A SHROPSHIRE LAD, published in 1896, evidences influences of traditional and classical ballads and verse. His poetry, such as LOVELIEST OF TREES, is deceptively simple and free of ornamentation.

LOVELIEST OF TREES

A. E. Housman
(1859-1936)

> Loveliest of trees, the cherry now
> Is hung with bloom along the bough.
> And stands about the woodland ride
> Wearing white for Eastertide.
>
> Now, of my threescore years and ten,
> Twenty will not come again,
> And take from seventy springs a score,
> It only leaves me fifty more.
>
> And since to look at things in bloom
> Fifty springs are little room,
> About the woodlands I will go
> To see the cherry hung with snow.

> George Santayana was Spanish by birth, but came to Boston when he was nine. He was educated in our country and taught at Harvard, but he always felt somewhat inadequate in English because, as he said, "I never drank in in childhood the homely cadences . . . which in pure spontaneous poetry set the essential key. . . ." However, as Louis Untermeyer points out, Santayana was unjustly critical of himself, his verse is "richly woven. His sonnets are particularly warm in phrase and deep in feeling. . . . they are among the finest contemporary examples of the form."

O WORLD

George Santayana
(1863-1952)

O world, thou choosest not the better part!
It is not wisdom to be only wise,
And on the inward vision close the eyes,
But it is wisdom to believe the heart.
Columbus found a world, and had no chart,
Save one that faith deciphered in the skies;
To trust the soul's invincible surmise
Was all his science and his only art.
Our knowledge is a torch of smoky pine
That lights the pathway but one step ahead
Across a void of mystery and dread.
Bid, then, the tender light of faith to shine
By which alone the mortal heart is led
Unto the thinking of the thought divine.

A poet of profound influence on twentieth century poetry
was William Butler Yeats, born near Dublin in 1865. His
life was devoted to a renascence of culture in Ireland. He
wrote dramas and lyrics, recreated folk tales, and examined
the Irishman in a world of psychological truth. As he grew
old, he despaired of ever seeing Ireland culturally aware and
wrote: "Romantic Ireland's dead and gone./ It's with
O'Leary in the grave." But no poet has been the subject of
more posthumous praise. W. H. Auden wrote a magnificent
poetic tribute which he called "In Memory of W. B. Yeats"
and in which he implored, "Earth, receive an honored
guest;/ William Yeats is laid to rest. . . ."
Few poems can match the musical and dreamlike quality
of these nostalgic verses. They are perfect for interpretation.

THE LAKE ISLE OF INNISFREE

William Butler Yeats
(1865-1939)

I will arise and go now, and go to Innisfree,
And a small cabin build there, of clay and wattles made;

Nine bean rows will I have there, a hive for the honey bee,
And live alone in the bee-loud glade.

And I shall have some peace there, for peace comes dropping
slow,
Dropping from the veils of the morning to where the cricket
sings;
There midnight's all a glimmer, and noon a purple glow,
And evening full of the linnet's wings.

I will arise and go now, for always night and day
I hear lake water lapping with low sounds by the shore;
While I stand on the roadway, or on the pavements gray,
I hear it in the deep heart's core.

WHEN YOU ARE OLD

William Butler Yeats

When you are old and grey and full of sleep,
And nodding by the fire, take down this book
And slowly read, and dream of the soft look
Your eyes had once, and of their shadows deep;

How many loved your moments of glad grace,
And loved your beauty with love false or true,
But one man loved the pilgrim soul in you,
And loved the sorrows of your changing face;

And bending down beside the glowing bars,
Murmur, a little sadly, how Love fled
And paced upon the mountains overhead
And hid his face amid a crowd of stars.

The English poet, Ralph Hodgson, was a fierce defender
of dumb animals, and waged furious battle to end the
practice of clipping dogs' tails and ears. Personally, however, he was reticent. He lectured on English literature in
Japan, but came later in life to the United States. His lyrics
such as TIME, YOU OLD GYPSY MAN, are ethereal in
their beauty.

TIME, YOU OLD GYPSY MAN

Ralph Hodgson
(1872-1962)

Time, you old gypsy man,
  Will you not stay,
Put up your caravan
  Just for one day?

All things I'll give you
Will you be my guest,
Bells for your jennet
Of silver the best,
Goldsmiths shall beat you
A great golden ring,
Peacocks shall bow to you,
Little boys sing,
Oh, and sweet girls will
Festoon you with may.
Time, you old gypsy,
Why hasten away?

Last week in Babylon,
Last night in Rome,
Morning, and in the crush
Under Paul's dome;
Under Paul's dial
You tighten your rein —
Only a moment,
And off once again;
Off to some city
Now blind in the womb,
Off to another
Ere that's in the tomb.

Time, you old gypsy man,
  Will you not stay,
Put up your caravan
  Just for one day?

Wallace Stevens was an insurance company executive in
Hartford, Conn., writing his brilliant poetry in spare time

and separating his business and poetic lives so completely that some of his colleagues knew nothing of the duality of his existence. In his writing he underlined the necessity of creatively transforming reality, making of a routine and drab life something that had meaning and inspiration through poetry. His collected poems filled a book of over 500 pages, and included many like THE POEMS OF OUR CLIMATE that appeal to the senses as well as to the intellect.

THE POEMS OF OUR CLIMATE

Wallace Stevens
(1879-1955)

I

Clear water in a brillant bowl,
Pink and white carnations. The light
In the room more like a snowy air,
Reflecting snow. A newly-fallen snow
At the end of winter when afternoons return.
Pink and white carnations — one desires
So much more than that. The day itself
Is simplified: a bowl of white,
Cold, a cold porcelain, low and round,
With nothing more than the carnations there.

II

Say even that this complete simplicity
Stripped one of all one's torments, concealed
The evilly compounded, vital I
And made it fresh in a world of white,
A world of clear water, brilliant-edged,
Still one would want more, one would need more,
More than a world of white and snowy scents.

III

There would still remain the never-resting mind,
So that one would want to escape, come back
To what had been so long composed.
The imperfect is our paradise.
Note that, in this bitterness, delight,
Since the imperfect is so hot in us,
Lies in flawed words and stubborn sounds.

Another poet who lived really two lives of great influence was William Carlos Williams, a medical doctor, who was filled with delight and affection for everything in his surroundings. He recorded his reactions in detail, vividly and realistically, as in SIGNS EVERYWHERE OF BIRDS NESTING, WHILE, at the same time practicing medicine for over 50 years. He left several volumes of poetry, novels, plays, and short stories. The Pulitzer Prize for poetry was awarded to him posthumously in 1963.

SIGNS EVERYWHERE OF BIRDS NESTING, WHILE

William Carlos Williams
(1883-1963)

Signs everywhere of birds nesting, while
in the air, slow, a crow zigzags
with heavy wings before the wasp-thrusts
of smaller birds circling about him
that dive from above stabbing for his eyes

Walking —

he leaves the path, finds hard going
across-field, stubble and matted brambles
seeming a pasture — but no pasture
— old furrows, to say labour sweated or
had sweated here

a flame,
spent.

The file-sharp grass

When! from before his feet, half tripping,
picking a way, there starts
a flight of empurpled wings!
— invisibly created (their
jackets dust-grey) from the dust kindled
to sudden ardor!

They fly away, churring! until
their strength spent they plunge
to the coarse cover again and disappear
— but leave, livening the mind, a flashing
of wings and a churring song .

AND a grasshopper of red basalt, boot-long,
tumbles from the core of his mind,
a rubble-bank disintegrating beneath a
tropic downpour

Chapultepec! grasshopper hill!

— a matt stone solicitously instructed
to bear away some rumor
of the living presence that has preceded
it, out-precedented its breath .

These wings do not unfold for flight —
no need!
the weight (to the hand) finding
a counter-weight or counter buoyancy
by the mind's wings .

He is afraid! What then?

Before his feet, at each step, the flight
is renewed. A burst of wings, a quick
churring sound :
                              couriers to the ceremonial of love!
— aflame in flight!
                    — aflame only in flight!
                              No flesh but the caress!
He is led forward by their announcing wings.

Elinor Wylie idolized Shelley and loved beauty with exquisite passion. Her verse was skillful, precise, and fastidious.
Have you ever heard a more perfect description of the
silence of snow than that in VELVET SHOES? Can you
interpret this poem with the delicacy it deserves?

VELVET SHOES

Elinor Wylie
(1885-1928)

Let us walk in the white snow
  In a soundless space;
With footsteps quiet and slow,
  At a tranquil pace,
  Under veils of white lace.

I shall go shod in silk,
  And you in wool,
White as a white cow's milk,
  More beautiful
  Than the breast of a gull.

We shall walk through the still town
  In a windless peace;
We shall step upon white down,
  Upon silver fleece,
  Upon softer than these.

We shall walk in velvet shoes:
  Wherever we go
Silence will fall like dews
  On white silence below.
  We shall walk in the snow.

Robinson Jeffers, a West Coast poet, son of a minister, is best known for his adulation of individualism, his affinity for the strong and primitive, his pessimistic attitudes. In Carmel, with the help of twin sons, he built a home of stone boulders, which became his tower of escape. One of his poems is called TO THE STONE-CUTTERS and in it he mentions the "honey of peace in old poems."

TO THE STONE-CUTTERS

Robinson Jeffers
(1887-1962)

Stone-cutters fighting time with marble, you fore-defeated
Challengers of oblivion
East cynical earnings, knowing rock splits, records fall down,
The square-limbed Roman letters
Scale in the thaws, wear in the rain. The poet as well
Builds his monument mockingly;

For man will be blotted out, the blithe earth die, the brave sun
Die blind and blacken to the heart:
Yet stones have stood for a thousand years, and pained
    thoughts found
The honey of peace in old poems.

One of the most lauded and influential poets of our century is Marianne Moore, whose 1951 COLLECTED POEMS won three outstanding awards: the Pulitzer Prize, National Book Award, and Bollingen Prize. Her verse, like that of some other modern poets, is oddly patterned, and modestly Miss Moore has said that anyone could do what she does, which she doubts is even poetry. Her metrical patterns demand careful preparation. Her appeal is intellectual. If you look into other of her poems, you will find she is often inspired by her fondness for animals.

WHAT ARE YEARS?

Marianne Moore
(1887-   )

What is our innocence,
what is our guilt? All are
    naked, none is safe. And whence
is courage: the unanswered question,
the resolute doubt —
dumbly calling, deadly listening — that
in misfortune, even death,
        encourages others
        and in its defeat, stirs

    the soul to be strong? He
seems deep and is glad, who
    accedes to mortality
and in his imprisonment, rises
upon himself as
the sea in a chasm, struggling to be
free and unable to be,
        in its surrounding
        finds its continuing.

    So he who strongly feels,
behaves. The very bird,
    grown taller as he sings, steels
his form straight up. Though he is captive,
his mighty singing
says, satisfaction is a lowly
thing, how pure a thing is joy.
        This is mortality,
        this is eternity.

Thomas Stearns (T. S.) Eliot, American-born English poet, critic, and dramatist, has had a revolutionary effect on poetry. He broke with tradition both in subject matter and in technique. For subjects, he drew upon his own experience and social background. His technical changes brought into poetry the idioms of natural speech. In later poetry, Eliot's conversion to the Anglican Church is reflected in his choice of subject. JOURNEY OF THE MAGI describes regret, despair, hope, and salvation in a vision of the past, symbolizing the soul's struggle for rebirth.

JOURNEY OF THE MAGI

T. S. Eliot
(1888-1965)

"A cold coming we had of it,
Just the worst time of the year
For a journey, and such a long journey:
The ways deep and the weather sharp,
The very dead of winter."
And the camels galled, sore-footed, refractory,
Lying down in the melting snow.
There were times we regretted
The summer palaces on slopes, the terraces,
And the silken girls bringing sherbet.
Then the camel men cursing and grumbling
And running away, and wanting their liquor and women,
And the night-fires going out, and the lack of shelters,
And the cities hostile and the towns unfriendly
And the villages dirty and charging high prices:
A hard time we had of it.
At the end we preferred to travel all night,
Sleeping in snatches,
With the voices singing in our ears, saying
That this was all folly.

Then at dawn we came down to a temperate valley,
Wet, below the snow line, smelling of vegetation;
With a running stream and a water-mill beating the darkness,
And three trees on the low sky,
And an old white horse galloped away in the meadow.
Then we came to a tavern with vine-leaves over the lintel.
Six hands at an open door dicing for pieces of silver,

And feet kicking the empty wine-skins.
But there was no information, and so we continued
And arriving at evening, not a moment too soon
Finding the place; it was (you may say) satisfactory.

And this was a long time ago, I remember,
And I would do it again, but set down
This set down
This: were we led all that way for
Birth or Death? There was a Birth, certainly,
We had evidence and no doubt. I had seen birth and death,
But had thought they were different; this Birth was
Hard and bitter agony for us, like Death, our death.
We returned to our places, these Kingdoms,
But no longer at ease here, in the old dispensation,
With an alien people clutching their gods.
I should be glad of another death.

Conrad Aiken's poetry has been compared by Untermeyer
to the "languid nocturnes" of Chopin and the "wavering
melodies" of Debussy, and perhaps this thought will help in
the interpretation of the strange images and indefinite movement of THIS IS THE SHAPE OF THE LEAF.

This Is the Shape of the Leaf
from PRIAPUS AND THE POOL

Conrad Aiken
(1889-   )

This is the shape of the leaf, and this of the flower,
And this the pale bole of the tree
Which watches its bough in a pool of unwavering water
In a land we never shall see.

The thrush on the bough is silent, the dew falls softly,
In the evening is hardly a sound. . . .
And the three beautiful pilgrims who come here together
Touch lightly the dust of the ground.

Touch it with feet that trouble the dust but as wings do,
Come shyly together, are still,
Like dancers who wait in a pause of the music, for music
The exquisite silence to fill. . . .

This is the thought of the first, and this of the second,
And this the grave thought of the third:
"Linger we thus for a moment, palely expectant,
And silence will end, and the bird

"Sing the pure phrase, sweet phrase, clear phrase in the twilight
To fill the blue bell of the world;
And we, who on music so leaflike have drifted together,
Leaflike apart shall be whirled

"Into what but the beauty of silence, silence forever? . . ."
. . . This is the shape of the tree,
And the flower, and the leaf, and the three pale beautiful
     pilgrims:
This is what you are to me.

Among the strongest of the Negro poets who have contributed richly to the cultural life of the United States was
Claude McKay, who inspired much literary activity in Harlem following his 1922 publication, HARLEM SHADOWS.
One of the loveliest of his poems for oral interpretation
is FLAME-HEART.

FLAME-HEART

Claude McKay
(1890-1948)

So much have I forgotten in ten years,
     So much in ten brief years! I have forgot
What time the purple apples come to juice,
     And what month brings the shy forget-me-not.
I have forgot the special, startling season
     Of the pimento's flowering and fruiting;
What time of year the ground doves brown the fields
     And fill the noonday with their curious fluting.
I have forgotten much, but still remember
The poinsettia's red, blood-red in warm December.

I still recall the honey-fever grass,
     But cannot recollect the high days when
We rooted them out of the ping-wing path
     To stop the mad bees in the rabbit pen.

I often try to think in what sweet month
  The languid painted ladies used to dapple
The yellow byroad mazing from the main,
  Sweet with the golden threads of the rose apple.
I have forgotten — strange — but quite remember
The poinsettia's red, blood-red in warm December.

What weeks, what months, what time of the mild year
  We cheated school to have our fling at tops?
What days our wine-thrilled bodies pulsed with joy
  Feasting upon blackberries in the copse?
Oh, some I know! I have embalmed the days,
  Even the sacred moments when we played,
All innocent of passion, uncorrupt,
  At noon and evening in the flame-heart's shade.
We were so happy, happy, I remember,
Beneath the poinsettia's red in warm December.

MacLeish has expended much of his poetic effort on political messages, often in the form of verse plays. He has been Librarian of Congress, director of the Office of Facts and Figures, assistant director of the Office of War Information, and assistant secretary of state. When he has not been writing socially or politically inspired poems and essays, he has composed such effective poems as IMMORTAL AUTUMN.

IMMORTAL AUTUMN
Archibald MacLeish
(1892-   )

I speak this poem now with grave and level voice
In praise of autumn of the far-horn-winding fall
I praise the flower-barren fields the clouds the tall
Unanswering branches where the wind makes sullen noise

I praise the fall it is the human season now
No more the foreign sun does meddle at our earth
Enforce the green and thaw the frozen soil to birth
Nor winter yet weigh all with silence the pine bough

But now in autumn with the black and outcast crows
Share we the spacious world the whispering year is gone
There is more room to live now the once secret dawn
Comes late by daylight and the dark unguarded goes

Between the mutinous brave burning of the leaves
And winter's covering of our hearts with his deep snow
We are alone there are no evening birds we know
The naked moon the tame stars circle at our eaves

It is the human season on this sterile air
Do words outcarry breath the sound goes on and on
I hear a dead man's cry from autumn long since gone

I cry to you beyond this bitter air.

E. E. Cummings has become more noted for his eccentricity of punctuation than for anything else. Actually his odd style was meant to contribute to the meaning and interpretation of rhythmic pattern. He was at times lyrical, bitter, satirical, and humorous, and used slang, dialect, and jazz beats in his poems. See if, in the following poem, the typography does not help you interpret the meaning, emphasis, and rhythms.

O SWEET SPONTANEOUS EARTH

E. E. Cummings
(1894-1962)

> O sweet spontaneous
> earth how often have
> the
> doting
>
>   fingers of
> prurient philosophers pinched
> and
> poked
>
> thee
> ,has the naughty thumb
> of science prodded
> thy

beauty   . how
often have religions taken
thee upon their scraggy knees
squeezing and

buffeting thee that thou mightest conceive
gods
    (but
true

to the incomparable
couch of death thy
rhythmic
lover

    thou answerest

them only with

      spring)

Hart Crane suffered from many things: instability of character, almost too much curiosity satiated only by experimentation, and a bewildering assortment of ideas which he tried to bunch together in his work, resulting in confusion rather than clarity. In his last years, however, he was working on a more disciplined volume of poetry in which ROYAL PALM was to have appeared. It indicates the genius which was lost to the world in his early death.

ROYAL PALM

Hart Crane
(1899-1932)

Green rustlings, more-than-regal charities
Drift coolly from that tower of whispered light.
Amid the noontide's blazed asperities
I watched the sun's most gracious anchorite

Climb up as by communings, year on year
Uneaten of the earth or aught earth holds,
And the gray trunk, that's elephantine, rear
Its frondings sighing in aethereal folds.

Forever fruitless, and beyond that yield
Of sweat the jungle presses with hot love
And tendril till our deathward breath is sealed —
It grazes the horizons, launched above

Mortality — ascending emerald-bright,
A fountain at salute, a crown in view —
Unshackled, casual of its azured height,
As though it soared suchwise through heaven too.

The fine quality of Stanley Kunitz's poetry is becoming more and more admired. His contribution to the American literary scene in the way of biographical dictionaries (BRITISH AUTHORS OF THE NINETEENTH CENTURY, AMERICAN AUTHORS: 1600-1900, TWENTIETH CENTURY AUTHORS, and BRITISH AUTHORS BEFORE 1800) which he has co-edited with Howard Haycraft, is appreciated by all students of literature.

In the following poems we see the diversity of Kunitz' poetic talent.

THE WALTZER IN THE HOUSE

Stanley Kunitz
(1905-   )

A sweet, a delicate white mouse,
A little blossom of a beast,
Is waltzing in the house
Among the crackers and the yeast.

O the swaying of his legs!
O the bobbing of his head!
The lady, beautiful and kind,
The blue-eyed mistress, lately wed,

Has almost laughed away her wits
To see the pretty mouse that sits
On his tiny pink behind
And swaying, bobbing, begs.

She feeds him tarts and curds,
Seed packaged for the birds,
And figs, and nuts, and cheese;
Polite as Pompadour to please
The dainty waltzer of her house,
The sweet, the delicate, the innocent white mouse.

As in a dream, as in a trance,
She loves his rhythmic elegance,
She laughs to see his bobbing dance.

THE ILLUSIONIST

Stanley Kunitz

My name is sand: I make
Dumbshows on windowshades;
Wring hands; dissolve; swirl back;
Play furious, grim charades.
In airless room confined,
Thick with the curds of night,
I live upon my mind,
Am six-foot parasite;
Am envy, like a vein
Run dry; am hypocrite,
Whose bonecase (melted down)
Shimmers with scaly wit.
What have I not permitted?
What flagrant postures taken?
Nor shown the head matted
Nor the white forehead broken,
But parodied my life,
Assumed eccentric forms,
Retreated into leaf,
Made branches of my arms;
Groveled; ah, clung in hiding
To my father's rotten wall.

Kneel, spirit. At this beheading
Thy spongy faces fall.

W. H. Auden is a poet, dramatist, and critic whose ideas and ideologies have changed over the years but who has not been afraid to rewrite and edit reprints of poetry to suit his newer political and religious beliefs. He has been widely diverse in his writing, his interests extending from opera librettos to popular music-hall verse, from critical essays to sonnets. In NOTHING IS GIVEN: WE MUST FIND OUR LAW, he turns philosopher.

NOTHING IS GIVEN: WE MUST FIND OUR LAW

W. H. Auden
(1907-   )

Nothing is given: we must find our law.
Great buildings jostle in the sun for domination;
Behind them stretch like sorry vegetation
The low recessive houses of the poor.

We have no destiny assigned us:
Nothing is certain but the body; we plan
To better ourselves; the hospitals alone remind us
of the equality of man.

Children are really loved here, even by police:
They speak of years before the big were lonely,
And will be lost.

                    And only
The brass bands throbbing in the parks foretell
Some future reign of happiness and peace.

We learn to pity and rebel.

Stephen Spender, friend and associate of Auden, covers his reactions to conditions of poverty, unemployment, injustice, and human suffering of all types in his poetry. AN ELEMENTARY SCHOOL CLASSROOM IN A SLUM is an excellent example of his passionate concern for the world's unfortunate people.

AN ELEMENTARY SCHOOL CLASSROOM IN A SLUM

Stephen Spender
(1909-   )

Far far from gusty waves, these children's faces.
Like rootless weeds the torn hair round their paleness.
The tall girl with her weighed-down head. The paper-seeming
boy with rat's eyes. The stunted unlucky heir
Of twisted bones, reciting a father's gnarled disease,
His lesson from his desk. At back of the dim class,
One unnoted, sweet and young: his eyes live in a dream
Of squirrels' game, in tree room, other than this.

On sour cream walls, donations. Shakespeare's head
Cloudless at dawn, civilized dome riding all cities.
Belled, flowery, Tyrolese valley. Open-handed map
Awarding the world its world. And yet, for these
Children, these windows, not this world, are world,
Where all their future's painted with a fog,
A narrow street sealed in with a lead sky,
Far, far from rivers, capes, and stars of words.

Surely Shakespeare is wicked, the map a bad example
With ships and sun and love tempting them to steal —
For lives that slyly turn in their cramped holes
From fog to endless night? On their slag heap, these children
Wear skins peeped through by bones and spectacles of steel
With mended glass, like bottle bits on stones.
All of their time and space and foggy slum
So blot their maps with slums as big as doom.

Unless, governor, teacher, inspector, visitor,
This map becomes their window and these windows
That open on their lives like crouching tombs
Break, O break open, till they break the town
And show the children to the fields and all their world
Asure on their sands, to let their tongues
Run naked into books, the white and green leaves open
The history theirs whose language is the sun.

Karl Shapiro has influenced poetry in America through his
work as critic and editor of such magazines as POETRY
and PRAIRIE SCHOONER. His best known poems con-

cern World War II. He has taken strong positions against stereotype thinking and social injustices. But he has a range of passion that extends even to an ecstatic appreciation of a beautiful car.

BUICK

Karl Shapiro
(1913-   )

As a sloop with a sweep of immaculate wing on her delicate spine
And a keel as steel as a root that holds in the sea as she leans,
Leaning and laughing, my warm-hearted beauty, you ride, you ride,
You tack on the curves with parabola speed and a kiss of goodbye,
Like a thoroughbred sloop, my new high-spirited spirit, my kiss.

As my foot suggests that you leap in the air with your hips of a girl,
My finger that praises your wheel and announces your voices of song,
Flouncing your skirts, you blueness of joy, you flirt of politeness,
You leap, you intelligence, essence of wheelness with silvery nose,
And your platinum clocks of excitement stir like the hairs of a fern.

But how alien you are from the booming belts of your birth and the smoke
Where you turned on the stinging lathes of Detroit and Lansing at night
And shrieked at the torch in your secret parts and the amorous tests,
But now with your eyes that enter the future of roads you forget;
You are all instinct with your phosphorous glow and your streaking hair

And now when we stop it is not as the bird from the shell that I leave
Or the leathery pilot who steps from his bird with a sneer of delight,

And not as the ignorant beast do you squat and watch me
    depart,
But with exquisite breathing you smile, with satisfaction of love,
And I touch you again as you tick in the silence and settle in
    sleep.

One of the few poets who could read aloud as well as write
poetry, Dylan Thomas, the Welsh genius, was brought to
an untimely death through uncontrollable drinking. But he
never ceased to vibrate to the nostalgic joys of youth.
FERN HILL recalls a happy picture of a boy's summer on
a Welsh farm.

FERN HILL

Dylan Thomas
(1914-1953)

Now as I was young and easy under the apple boughs
About the lilting house and happy as the grass was green,
   The night above the dingle starry,
     Time let me hail and climb
   Golden in the heydays of his eyes,
And honoured among wagons I was prince of the apple towns
And once below a time I lordly had the trees and leaves
     Trail with daisies and barley
   Down the rivers of the windfall light.

And as I was green and carefree, famous among the barns
About the happy yard and singing as the farm was home,
   In the sun that is young once only,
     Time let me play and be
   Golden in the mercy of his means,
And green and golden I was huntsman and herdsman, the
         calves
Sang to my horn, the foxes on the hills barked clear and cold,
    And the sabbath rang slowly
   In the pebbles of the holy streams.

All the sun long it was running, it was lovely, the hay —
Fields high as the house, the tunes from the chimneys, it was air
   And playing, lovely and watery
     And fire green as grass.
   And nightly under the simple stars

As I rode to sleep the owls were bearing the farm away,
All the moon long I heard, blessed among stables, the nightjars
  Flying with the ricks, and the horses
    Flashing into the dark.

And then to awake, and the farm, like a wanderer white
With the dew, come back, the cock on his shoulder: it was all
  Shining, it was Adam and maiden,
    The sky gathered again
  And the sun grew round that very day.
So it must have been after the birth of the simple light
In the first, spinning place, the spellbound horses walking warm
  Out of the whinnying green stable
    On to the fields of praise.

And honoured among foxes and pheasants by the gay house
Under the new made clouds and happy as the heart was long,
  In the sun born over and over,
    I ran my heedless ways,
  My wishes raced through the house-high hay
And nothing I cared, at my sky blue trades, that time allows
In all his tuneful turning so few and such morning songs
  Before the children green and golden
    Follow him out of grace,

Nothing I cared, in the lamb white days, that time would take
    me
Up to the swallow thronged loft by the shadow of my hand,
  In the moon that is always rising,
    Nor that riding to sleep
  I should hear him fly with the high fields
And wake to the farm forever fled from the childless land.
Oh as I was young and easy in the mercy of his means,
    Time held me green and dying
  Though I sang in my chains like the sea.

Cornel Adam, novelist and historian, musician, college professor, and poet, has been involved in a number of interesting cultural and social projects. His verse drama, THE ATOM CLOCK, won the Maxwell Anderson award in 1950. His historical novel, FOUR DAYS IN JULY, was widely acclaimed. His earliest published writings at the age of 18 and his latest work are in the field of poetry. LINES FOR TERESA is a sonnet from his 1965 publication, FIFTY POEMS.

LINES FOR TERESA

Cornel Adam
(1915-   )

> I never claimed to make your beauty deathless:
> Your loving self will long outlast my rhyme.
> Of words I built no cage to trap a breathless
> Bird song, unbetrayable by time.
> I never vowed my love would prove immortal:
> The pyramids are crumbling with the moon.
> Time's trampling feet will find the smallest portal
> And hide with sand the flowers of night or noon.
>
> We climbed our hills above the clouds one evening
> And ate red apples by a pool of Mars
> Or Venus: as blind young gods set worlds a-wheeling,
> We flung our apple cores among the stars.
> And since I could not catch eternities,
> I caught but that one moment: here it is.

Looking at poetry with traditional attitudes, one does not always appreciate at first some of the exciting things that are being done as contemporary poets experiment with fresh images and unusual techniques of putting down their thoughts. May Swenson is writing in a purely individual style. Her attitudes are motivated by a delight in living and she is perceptually aware of natural phenomena that escape the less curious and thoughtful person. Have you, for example, ever really considered how it might feel to be a bird for a while — to "feel like a bird"? The lines are arranged to help communicate the ideas. Read them thoughtfully.

FEEL LIKE A BIRD

May Swenson
(1919-   )

> feel like A Bird
> understand
> he has no hand

instead A Wing
close-lapped
mysterious thing

in sleeveless coat
he halves The Air
skipping there
like water-licked boat

lands on star-toes
finger-beak in
feather-pocket
finds no coin

in neat head like
seeds in A Quartered
Apple eyes join
sniping at opposites
stereoscope The Scene
Before

close to floor giddy
no arms to fling
A Third Sail
spreads for calm
his tail

hand better
than A Wing?
to gather A Heap
to count
to clasp A Mate?

or leap
lone-free and mount
on muffled shoulders
to span A Fate?

Richard Wilbur, like many of our influential modern poets, has taught on collegiate levels. His work is usually rhymed and metered. With thoughtful preparation, it reads aloud easily and well.

AFTER THE LAST BULLETINS

Richard Wilbur
(1921-   )

After the last bulletins the windows darken
And the whole city founders easily and deep,
Sliding on all its pillows
To the thronged Atlantis of personal sleep,

And the wind rises. The wind rises and bowls
The day's litter of news in the alleys. Trash
Tears itself on the railings,
Soars and falls with a soft crash,

Tumbles and soars again. In empty lots
Our journals spiral in a fierce noyade
Of all we thought to think,
Or caught in corners cramp and wad

And twist our words. And some from gutters flail
Their tatters at the tired patrolman's feet
Like all that fisted snow
That cried beside his long retreat

Damn you! damn you! to the emperor's horses' heels.
Oh none too soon through the air white and dry
Will the clear announcer's voice
Beat like a dove, and you and I

From the heart's anarch and responsible town
Rise by the subway-mouth to life again,
Bearing the morning papers,
And cross the park where saintlike men,

White and absorbed, with stick and bag remove
The litter of night, and footsteps rouse
With confident morning sound
The songbirds in the public boughs.

HEART'S NEEDLE, first volume of poetry by W. D. Snodgrass, was awarded the Pulitzer Prize in 1959. His deeply
personal poetry, among the finest being written by the
younger generation of poets, is polished and influenced by

traditional forms, but the ideas and concepts are often surprising and almost sensational. THE OPERATION, one of his best, sends chills up the spine as you read it.

THE OPERATION

W. D. Snodgrass
(1926-   )

From stainless steel basins of water
They brought warm cloths and they washed me,
From spun aluminium bowls, cold Zephiran sponges,
    fuming;
Gripped in the dead yellow glove, a bright straight razor
Inched on my stomach, down my groin,
Paring the hair off. They left me
White as a child, not frightened. I was not
Ashamed. They clothed me, then,
In the thin, loose, light, white garments,
The delicate sandals of poor Pierrot,
A schoolgirl first offering her sacrament.

I was drifting, inexorably, on toward sleep.
In skullcaps, masked, in blue-green gowns, attendants
Towed my cart, afloat in its white cloths,
The body with its tributary poisons borne
Down corridors of the diseased, thronging:
The scrofulous faces, contagious grim boys,
The huddled families, weeping, a staring woman
Arched to her gnarled stick, — a child was somewhere
Screaming, screaming — then, blind silence, the elevator rising
To the arena, humming, vast with lights; blank hero,
Shackled and spellbound, to enact my deed.

Into flowers, into women, I have awakened.
Too weak to think of strength, I have thought all day,
Or dozed among standing friends. I lie in night, now,
A small mound under linen like the drifted snow.
Only by nurses visited, in radiance, saying, Rest.
Opposite, ranked office windows glare; headlamps, below,
Trace out our highways; their cargoes under dark tarpaulins,
Trucks climb, thundering, and sirens may
Wail for the fugitive. It is very still. In my brandy bowl
Of sweet peas at the window, the crystal world
Is inverted, slow and gay.

Poet Ralph S. Pomeroy is a member of the Department of Dramatic Art and Speech faculty at the University of California at Davis. His publications include a volume of poetry, A PREY OF DIVERSE' COLORS, from which this selection and a later one are taken. Pomeroy's poetry is written to be read aloud. Much can be contributed by the interpreter.

THREE BEFORE BEDTIME

Ralph S. Pomeroy
(1926-   )

Will work, will surely work,
Will tranquilize, you say?
Why then I'll try
The prescribed number at
The prescribed times.
Or more. Or oftener. Or both.

For my friends assure me
That my mind needs freeing —
Needs to lose or banish,
Somehow send away
Those reds, hectic reds
And frantic greens of being:

Each one a knob, nub, hub
Hasp, helm, helve
By which we grasp
Ourselves, unseeing,
Webbed in pale structures
Of our panic days.

Versatility marks the writing of John Updike, better known for his novels, but who has written a number of short stories, and whose first published book in 1958 and whose 1963 publication, TELEPHONE POLES AND OTHER POEMS, place him among the most promising younger poets. Updike writes not only serious poetry, but has the wit and facility to turn out exceptionally fine light verse (usually

with serious undertones). THOUGHTS WHILE DRIVING
HOME like these have plagued many a young man.

THOUGHTS WHILE DRIVING HOME

John Updike
(1932-   )

Was I clever enough? Was I charming?
Did I make at least one good pun?
Was I disconcerting? Disarming?
Was I wise? Was I wan? Was I fun?

Did I answer that girl with white shoulders
Correctly, or should I have said
(Engagingly), "Kierkegaard smolders,
But Eliot's ashes are dead"?

And did I, while being a smarty,
Yet some wry reserve slyly keep,
So they murmured, when I'd left the party,
"He's deep. He's deep. He's deep"?

Frank B. Smith is representative of many deeply motivated
young poets working and studying on American campuses.
He has been writing under the direction of Philip Levine
at Fresno State College, and William Dickey at San Francisco State College in California.

PEREGRINE

Frank B. Smith
(1944-   )

I schooled her in the dark, hooded, to blind
And keep her tame. She seemed to know the glove,
And settled on my hand as if resigned.

Later, I felt her fight when her winged shove
Against the air drove her claws tight, fighting the bind
Of the jesses that held her from the air above.

When I let her jesses go, she seemed to find
Her old life again, where meat of dove,
Duck, and rabbit were found, and quickly won.

Today, I found her lying by the field,
Her breast ripped up by buckshot, her bloody talons
Holding a fat dove that she would not yield.

developing an understanding
of the uses of drama
in oral interpretation

Most actors before each performance put on costumes and make-up. . . . But they forget the most important part, which is the inner preparation. . . . Why do not they put make-up and a costume on their souls?

From *An Actor Prepares*
Constantin Stanislavski

This, then, is the reason that . . . dramas . . . exist: to convey such propositions as "Life is tragic" or "Susanna is beautiful" . . . by putting us through a whole series of experiences that make us feel toward life . . . as the author did.

From *Language in Thought and Action*
S. I. Hayakawa

Some of the finest material available to the oral interpreter is to be found in dramatic literature. Drama, as suggested by the above quotations, gets to the heart and soul of life. It is the closest we can come in literature to firsthand experience. A skilled playwright is able to shape characters who speak and react convincingly; he plots experiences which explain fundamental truths about life. The skilled interpreter is able to communicate to his audience the essence of the playwright's message.

Plays, of course, are written primarily for oral performance, although some are written to be read silently. Many plays contain moving selections of prose and poetry, and readings taken from them do not necessarily need to be explained in terms of the total play. Others, skillfully cut and presented, may afford an interpreter an ideal vehicle for a complete performance.

Most dramatic literature has built-in audience appeal, for it tells a story devoid of description and comment. Drama, therefore, is even more direct than story-telling.

three myths about interpretation of drama

In facing the prospect of interpreting dramatic literature, most students who have not been on the stage in an actual play feel overwhelmed by lack of what they so often label "talent" and "experience." Others, who have appeared frequently in school or community plays, often experience a confidence which may be their undoing in facing the responsibilities of an interpreter. Let us put these misconceptions into focus by stating them as myths.

Myth I: "You are talented or you are not talented in acting. It is necessary to be talented in acting before you can become an interpreter able to perform a reading from a play. You are a 'born actor' or you aren't. Therefore, if you haven't already shown that you are endowed with acting talent, you might as well avoid the whole area of dramatic reading."

Myth II: "You can't read from plays unless you have already had experience by being in them. Only the *experienced actor* can successfully interpret a play." This myth goes on to the conclusion that acting in a play is a frightening experience (it is, viewed in the abstract) and therefore interpreting scenes from a play is a frightening experience.

Myth III: This myth, enjoyed by the so-called talented and experienced actor, might read like this: "Ever since I was a small child I have shown great talent. My parents noticed it from the beginning. I've been in plays and plays. I have no trouble memorizing lines and taking parts. Therefore, I am a 'natural' when it comes to interpreting dramatic literature."

Of the three myths, the THIRD is the hardest to deal with in classes in interpretation. As we look a little closer at the unique attitudes and skills involved in interpretation as opposed to acting, we will see they differ considerably; therefore, a great amount of talent *and* skill in acting is not necessarily the best preparation for interpretation. It is often exceedingly difficult for trained actors to bring cooperative attitudes to the unique problems involved in *interpreting* a play, or scenes from a play, as opposed to *acting* them. The interpreter views the play as a piece of literature which he is to communicate as a whole, in most cases. The affectations of diction, gesture, voice, and movement which distinguish individual performances in acting very often are entirely inappropriate to the interpretation of a play and serve to interfere with the communication process. The trained, experienced actor is used to playing the part of one character. The interpreter must be capable of suggesting several characters, assuming from time to time his own personality as commentator in order to explain action or plot not depicted, lapses of time, and changes of setting. To ask a highly trained and experienced actor to step into the role of interpreter is very much like asking the concertmaster of an orchestra to take over the job of director. He may be able to do it very well, but in taking up the baton and putting down the bow he is going to have to view the performance of the orchestra from an entirely different perspective.

In approaching the interpretation of dramatic material then, it is well to review the myths which may be limiting you. Perhaps you are suffering from one of the three suggested. You may be dominated by others — your voice isn't loud enough, your appearance isn't sufficiently dramatic, you haven't seen enough legitimate drama to know what it's all about.

Remember, the interpretation of dramatic literature is very much like the reading of any other good literary material. The interpreter's problems are almost the same. He is aiming to get others to feel and understand as he thinks the author intended. He aims to communicate. He is working for response, clear and direct. His job is to understand the ESSENCE of the play selection or character and, by careful attention to intonation, inflection, and attitudes, to transmit that ESSENCE to his listeners.

the challenge of interpreting dramatic literature

While many students will seek to avoid dramatic literature because of myths about their competence in interpretation, we do not mean to infer that a good performance in this area is easy. Perhaps a really fine reading of a dramatic selection is the greatest of all interpretative assignments. Not only does it require that the performer be able to suggest how a character acts and thinks — he will have to do this without benefit of props, stage set, or costume. If he uses any of these, they will be mere suggestions of what one would see in a staged play.

An interpretation of dramatic material also requires at times that the performer be able to switch from character to character with clarity and facility. It requires that the interpreter "become himself" at times, and this, very often, is the most difficult thing for a trained actor to do.

As the oral interpreter approaches the use of dramatic material, he must be able to throw off almost totally the words, ideas, prejudices, and concepts which control him as an individual. He must be flexible.

Only an interpreter who has taken time to thoroughly understand the roles he must project, the motives and aims of the playwright, and the total play itself will be able to handle a successful reading, delivering it with authority and conviction.

differences beween acting and interpretation

We have suggested in our discussions a number of differences between acting and interpretation. Let us continue, exploring a bit more in detail what these differences are. Understanding them will serve to dispel the validity of myths which tend to inhibit students from exploring the world of dramatic literature.

In relation to physical aspects, the staged play requires scenery, costuming, make-up, and different people for different characters. An oral interpretation of that same play by one individual means little or no scenery, costuming, and make-up, and very little moving about. Lines in a staged play are memorized. Lines in an interpretation are seldom memorized. It is considered preferable nowadays for the interpreter to hold or have a script or book plainly in sight, even though he may have almost memorized a play reading. This establishes him as an interpreter or middleman between author and listener.

Instead of acting a part, the interpreter SUGGESTS characterizations.

In summarizing the differences between acting and interpreting dramatic selections, it might help to picture the interpreter as an artist who paints abstractions and the actor as one who strives for photographic likenesses. It is entirely possible that the abstraction of a character will be even more meaningful in the minds of listeners than the closer resemblance to reality in the acted character. The interpreter must emphasize the significant and unique qualities of the characters he suggests, while the actor displays the full spectrum of individual differences.

differences between interpretation and impersonation

Between acting and interpretation, as we have seen, there are basic differences in preparation and performance. What about impersonation and interpretation? Here the line of demarcation narrows.

For many years, America has had impersonators. Today we frequently see on stage, in night clubs, and on television people who are gifted at stepping into the role of another person — taking on his appearance, speaking with his voice, saying the type of thing he would say. These are impersonators; usually they perform with little or no props. The impersonator is coming closer to acting than the interpreter ordinarily does.

Impersonators sometimes do affect costumes, props (limited), and some scenery. In this case, especially when the performer continues in a role for a substantial length of time, we call him a monologist or mono-actor. Some of the more famous monologists of recent times have been Ruth Draper, Cornelia Otis Skinner, and — more specialized in his approach — Hal Holbrook, who limits himself on occasions to impersonating Mark Twain. The monologist is really more an actor than interpreter.

interpreting drama with taste and restraint

There is a danger in approaching the interpretation of dramatic material that the accouterments of acting will get in the way of tasteful performance. By accouterments we mean the physical affectations of the actor. It is considered in rather poor taste to indulge too freely in the changes of voice, posture, and appearance which distinguish characters in a play production. The art of oral interpretation is to SUGGEST such changes rather than to SHOW them. In other words, the practice of shaking, bending over, and limping to depict an old man is to be frowned upon. A mere suggestion of the infirmities of age in voice and diction is enough to get the idea across. As in dressing well, to err on the side of being understated is better than to be too obvious. However, it is well not to rely too completely on the imagination of your listeners. Your suggestion of characterization must be sufficient to reach out and communicate with the audience.

types of drama suitable for oral interpretation

The oral interpreter will find in dramatic literature very exciting material. Some plays actually read aloud better than they perform. Others demand performance to be understood. It is up to the interpreter to develop some skill in selecting suitable readings.

What types of drama are there?

Traditionally, drama has been divided into "Tragedy" and "Comedy," but these are misnomers in our time. Tragedy has meant conflict (conflict between man and a foe, between man and another man or men, between man and a social evil or some flaw in his character) which ends in defeat. In Tragedy, man is the loser. Comedy has simply meant conflict in which man was the winner. Comedy, then, has not always meant something funny. Tragedy has not necessarily meant bloodshed and death.

Other labels which have been applied to types of drama include melodrama (overdone sentiment, heightened action, or thrills), farce (emphasis on the ridiculous, broad humor), and burlesque ("making fun of," often cheap). Among the types of drama currently in vogue are fantasy and realism. We see both on the stage, in movies, and on television.

An extreme form of play which has found its way onto modern stages and imposed itself in modern dramatic literature is the "journalistic play." Often this type goes too far in spilling blood, stirring up controversy, and picturing man at his worst. Theatrical illusion is shattered.

A baffling form of drama which has increased in popularity over the past ten years is the play being written for the "theatre of the absurd." Such writers as Samuel Beckett, Eugene Ionesco, and Edward Albee have displayed a fascinating power over public taste in writing plays which specialize in ambiguity. For example, a passage from Beckett's much-performed WAITING FOR GODOT reads:

> . . . the practice of sports such as tennis football running cycling swimming flying floating riding gliding conating camogie skating tennis of all kinds dying flying sports of all sorts autumn summer winter tennis of all kinds hockey of all sorts penicilline and succedanea in a word I resume.
> . . .

As pointed out by drama critic Walter Kerr,[1] the IMPOSSIBILITY OF COMMUNICATION between humans is at the basis of much "absurd" drama. "In many plays," he says, ". . . much is made of the fact that words are slippery, unstable tools, not to be trusted as tokens of meaning." Other recurring themes are the "incrustation of conformity" or the effects of "herd behavior" and "loss of identity" in which we enter a blank world such as that created by Beckett, where waiting for nothing takes up a whole evening. It is an interesting type of drama to look into and presents some possibilities for interpreters who are willing to mine an ore which hasn't yet proved either its worth or its total worthlessness.

Looking at the various types of drama we have discussed, it is obvious that a discriminating interpreter can find readings of considerable variety.

---

[1]Walter Kerr, "Making A Cult of Confusion," *Horizon,* September, 1962.

Some periods in drama's history have left us with material which has proved its worth, and it is from this heritage that we do well to select readings in this class, although a foray into contemporary drama and even the "theatre of the absurd" is not to be discouraged for more venturesome souls!

some outstanding periods of drama

1. The Greek Theatre: Poetry is conceded to be the earliest literary form of the Greeks, but much of this was essentially dramatic. The great religious festivals of the Greeks introduced poetic drama. Celebrating in honor of Dionysius, god of wine, choruses of 50 men were heard in contrast to perhaps ONE voice which carried on a type of dialogue with the chorus. This probably stimulated the idea of plays with several voices or parts being heard in the delineation of a story. Some of the greatest Greek dramatists, whose works offer possibilities for oral interpretation, are Sophocles (*Antigone* and *Electra*), Euripides (*Medea*), and Aristophanes (*Lysistrata*).

2. Renaissance Drama: Among the dramatists who influenced writers of the following centuries, none was more important than Molière, whose real name was Jean Baptiste Poquelin, master of French comedy. In his ability as a writer and influence on his successors, Molière has been compared to Shakespeare. His rare talent for characterization, both with respect to individuals and to types, and his ability to suggest a moral without moralizing still make his plays lively reading. Among those which offer possibilities for oral interpreters are: *Tartuffe, Le Misanthrope,* and *The Imaginary Invalid.*

3. The Elizabethan Era: This is perhaps the greatest of all dramatic periods. From this outstanding age William Shakespeare's many works are filled with material for oral interpretation. We won't endeavor to list them.

Others who lived during this era and whose works offer material for readings include Christopher Marlowe (*Tamburlaine the Great, Doctor Faustus*) and John Dryden, whose best known play is *All for Love.*

4. Eighteenth Century Drama: Among the writers who left perennially popular plays are Oliver Goldsmith (*She Stoops to Conquer*) and Richard Brinsley Sheridan, master of dialogue and characterization. Some of his better known plays from which selections may be taken are *The Rivals* and *The School for Scandal.*

5. Modern Drama: The playwright credited with ushering in modern drama is the eminent Norwegian, Henrik Ibsen, who conceived of drama

as an instrument of social reform and protest against hypocrisy. His plays which offer excellent interpretative material include *A Doll's House, Peer Gynt, Ghosts, Hedda Gabler, The Wild Duck,* and *The Master Builder.* George Bernard Shaw produced such plays as *Candida, Pygmalion,* and *Saint Joan,* with much material for interpretation. Edmond Rostand wrote a poetic drama, *Cyrano de Bergerac,* in which stunning excerpts for interpretation can be found.

6. Contemporary Drama: Among the many more contemporary playwrights who have produced dramas that lend themselves to individual interpretation are Tennessee Williams (*The Glass Menagerie, Summer and Smoke*), Arthur Miller (*Death of A Salesman*), Christopher Fry (*The Lady's Not For Burning*), and George S. Kaufman and Moss Hart (*The Man Who Came to Dinner*). There are many more fine contemporary dramatists and plays from which you may take reading selections.

summary

Dramatic literature is rich in material for oral interpretation since drama is close to the heart and soul of life, or direct experience. But we need to approach the interpretation of dramatic material in a different manner than does the actor; hence we do not need to feel limited by so-called lack of acting talent, stage voice, and distinguished physical bearing. An overreliance on acting experience may work detrimentally to the realization of fine interpretative performance.

Basic to interpretation of dramatic literature, again, is the concept of communication. Flexibility in performance is imperative in an interpreter, whereas it may work against an actor.

The differences between acting and interpreting dramatic selections can be likened to differences in the approach of an artist depicting realistic scenes as opposed to the approach of an artist painting an abstract of those scenes. The impersonator comes closer to acting than does the interpreter, at times using some props, costumes, and other devices of the actor.

Drama must be interpreted with taste and restraint. Age, sex, and characterization should be suggested rather than shown.

The dramatic literature at our disposal ranges over a wide variety of styles, from early Greek tragedy to contemporary "theatre of the absurd." The discriminating interpreter may find exciting readings from dramatists of all ages and styles.

applications: _____

1. Compose a statement relative to your own feelings about your readiness for interpreting dramatic material. Examine your feelings carefully to discover if they are warped by "myths" concerning your talent and experience.
2. List as many similarities as you can think of between the interpreter's problems in reading poetry and his problems in reading drama. Are there any differences of substantial nature?
3. Read the selections given at the end of this chapter.
4. Discover on your own, from any one of the periods outlined in this chapter, a dramatic reading which seems to suit your needs. Give your reasons for the selection.

preview of chapter 8:

SELECTING, EVALUATING, AND
PREPARING MATERIAL

In the next chapter, we will be discussing the Personal Anthology and its value to the motivation of your search for new reading materials and to the development of your powers of evaluation.

We also will be considering certain methods of preparing readings, which have been used by interpreters without too much attention to their validity. We will endeavor to suggest some generally valid steps of preparation which can be adapted to individual needs.

an understanding of drama use in oral interpretation

selections for study and interpretation

In the following selections, some of the finest material from dramatic literature is excerpted for study and practice to motivate the best of which you are capable in interpreting emotion and character. These selections have been chosen because they emphasize various aspects of human character — nobility, loyalty, virtue, courage, and compassion — as well as many emotional responses of human nature — regret, ridicule, hope, fear, anger, and joy. Think of these as you start your preparation of any of the following selections, and establish first the *essence* of the character you are to portray.

In a careful preparation for public performance of any selection you need to gather all the information you can about the play from which an excerpt is taken; of the dramatist; of the period in which it was written. All of this information is necessary to understand the character whose role you are stepping into, however briefly.

And, of course, no preparation can overlook the attention which must be given to vocal and physical skills required in suggesting characters in their many aspects.

selections for one male

1. **Mark Antony's speech, "Friends, Romans, countrymen," from JULIUS CAESAR by Shakespeare.**

   (*This funeral speech calls upon all the powers of wit and persuasaion of Mark Antony, magnificently loyal to the slain Caesar, as he inflames the Roman populace against the conspirators, Brutus and Cassius.*)

MARK ANTONY:

Friends, Romans, countrymen, lend me your ears;
I come to bury Caesar, not to praise him.
The evil that men do lives after them;
The good is oft interred with their bones:
So let it be with Caesar. The noble Brutus
Hath told you Caesar was ambitious.
If it were so, it was a grievous fault,

And grievously hath Caesar answered it.
Here, under leave of Brutus and the rest —
For Brutus is an honourable man;
So are they all, all honourable men —
Come I to speak in Caesar's funeral.
He was my friend, faithful and just to me —
But Brutus says he was ambitious;
And Brutus is an honourable man.
He hath brought many captives home to Rome,
Whose ransoms did the general coffers fill.
Did this in Caesar seem ambitious?
When that the poor have cried, Caesar hath wept;
Ambition should be made of sterner stuff.
Yet Brutus says he was ambitious;
And Brutus is an honourable man.
You all did see that on the Lupercal
I thrice presented him a kingly crown,
Which he did thrice refuse. Was this ambition?
Yet Brutus says he was ambitious;
And, sure, he is an honourable man.
I speak not to disprove what Brutus spoke,
But here I am to speak what I do know.
You all did love him once, not without cause.
What cause withholds you then, to mourn for him?
O judgement! thou art fled to brutish beasts,
And men have lost their reason. Bear with me,
My heart is in the coffin there with Caesar,
And I must pause till it come back to me.

> (*Here, various citizens begin to mumble that there is "much
> reason in his sayings" and one says "There's not a nobler man
> in Rome than Antony." He continues. . .*)

But yesterday the word of Caesar might
Have stood against the world; now lies he there,
And none so poor to do him reverence.
O masters, if I were disposed to stir
Your hearts and minds to mutiny and rage,
I should do Brutus wrong, and Cassius wrong,
Who, you all know, are honourable men.
I will not do them wrong; I rather choose
To wrong the dead, to wrong myself and you,
Than I will wrong such honourable men.

> (*At this point, Antony speaks of Caesar's will, which he says
> he doesn't mean to read but which he assures the populace
> bequeaths them a "rich legacy." But the people insist on hearing
> it. Antony says to read it would be to "inflame" them, to make*)

> them "mad." They cry, "The will! The testament!" so Antony
> continues. . .)

You will compel me, then, to read the will?
Then make a ring around the corpse of Caesar,
And let me show you him that made the will.
Shall I descend? And will you give me leave?

> (*He descends as they whisper, "Room for Antony, most noble
> Antony!"*)

If you have tears, prepare to shed them now.
You all do know this mantle. I remember
The first time ever Caesar put it on;
'Twas on a summer's evening, in his tent,
That day he overcame the Nervii.

> (*Cleverly, Antony draws their attention to the wounds and rents
> left by the conspirators' daggers; describes the fall of the noble
> and mighty Caesar; entreats them not to be stirred up to mutiny,
> but to remember that they who had done this deed were "hon-
> ourable men." By now, the populace is full of anger, and Antony
> calls to them to stay — they have forgotten the will! They all
> shout, "Most true. The will! Let's stay and hear the will."*)

Here is the will, and under Caesar's seal.
To every Roman citizen he gives,
To every several man, seventy-five drachmas.

. . . .

Moreover, he hath left you all his walks,
His private arbours and new-planted orchards,
On this side Tiber. He hath left them you,
And to your heirs for ever, common pleasures,
To walk abroad, and recreate yourselves.
Here was a Caesar! When comes such another?

Act III, Scene II.

2. **Cyrano's speech from CYRANO DE BERGERAC by Edmond Rostand:**
   "What would you have me do?"[2]

> (*One of the brilliant plays of the nineteenth century,
> CYRANO DE BERGERAC enthralled Parisians on its*

---

[2]from CYRANO DE BERGERAC by Edmond Rostand, Brian Hooker
translation. Copyright 1923 by Holt, Rinehart and Winston, Inc. Copyright 1951 by Doris C. Hooker. Reprinted by permission of Holt,
Rinehart and Winston, Inc.

opening night, December 28, 1897. Its author, Edmond Rostand, only 29, was unknown outside the city. Paris was entranced by the story of the swaggering poet of the preposterous nose, Cyrano, whose lyric speeches, uttered in the dark, won for his handsome tongue-tied friend the love of fair Roxanne. Several poor translations into English were attempted, but Brian Hooker finally brought the play to the American stage with his beautiful translation. In it, we can see why CYRANO, like certain of Shakespeare's plays, has been called a drama "not of an age but for all time.")

CYRANO:

What would you have me do?
Seek for the patronage of some great man,
And like a creeping vine on a tall tree
Crawl upward, where I cannot stand alone?
No, thank you! Dedicate, as others do,
Poems to pawnbrokers? Be a buffoon
In the vile hope of teasing out a smile
On some cold face? No, thank you! Eat a toad
For breakfast every morning? Make my knees
Callous, and cultivate a supple spine, —
Wear out my belly grovelling in the dust?
No, thank you! Scratch the back of any swine
That roots up gold for me? Tickle the horns
Of Mammon with my left hand, while my right,
Too proud to know his partner's business,
Takes in the fee? No, thank you! Use the fire
God gave me to burn incense all day long
Under the nose of wood and stone? No, thank you!
Shall I go leaping into ladies' laps
And licking fingers? — or — to change the form —
Navigating with madrigals for oars,
My sails full of the sighs of dowagers?
No thank you! Publish verses at my own
Expense? No, thank you! Be the patron saint
Of a small group of literary souls
Who dine together every Tuesday? No
I thank you! Shall I labor night and day
To build a reputation on one song,
And never write another? Shall I find
True genius only among Geniuses,
Palpitate over little paragraphs,

> And struggle to insinuate my name
> Into the columns of the *Mercury?*
> No, thank you! Calculate, scheme, be afraid,
> Love more to make a visit than a poem,
> Seek introductions, favors, influences? —
> No, thank you! No, I thank you! And again
> I thank you! — But . . .
> To sing, to laugh, to dream,
> To walk in my own way and be alone,
> Free, with an eye to see things as they are,
> A voice that means manhood — to cock my hat
> Where I choose — At a word, a *Yes,* a *No,*
> To fight — or write. To travel any road
> Under the sun, under the stars, nor doubt
> If fame or fortune lie beyond the bourne —
> Never to make a line I have not heard
> In my own heart; yet, with all modesty
> To say: "My soul, be satisfied with flowers,
> With fruit, with weeds even; but gather them
> In the one garden you may call your own."
> So, when I win some triumph, by some chance,
> Render no share of Caesar — in a word,
> I am too proud to be a parasite,
> And if my nature wants the germ that grows
> Towering to heaven like the mountain pine,
> Or like the oak, sheltering multitudes —
> I stand, not high it may be — but alone!

Act II

selections for one female

1. Portia's "quality of mercy" speech from Shakespeare's **MERCHANT OF VENICE.**

   (*Few dramatic parts for women surpass the magnificent role of Portia in Shakespeare's MERCHANT OF VENICE. Probably one of the most beautiful speeches ever written is "the quality of mercy" speech. In Shakespeare's time, boys were trained to take the part of young women, and Portia's speeches were written to make the most of the attributes of a talented boy-actor. It is a difficult speech to interpret, not only because it has been done so much that it is almost hackneyed, but because it takes an interpreter who can suc-*

cessfully assume the masquerade of a boy without totally
destroying the credibility of Portia's being female.)

PORTIA:

The quality of mercy is not strained,
It droppeth as the gentle rain from heaven
Upon the place beneath. It is twice blest:
It blesseth him that gives and him that takes.
'Tis mightiest in the mightiest; it becomes
The throned monarch better than his crown;
His sceptre shows the force of temporal power,
The attribute to awe and majesty,
Wherein doth sit the dread and fear of kings.
But mercy is above this sceptred sway;
It is enthroned in the hearts of kings,
It is an attribute to God himself;
And earthly power doth then show likest God's
When mercy seasons justice.

Act IV, Scene I

2. Joan's speech, "You promised me my life; but you lied," from SAINT
   JOAN by George Bernard Shaw.[3]

   (*SAINT JOAN, by Shaw, first produced in 1923, three years*
   after the canonization of St. Joan of Arc, tells the story of
   a radically nationalistic teen-ager, burnt for witchcraft and
   sorcery in 1431. Joan died because her new ideas were a
   threat to the Church and society of her day. In an epilogue,
   she is surprised to find she has been made a saint, but when
   she offers to return to earth, she is rejected — "The heretic
   is always better dead. And mortal eyes cannot distinguish
   the saint from the heretic. Spare them," she is advised. At
   the end of the play, Joan faces her inquisitors at court, who
   beg her to renounce her convictions, and promise to spare
   her life if she will. But she discovers they intend to give her,
   instead of freedom, perpetual imprisonment!)

JOAN:

. . . You promised me my life; but you lied. . . . You think that life is nothing
but not being stone dead. It is not the bread and water I fear: I can live on

---

[3]From the play SAINT JOAN by Bernard Shaw. Reprinted by permission from The Public Trustee and The Society of Authors, 84
Drayton Gardens, London SW. 10.

bread: when have I asked for more? It is no hardship to drink water if the water be clean. Bread has no sorrow for me, and water no affliction. But to shut me from the light of the sky and the sight of the fields and flowers; to chain my feet so that I can never again ride with the soldiers nor climb the hills; to make me breathe foul damp darkness, and keep from me everything that brings me back to the love of God when your wickedness and foolishness tempt me to hate Him: all this is worse than the furnace in the Bible that was heated seven times. I could do without my warhorse; I could drag about in a skirt; I could let the banners and the trumpets and the knights and soldiers pass me and leave me behind as they leave the other women, if only I could still hear the wind in the trees, the larks in the sunshine, the young lambs crying through the healthy frost, and the blessed blessed church bells that send my angel voices floating to me on the wind. But without these things I cannot live; and by your wanting to take them away from me, or from any human creature, I know that your counsel is of the devil, and that mine is of God.

Scene VI

selection for one male and one female

There are many selections which might be suggested for oral interpretation by two characters, one male and one female. Shakespeare is full of them; Ibsen offers many possibilities, particularly in THE DOLL'S HOUSE. J. M. Barrie's plays present surprising and entertaining scenes of character contrast. One of the most tense situations in dramatic literature occurs in **DARK VICTORY by George Brewer, Jr., and Bertram Bloch.**[4]

> (*Dr. Steele, noted brain surgeon, is calling on Judith Traherne, on whom he has recently successfully operated for brain tumor. During the period of her recovery these two widely divergent persons — Steele, a taciturn Vermonter, and Judith, a vivacious socialite — have fallen in love. Contrasting characters and deep emotional responses reach a dramatic intensity in the following scene.*)

JUDITH *is a little shy at first, a little breathless with eagerness and excitement.*
JUDITH.   Hello. . . .
STEELE.   Hello. . . . I'm not putting you out?
JUDITH.   You're not putting me out.
STEELE.   I like you in those things. You look fit — ready to work.

---

[4]From the play DARK VICTORY by George Brewer, Jr. and Bertram Bloch. Copyright, 1932, 1939, by George Emerson Brewer, Jr. Reprinted by permission of Dramatists Play Service, Inc.

JUDITH.   Sit down, Fred. . . . Something to drink?

STEELE.   Un-hunh . . . by and by maybe. How have you been?

JUDITH.   Splendid.

STEELE.   Let's have a look at you. . . . [*Pushes back her hair and looks at the scar.*] No headache?

JUDITH.   None. . . . You haven't been near me for three days.

STEELE.   Sleeping well?

JUDITH.   Beautifully. . . .Have you been busy?

STEELE.   Very. . . . Appetite good?

JUDITH.   Marvelous. . . . All things according to Hoyle.

STEELE.   Good. Now stand with both feet together. . . . Close your eyes. . . . [*She poses elaborately.*] How's the balance?

JUDITH.   Perfect. . . . You see I know all the answers.

STEELE.   I find nothing wrong.

JUDITH.   There isn't anything.

STEELE.   [*Smiles.*] Patient dismissed.

[*Pause.*]

JUDITH.   [*Thoughtfully — uneasily.*] So you're off tomorrow?

STEELE.   Unless the heavens fall.

JUDITH.   I have no luck with heaven.

STEELE.   Hmm . . . I'm already a month late, Judith.

JUDITH.   I didn't realize until Dr. Parsons told me that you'd given up all your plans for me. . . . How can I ever thank you?

STEELE.   Don't let's talk of thanks.

JUDITH.   But I owe you — everything.

STEELE.   Just seeing you as you stand there has repaid me a thousand times for anything I've done.

JUDITH.   I'd like to believe that.

STEELE.   You must. Because I don't want you ever to feel under any obligation to me.

JUDITH.   I think that's the nicest thing anyone ever said to me. Are you so generous to all your patients?

STEELE.   Judith — you know what I mean.

JUDITH.   Perhaps I do — perhaps I don't. How much of what you mean do you ever say?

STEELE.   [*Very seriously.*] Then let me say that I care so much that I'll come to you half across the earth, whenever you call me. . . . Is that better?

JUDITH.   [Vaguely disturbed at something in his tone.] You sound awfully serious.

STEELE.   It was a serious speech.

JUDITH.   [*Thinking through.*] It had such — finality. [*She searches his face.*] Fred, what's disturbing you?

STEELE.   Nothing.

JUDITH.   Yes, there is.

STEELE.   What makes you think so?

JUDITH.   Why did you choose just those words — "whenever you call me"?

STEELE.   I was trying to fit the role you picked for me.

JUDITH.   You're not telling me the truth. [*Pause.*] . . . So you're really going to be an old-fashioned country doctor?

STEELE.   Hideously old-fashioned.

JUDITH.   You'll get down here — occasionally?

STEELE.   Not often. I expect they'll keep me pretty busy.

JUDITH.   I expect so. . . . And you'll really love it; you'll have no regrets; — not one? . . .

[*Pause.*]

STEELE.   [*Goes to window and looks out. Pause.*] Judith . . . do you think anything worth saving was ever saved by running away from it?

JUDITH.   Do you?

STEELE.   I want to know what *you* think.

JUDITH.   [*After a pause.*] No, Fred, I don't.

STEELE.   [*Turning to her.*] Do you remember the drive we took the morning of the operation, when we saw the first sun on the Palisades?

JUDITH.   Yes.

STEELE.   Remember what you said?

JUDITH.   Tell me.

STEELE.   You said that till that moment you'd never realized how magnificent they were; that it was almost as though you were seeing them for the first time with new eyes.

JUDITH.   The world was very simple and clear that morning in spite of what I knew was in store for me.

STEELE.   I think, *because* of it, Judith. It's apt to be that way when you know exactly what you're facing and you aren't afraid.

JUDITH.   People don't show fear in front of you, Fred. They're ashamed to.

STEELE.   It was a challenge, and you accepted it with perfect courage — almost with eagerness.

JUDITH.   But I was glad you were beside me.

STEELE.   If you knew I'd always be beside you . . . do you . . . do you think you'd ever be afraid of anything?

JUDITH.   Only of one thing — of you.

STEELE.   What do you mean by that, Judith?

JUDITH.   How can I put it? . . . It's the iron core in you . . . that unyielding something that would never let you flinch at pain, would never let you compromise with an ideal. It's what gives you your strength; but it frightens me.

STEELE.   [*Troubled.*] Why?

JUDITH.   Because I know I can't make any impression on it. I can't bend it — even the fraction of an inch. It's stronger than I am — it's even stronger than you.

STEELE.   [*Gently.*] You mustn't be afraid.

JUDITH.   You don't understand because you've never known fear, Fred.

STEELE.   I've known loneliness, Judith. In fact, I've never known anything else
— and that's a *kind* of fear.

JUDITH.   Oh, Fred . . . we're getting in deep water. Before it's too late I've
got to make you understand this: you're a very great person; I'm not. I'm
shallow. You have a great purpose and a great faith — I have neither. . . .
Believe in your work, Fred; believe in yourself — but leave me out of your
belief — I'd only let you down.

STEELE.   I know that isn't true.

JUDITH.   I've warned you.

STEELE.   I once asked you for something very important — your complete faith.
Have I still got it?

JUDITH.   [*Unable to stem the tide, swept on by it.*] You still have it.

STEELE.   [*Deeply moved, takes her hand a little awkwardly.*] That means — er
— that means almost everything to me —

JUDITH.   [*Softly.*] What do you mean, Fred — "almost"?

STEELE.   I mean — Judith! Can't you see it? I — I want — I must have your love,
dear.

JUDITH.   Oh, Fred . . . I've wanted you to say that for so long. . . . Couldn't
you tell?

STEELE.   You see, I've never felt anything like this before. I never thought it
could happen to me, but it has. I know now that, without you, I'm no longer
anything — I'm incomplete — I'm nothing.

JUDITH.   I know — in spite of all your strength, all your greatness, you've never
been happy. Do you really think I can make you happy?

STEELE.   [*After a pause.*] We're starting on a very strange and beautiful adventure, my dear.

JUDITH.   There have been millions of others in love.

STEELE.   But not quite like us; none that had such need for each other [*Smiles.*]
and such need for courage.

JUDITH.   You make it sound so perilous, Fred.

STEELE.   It is, and yet if we're sure of our love that needn't matter.

JUDITH.   Are *you* sure?

STEELE.   I am!

JUDITH.   And yet you've never been in love before?

STEELE.   [*In a higher key.*] It's a completely new experience.

JUDITH.   [*Simply — naively.*] Don't you want to kiss me? [*Steele smiles.*] Then
you'd better do it. . . . [*Steele kisses her simply, and a little awkwardly.
She laughs gaily.*] I'm afraid I'm going to have to teach you an awful lot,
Fred.

STEELE.   I suspect you will.

JUDITH.   It'll be fun teaching you.

STEELE.   It'll be fun learning. . . .

JUDITH.   Fred — I never thought! How do you take your coffee in the morning?

STEELE.   Black, strong, no sugar. . . .

JUDITH.   How utterly revolting.

STEELE.   Horrible. . . .

JUDITH.   But you'll insist upon it — and upon what else? You see, I know so
little, Fred. . . . I won't have to eat cold applie pie for breakfast . . . will I?

STEELE.   No. Word of honor.

JUDITH.   But I suppose you'll want me to entertain all your grateful patients?

STEELE.   All.

JUDITH.   And pay the bills on time?

STEELE.   Un-hunh.

JUDITH.   And run the house on a budget?

STEELE.   Miss Jenny will see to that.

JUDITH.   I'd forgotten about her. Your housekeeper? The one who taught you at
school?

STEELE.   That's the one.

JUDITH.   I'm a little afraid of her.

STEELE.   You'd better be!

JUDITH.   Oh, Fred, I'm going to love it — every minute of it . . . and we'll
have a garden — of course you'll want that . . . and babies . . . ? What's
the matter, Fred!

STEELE.   Nothing, dear — I —

JUDITH.   What's going on in your mind? . . . What are you afraid of?

STEELE.   What is there to be afraid of, if we're together?

JUDITH.   [*Thoughtfully.*] Parting, I suppose.

STEELE.   As I think of it, parting isn't terrible. The only terrible thing is — not
to have lived.

JUDITH.   Dear God, thank you for letting me be — young — and alive! . . .
[*Turning to Steele with all eagerness.*] Oh, Fred, I love this earth and all the
good things on it.

STEELE.   [*Too solemnly.*] I'm going to help you find them, if I can.

JUDITH.   [*Searching him.*] That strange solemn note whenever you talk about
my future. . . . I've noticed — What are you trying to keep from me?

STEELE.   Nothing.

JUDITH.   Don't, dear.

STEELE.   You trust me?

JUDITH.   You — not your words. Ever since the first day in this room I've felt
that you were keeping something from me. . . . I've sensed it a hundred
times since.

STEELE.   Imagination, dear.

JUDITH.   No . . . it's not. . . . All those carefully guarded phrases . . . [*Long
pause as she tries to remember them.*] "A complete *surgical* recovery" . .
and "I'll come to you half way across the earth — *whenever you call me.*"
[*She walks to the piano and stands there quietly for a moment — thinking.
Then she speaks very levelly but quietly.*] Fred . . . I'm going to ask you a
very simple question and I want you to answer it. . . . Is there anything
wrong with me?

STEELE.   [*Pause.*] I've told you, Judith, you may do anything you want now.

JUDITH.   That won't do. I shan't let you evade this time. . . . It has something
to do with the operation. . . . What is it? . . .Don't lie. . . . You have
no right to play God; no right to do that. . . . Fred, I'm asking for the
truth — and I'm entitled to it.

STEELE.   You are entitled to it. . . . Judith, I'd hoped with all my soul this
wouldn't happen, but it has; — so we'll face it. [*He leads her to sofa and they
sit down.*] We *can* now, can't we? Now, hold my hand while I tell you. . . .
As far as surgery can go you're cured — absolutely. But there are some things
surgery can't do. I shan't be technical, but when I took that thing out of your
head there was a tiny part of it that couldn't be reached. . . . It's what we
call an infiltration

JUDITH.   [*Very quietly.*] So you didn't get it all out?

STEELE.   All that I could see, but not quite all there was.

JUDITH.   Then the operation . . . didn't cure me?

STEELE   It did. . . . This thing isn't doing you any harm — at the moment.
. . . You see for yourself you're perfectly well.

JUDITH.   For the moment.

STEELE.   I'm not worried about you now . . . but in time — it will grow.

JUDITH.   Then this horrible thing is coming back again . . . and that means
another opera . . . ? [*She reads his face.*] No? . . . You mean that . . .
wouldn't do any good? . . . I see. . . . Give me a cigarette, will you, please?
. . . [*He does so and she lights it.*] Thanks . . . [*She draws on it deeply.*]
and I'll have to face those headaches and that ghastly confusion all over
again. . . .

STEELE.   No, dear. You won't. That's all behind you. I promise you that; promise
you that there'll be no suffering and no invalidism of any kind.

JUDITH.   But . . . how will it happen?

STEELE.   As quietly as going to sleep.

JUDITH.   God's last small mercy! . . . I mustn't forget to thank Him for that
when I see Him! . . . You say I'll be perfectly well up to the — last?

STEELE.   As well as you are this moment.

JUDITH.   Then — how will I know! How will I know!

STEELE.   Why go into all this now, Judith?

JUDITH.   But I want to know if I'll have any warning — some chance to be
ready?

STEELE.   There will be a moment when you won't be able to — to — see as usual
— that's all.

JUDITH.   You mean I'll go *blind?*

STEELE.   Just for a moment. Then you'll be perfectly all right again . . . but
after a few hours, two or three . . . you . . . well, you will go to sleep.

JUDITH.   [*Pause.*] I see. . . . How much time have I. . . . ? [*Insistently.*]
How long have I before the — the end?

STEELE.   Judith, dear — let that be my secret.

JUDITH.   No! . . . You've had too many secrets! . . . Go on, tell me how long?
. . .Five years? — One year? — Six months? . . .

an understanding of drama use in oral interpretation

STEELE. Possibly more. One can't be certain — six — ten months, say.

JUDITH. That's not so very long.

STEELE. After all, time is only an illusion.

JUDITH. What does that mean?

STEELE. My dear, that we're on an adventure that can't be measured by time — because it's eternal. . . . Your birth was part of it, Judith; your beauty is part of it; and your death will be part of it. If you and I can reach the peak, what difference do a few hours make? What we are — the thing that's happened to us — our love — can't be revoked and can't be destroyed.

JUDITH. [*Gravely.*] You put it so eloquently . . so clearly thought out. . . . [*Pause.*] So you knew this all along? From the very first?

STEELE. Yes.

JUDITH. And you're offering to marry me and take me to Felsboro. . . . [*A short dry little laugh, of despair and disillusion.*] That's very chivalrous of you, Fred . . . very chivalrous . . . so like you. [*Steele puts his arm about her. She removes it.*] I'd rather you didn't touch me just now . . . do you mind? . . . It's still daylight . . . it seemed funny for a moment, that's all.

STEELE. I'd give you my own life if I could.

JUDITH. I know that, and I believe you . . . and I'm glad you told me. . . . Oh, you're so square and so strong and so unflinching . . . but I'm not. . . . [*Suddenly alert and bitter.*] God gives me something with one hand and takes it away with the other. . . . I was just thinking of us and the terrible difference between us — thinking how time would bring us together and now there is no time — even that has been taken away, and I can't have you. . . . I couldn't get used to this — this thing in six months . . . I couldn't stand it. . . . I'll stay here with what I know, where I can be safe — where I can forget, for that's all I want now, just to forget and then be forgotten.

STEELE. You're coming with me to Felsboro as my wife.

JUDITH. I'm staying right here, and I'm going to live so fast and so hard that I won't be able to think.

STEELE. Where will that lead?

JUDITH. Where all roads lead in six months. . . . Only I haven't time to go exploring. . . . I'll stick to the only life I know.

STEELE. You said you loved me.

JUDITH. I didn't know what I was saying — you fooled me for a minute . . . but I've put the pieces all together now. . . . I understand — all the carefully laid preparations — how you weighed each step — planned each move — even to marrying me. — Oh, I know why you did it, and, Fred, I want you to know I'm terribly, terribly grateful.

STEELE. Why? — I love you.

JUDITH. You're only sorry for me, Fred. If you really loved me you'd have held me in your arms and comforted me, instead of that you stand there and make speeches. . . . It's not your fault — it's the way you're made — what you feel is pity — intellectual pity, and it's no good. . . . I don't want it. . . . I want something that's alive and warm.

STEELE. Judith, you're not seeing things straight. . . . You can't see all the implications in this in a moment. Your world has crashed — but we're going to rebuild it together.

JUDITH. [*Covering her ears.*] I don't even hear what you're saying! I'm discovering that I'm just as hard and stubborn as you. Go away, Fred — forget about me, give yourself to your work and be happy.

STEELE. I have no life left. Don't you see that *I* need *you?* I'm holding on to you because I'm no good without you. . . . Judith, won't you help me?

JUDITH. No, I won't. I don't want to help you . . . I won't accept your way of life: It's too cold, too demanding. You're like those granite hills of yours. — I admit it was generous of you, but you'd never have offered this if you hadn't known. . . . I tell you I have no use for your pity . . . I don't ever want to see you again. Go to Vermont and let me die my own way. . . . If you must think of me, then think of me as your patient. Ten years from now you can look the case up in your files: . . . "Traherne, — Judith — aged twenty-seven — diagnosis March tenth — operation March fourteenth — patient made brilliant recovery — died six months later."

STEELE. Stop it, Judith!

JUDITH. This isn't going the way you expected! Beautiful Judith Traherne isn't acting up to your sentimental picture of her. . . . [*Pause.*] Why do you stand there and say nothing? That beautiful scientific mind judging me. . . . Well, what do you think of this exhibition? What do you think of me now?

STEELE. What I've always thought. I only want you to have the same faith in yourself that I have in you.

JUDITH. You've never had faith in me. *Hopes,* yes, but not faith. You thought there were too many bad spots. Oh, Fred, you're so easy for a woman to read. You despise everything I stand for in life — my set — my friends — my world. Well, thank God for that world now. . . . My friends — will help me forget — at least they know how to be amusing, and that's all I want — it's good enough for six months. . . .

STEELE. It won't work, Judith, you'll never be satisfied with that. You need so much more than your friends can possibly give you.

JUDITH. He takes away my life and offers me — what? Extinction in six months. Six long months. . . . Oh, God, how long they seem. . . . But don't worry — I'll fill them — I'll cram them full of living! There'll be plenty of action from now on — I'll show whoever runs this rotten world some merry hell before I've finished. . . . You didn't know I was like this, but you've never known me — not the real me. I'm not sweet and generous. I'm a bitter, angry woman and hard — hard as nails. . . . Well, why do you stand there? . . . Why don't you go? I've turned myself inside out for you — what more do you want?

STEELE. Sit down, Judith!

JUDITH. This isn't your office now! It's my home and I'll do in it as I like! . . . Please go away. My friends can lift me out of this, but you — you mean defeat, futility — death — always and always that. I mustn't ever see you again — ever. . . . [*Moves to the telephone.*] I'm calling Alden. . . . It's clear out and warm. I can wear my new dress. . . . 443 please. . . . My house-keeper will give you dinner. . . . Hello, Alden . . . Alden darling — I'm coming to the party after all — if you want me. . . . Oh, thanks — thanks, I'd love to . . . that's just what I want — a chance to celebrate and plenty to drink. — Alden, Alden, I'll be there with bells on!

selecting, evaluating, and preparing material

One of the things that is a very interesting thing to know is how you are feeling inside you to the words that are coming out to be outside of you.
Gertrude Stein

Literature is news that stays news.
Ezra Pound

Two things cause each of us to react to literary stimuli in individual ways. One of these is the nature of the material itself. "Literature is news that stays news," said Ezra Pound, suggesting that lifeless writing will die a natural death.

The second thing is ourselves. "How you are feeling inside," as Gertrude Stein put it, influences your reaction to literature. It isn't necessarily bad writing because you don't like it, nor is it necessarily good writing because you do, but if you don't like it, for you it probably won't be significant.

Any teacher of interpretation who insists on imposing his standards on his students is in serious error. You will have to be the judge of what selections you elect to make a permanent part of your collection.

the personal anthology

As students of interpretation, one of the most helpful aids to your development is the building up of a Personal Anthology.

There are a number of excellent anthologies available from which to select readings. You are encouraged to go to original sources on your own, to search the shelves of fiction and nonfiction and periodicals in the library and in your home. From these sources you will compile your Personal Anthology.

Clifton Fadiman, in a preliminary talk with the reader of his book, *The Lifetime Reading Plan*, says that he is merely pointing out to the reader "some of the liveliest talkers our civilization has produced," but that it is up to each reader to "make friends" all by himself. In this class, a Personal Anthology can be the basis of a "lifetime of conversation," a means of "making friends" with poets, essayists, speakers, storytellers, and playwrights who have inspired or delighted you. Your Personal Anthology will mean much more to you than any other anthology, no matter how good that other anthology may be.

The Personal Anthology should become your basis for selecting and programming material to use in performance situations. You will find it a constant motivation to the search for new material and a means of relating new discoveries to what you have already made a part of you.

There are no rules concerning the format of a Personal Anthology. How could there be? Since it is a personal thing, you will decide how you wish to prepare it and keep it up. You may wish to arrange your selections in categories: Humor, Philosophy, Inspiration, etc.; or Poetry, Prose, Drama, etc., or Greek, Middle Ages, Renaissance, etc. You may wish to keep your selections arranged according to author, title, or by first lines. You may wish to type them out. You may prefer to write them by hand in a notebook. You may wish to establish a clipping anthology. You may wish to keep your selections in a folder or in a card file.

The important thing is to *have* a Personal Anthology, arranged in some manner which allows for yearly growth and expansion and some means of finding a selection when you want it. Established now, such an anthology will be of constant use to you throughout a lifetime.

evaluation of literary selections

Your evaluation of literature will depend considerably on your cultural background, your personal taste, and your deliberate efforts to understand and appreciate the many types and varieties of writing that form our literary heritage. Standards of evaluation can not be imposed on people, as we have said before, although improvement of literary taste usually results from wide reading and from classes such as this in interpretation.

You have been given "a map of the territory" of literary heritages in previous chapters. We have reviewed outstanding writing available to us from various cultures and periods of history. We have suggested sources for you to check to discover good material from the current tremendous flow of publication. It is up to you to study the map and become acquainted with the territory, past and present.

three faulty methods of analysis and preparation of selections

Analysis and preparation of selections go hand in hand. In some instances, analysis overbalances preparation of a more oral nature. In other instances, oral preparation so far outweighs analysis that the interpreter has very little idea of what he is saying. At times, the interpreter may lack both analysis and oral preparation, expending his energies on fringe preparation which hasn't much influence on performance. Let us look at three faulty methods of analysis and preparation which frequently are used by interpreters and which we should seek to avoid:

1. The first faulty method might be compared to the clinical approach. It consists of so-called analysis of a selection by breaking it up into all sorts of separate parts — words, phrases, sentences. While it is valuable to consider the meaning of words we don't recognize (endeavoring to understand the meaning given to them by the author, not necessarily the dictionary), we should not overdo this detailed effort. Analysis of style is of value, but is of more concern to the literary critic than to the interpreter. An inspection of detailed components of a literary selection is somewhat dangerous to the audio-minded person. It may kill inspiration and emphathy to the total meaning of a piece. Focussing on intricacies of phrasing, structure and rhythm enables some to appreciate an author's artistry, but such study, when not balanced by an equal amount of attention to the over-all impact, may result in a meaningless uncommunicative interpretation.

2. The second faulty method might be compared to the detective approach, in which the interpreter becomes absorbed in accumulating all the details *about* a selection instead of concentrating on the selection itself. Facts and information pertinent to a piece, an author, or a style of writing are interesting and often shed informative light. But accumulating a stack of biographical information, encyclopedic fact, and critical comment cannot substitute for well balanced preparation.

3. The third faulty method, which has been used by many students in the past but which we would certainly not condone, is what might be called the mimic approach. Hearing a selection read beautifully often gives a clever mimic all he needs to go and do likewise. The obvious faults of this method are too numerous to list, but such an approach allows no room for personal growth in the art of interpretation.

In practice, experienced interpreters employ various methods, depending upon the nature of the material to be performed. Your method of analysis and preparation of literary selections will depend greatly on your personal attitudes toward study. You may have considerable background in written English, in which case you will take delight in the analysis of construction and composition. Others will approach preparation by depending more completely on opinions of experienced critics. It is to be hoped that you will endeavor to perfect a balance in various avenues to understanding so that your total preparation will result in true appreciation of your chosen literary selection.

suggested steps in preparation of a selection

In almost all cases there are certain steps which should be taken in the analysis and preparation of material for performance. Individuals will vary in the value placed on each of these steps, but we present them as valid approaches:

1. *Preliminary reading, both silent and aloud.* In silent reading you may want to read quickly, almost scanning at first, to get the general impact of the thing. Some stories almost demand this type of reading. To stop and ponder phrasing and individual words in a first reading is frustrating and often wasteful.

Depending on the material, you may want to read it over silently a number of times before you try it orally.

When you feel sufficiently acquainted with the material you may want to read it aloud, experimenting with vocal quality, word pace, and perhaps gesture, in order to get the feel of it and somewhat anticipate the problems ahead.

2. *Familiarizing yourself with pertinent facts and data concerning the selection and author.* It is usually quite helpful to find out something about the author and his attitudes toward life. Often it is absolutely essential to know something about the author to make sense of what he is saying. At times, a knowledge of the author will open up a whole new area of understanding about his writing. Knowing something of the era in which a piece

was written is at times essential to its interpretation. Knowing what competent critics have felt about writers and their writing may help you to form reasonable attitudes, although you should not depend on the judgment of critics to develop your own tastes. An audience is always more interested in what insight you may give from your own understandings than in hearing what critics have said.

3. *Comprehending the author's theme, meaning, and attitude.* This is seldom an easy task. Naturally you must look up words you don't recognize. To understand what an author meant by a word, however, involves more than a dictionary definition. There are always shades of inference, implied conclusions, and assumptions in words as they are used by different authors.

John Ciardi has said, "When a poem fails to communicate, the failure may as reasonably be charged against the reader as against the poet." When any literary selection fails to communicate, it may be charged against a poor effort at understanding on the part of reader. It is work, it takes imagination, and it is often a frustrating process to understand what an author is endeavoring to communicate, but you must be sure you understand the author's intention if you are going to interpret his selection. (It may be, of course, as in the case of some poetry, that he means to communicate emotion, nothing more.)

At times there are different levels of understanding to be arrived at in relation to a selection. It is quite simple to read and understand *Gulliver's Travels,* Jonathan Swift's masterpiece, as a fantastically enchanting fairy tale in which a ship's physician journeys to a land of tiny Lilliputians, to a country of giants, to a flying island of "wise men," and to the home of Houyhnhnms and Yahoos. It is considerably more difficult to read this work as social satire, as allegory, as a denunciation of mankind for the corruption of his greatest possession, reason.

If, after conscientious study, you do not trust your judgment of an author's theme, meaning, and attitude, seek the help of a competent librarian in directing you to written criticisms by others. Your insight will be enlarged by comparison of your conclusions with those of professionals.

4. *Examining a selection's structure or framework.* It goes without saying that it is necessary and helpful to put a literary work in some category — prose, poetry, or drama. At times a subcategory such as lyric (in the case of poetry) will enable you to make more sensitive judgments. Within this framework or structure, examine the author's theme, underlying organization of ideas (if, indeed, he has specific ideas), his key words, and his climax or climaxes.

5. *Indicating your desired interpretative inflections.* Knowing by now what you believe the author intended to communicate, you may indicate

on your copy by your own system of underlining or circling or by use of colored pencil markings, words you intend to emphasize, sentences you intend to build to climaxes, pauses you wish to observe for creating suspense before a climax or for reinforcing the emotional or inspirational quality of an idea. You may also wish to indicate degrees of vocal intensity.

6. *Reading material aloud.* This step, reading aloud, may occur all along in various stages of your preparation, or you may be the type of person who prefers to wait until you have thoroughly mastered the printed page. Generally it is better to read aloud frequently during your preparation, introducing at each reading new elements of your learning. In any case, allow plenty of time for adequate oral practice, for polish, and for thorough familiarity with your selection before you endeavor to present it in front of an audience.

summary

The Personal Anthology is a project which all students of interpretation should undertake as a means of extending, improving, and intensifying literary appreciation. Established now, your Personal Anthology can serve a lifetime of usefulness.

Literary evaluations are influenced by personal tastes, cultural background, and study. They are difficult, if not impossible, to impose on others. Three faulty methods of analyzing and preparing selections for performance are discussed, but it is important, in approaching these processes appropriately, to include the following steps: (1) A preliminary reading to estimate the scope of the project of preparation; (2) familiarizing yourself with pertinent facts and data; (3) studying the author's theme, meaning, and attitude; (4) examining a selection's structure; (5) indicating on the script desired interpretative inflections; and (6) practicing oral interpretation until you are entirely comfortable with the selection prior to performance.

applications: ───────────────────────

1. Outline your plans and expectations for a Personal Anthology if you do not have one already started. If you have started one, outline your project and evaluate your progress so far.
2. List your strengths and weaknesses in cultural background which may influence your evaluation of literary selections. What deliberate steps have you taken so far this semester to improve your weaknesses?

3. Select a piece of literature in any category of your personal choice and prepare it within the framework of steps suggested in this chapter. As you prepare it, keep a record of the specific things you do — silent reading, silent thought and contemplation, library research, oral practice, and such.

4. Read the selections given at the end of this chapter and establish on paper a preparation schedule which you might follow in readying three of these or others in this text for public performance. Now, take one of these selections and carry out your schedule. When you have your selection ready, present it for the class or, better yet, some group to which you belong.

preview of chapter 9:
PROGRAMMING CREATIVELY

In programming there is an opportunity for creative adaptations of reading selections to audience situations. Areas in which creativity enters include program formats, introductions, bridges or transitions, central program sections, and conclusions. Creative planning may go into programs for specific groups and special occasions. We will be discussing examples of these.

selections for study and interpretation

THE WRITER'S DUTY

William Faulkner
(1898-1962)

> *Excerpt from acceptance of the Nobel Prize for Literature, December 14, 1950.*

Our tragedy today is a general and universal physical fear so long sustained by now that we can even bear it. There are no longer problems of the spirit. There is only the question: when will I be blown up? Because of this, the young man or woman writing today has forgotten the problems of the human heart in conflict with itself which alone can make good writing because only that is worth writing about, worth the agony and sweat.

He must learn them again. He must teach himself that the basest of all things is to be afraid: and, teaching himself that, forget it forever, leaving no room in his workshop for anything but the old verities and truths of the heart, the old universal truths lacking which any story is ephemeral and doomed — love and honor and pity and pride and compassion and sacrifice. . . . His griefs grieve on no universal bones, leaving no scars. He writes not of the heart but of the glands.

Until he relearns these things, he will write as though he stood among and watched the end of man. I decline to accept the end of man. It is easy enough to say that man is immortal simply bcause he will endure. . . . I believe that man will not merely endure: he will prevail. He is immortal, not because he alone among creatures has an inexhaustible voice, but because he has a soul, capable of compassion and sacrifice and endurance. The poet's, the writer's duty is to write about these things. It is his privilege to help man endure by lifting his heart by reminding him of the courage and honor and hope and pride and compassion and pity and sacrifice which have been the glory of his past. The poet's voice need not merely be the record of man, it can be one of the props, the pillars that help him endure and prevail.

some words about words

Every epoch in history, every stage of personal development, every school and coterie has its own little dictionary of depreciation, list of words to be used as missiles to terrify the timid; and hold the loyal in line: bourgeois, old-fashioned, modernist, fascist, heretic, reactionary, unscholarly, superficial, unscientific, authoritarian, radical and the rest.

Francis Meehan

The paradox of language is this: the word is present only so long as it is heard; as it is spoken, it vanishes; but the truth which the word carries stays on. . . .

Max Picard

It is as dangerous for people unaccustomed to handling words and unacquainted with their technique to tinker about with these heavily charged nuclei of emotional power as it would be for me to burst into a laboratory and play about with a powerful electromagnet or other machine highly charged with electrical force. . . . very few of our people have been taught to understand and handle language as an instrument of power.

Dorothy Sayers

He who wants to persuade should put his trust not in the right argument, but in the right word. . . . you cannot fail to see the power of mere words; such words as Glory, for instance, or Pity. . . . Shouted with perseverance, with ardor, with conviction, these two by their sound alone have set whole nations in motion and upheaved the dry, hard ground on which rests our whole social fabric.

Joseph Conrad

The intellectual is constantly betrayed by his own vanity. Godlike, he blandly assumes that he can express everything in words; whereas the things one loves, lives and dies for are not, in the last analysis, completely expressible in words. . . . The writer . . . must fit his unhappy guests, his ideas, to his set bed of words. And in the process, it is inevitable that the ideas have their legs chopped off, or pulled out of joint, in order to fit the rigid frame.

Anne Morrow Lindberg

BEAUTY IN WORDS
from Literary Frontiers

J. Donald Adams
(1891-   )

Think of words like *dawn* and *dusk*. They are beautiful in themselves, and still, after long centuries of wide and continual use, untouched by time, as fresh as the day when they were minted. There is slowly spreading light in the word *dawn*, both in the sound and the look of it. And the soft and stealthy darkening that is conveyed by *dusk* is not merely the mental reflex occasioned by the sight or sound of the accustomed symbol. As you look at it, as you hear it, you are aware of the perfect appropriateness of the word. . . .

We never tire of the words which man in his folly and stupidity cannot smirch and debase. Words like those I have mentioned and many others like them never grow drab or stale. It is, for the most part, the words which express mental concepts that we tire of, that we come to use with misgiving or distaste — the words that we have sullied or betrayed, words like *liberty* and *honor*, *freedom* and *democracy*, *faith* and *glory*. These are the words that need renewal and repair from time to time, and that need to be thought about as we use them.

THE VITALITY OF WORDS
from Literary Frontiers

J. Donald Adams

Words, as a subject for talk or written comment, are almost on a par with the weather in their universality of appeal. We all use them, poorly or well, and for good or ill; even the least articulate among us have some interest in them. They are one of the most living things of man's creation; one might argue, indeed, that they possess more vitality than anything else the race has fashioned: what else is there that man has made which leads an independent life? Words do; they gather strength and lose it; they become blurred as do the eyes of an old man, yet keeping in them something of life; they gather evil about them, like some persons, or like others, prod our wits or lift our hearts. They pursue their own ends with what sometimes seems a dogged intention, and when they are utterly spent, and divorced from the common tongue, not all the grammarians and lexicographers can put Humpty Dumpty together again. . . .

They depend not at all upon material aids, though they may use them, for their effectiveness, as do all other fruits of the human mind. Architecture, painting, sculpture, music, science — all demand a material intermediary of some sort; words alone are as disembodied as when man first drew them from his stream of thought.

> For years, interpreters have been using THE FOOL'S PRAYER by Roland Sill in programs of readings. It has undeniable appeal to most audiences who not only enjoy the dramatic quality inherent in the contrast between jester and King, but easily understand and appreciate the message it conveys.

THE FOOL'S PRAYER

Edward Roland Sill
(1841-1887)

> The royal feast was done; the King
>   Sought some new sport to banish care,
> And to his jester cried: "Sir Fool,
>   Kneel now, and make for us a prayer!"
>
> The jester doffed his cap and bells,
>   And stood the mocking court before;
> They could not see the bitter smile,
>   Behind the painted grin he wore.

He bowed his head, and bent his knee
    Upon the monarch's silken stool;
His pleading voice arose: "O Lord,
    Be merciful to me, a fool!

"No pity, Lord, could change the heart
    From red with wrong to white as wool,
The rod must heal the sin; but Lord,
    Be merciful to me, a fool!

" 'Tis not by guilt the onward sweep
    Of truth and right, O Lord, we stay;
'Tis by our follies that so long
    We hold the earth from heaven away.

"These clumsy feet, still in the mire,
    Go crushing blossoms without end;
These hard, well-meaning hands we thrust
    Among the heart-strings of a friend.

"The ill-timed truth we might have kept —
    Who knows how sharp it pierced and stung?
The word we had not sense to say —
    Who knows how grandly it had rung?

"Our faults no tenderness should ask,
    The chastening stripes must cleanse them all;
But for our blunders — oh, in shame
    Before the eyes of heaven we fall!

"Earth bears no balsam for our mistakes;
    Men crown the knave and scourge the tool
That did his will; but Thou, O Lord,
    Be merciful to me, a fool!"

The room was hushed; in silence rose
    The king and sought his gardens cool,
And walked apart, and murmured low,
    "Be merciful to me, a fool!"

Edwin Arlington Robinson created (in poetry) a gallery of misfits and outcasts. Harvard-educated but unrecognized and unsuccessful himself as a poet, he chose as his subjects men who like Richard Cory had despair behind a façade of poise and self-esteem.

RICHARD CORY

Edwin Arlington Robinson
(1869-1935)

Whenever Richard Cory went down town,
  We people on the pavement looked at him:
He was a gentleman from sole to crown,
  Clean favored, and imperially slim.

And he was always quietly arrayed,
  And he was always human when he talked;
But still he fluttered pulses when he said,
  "Good-morning," and he glittered when he walked.

And he was rich — yes, richer than a king —
  And admirably schooled in every grace:
In fine, we thought that he was everything
  To make us wish that we were in his place.

So on we worked, and waited for the light,
  And went without the meat, and cursed the bread:
And Richard Cory, one calm summer night,
  Went home and put a bullet through his head.

MINIVER CHEEVY

Edwin Arlington Robinson

Miniver Cheevy, child of scorn,
  Grew lean while he assailed the seasons:
He wept that he was ever born,
  And he had reasons.

Miniver loved the days of old
  When swords were bright and steeds were prancing;
The vision of a warrior bold
  Would set him dancing.

Miniver sighed for what was not,
  And dreamed, and rested from his labors;
He dreamed of Thebes and Camelot,
  And Priam's neighbors.

Miniver mourned the ripe renown
  That made so many a name so fragrant;
He mourned Romance, now on the town,
  And Art, a vagrant.

Miniver loved the Medici,
  Albeit he had never seen one;
He would have sinned incessantly
  Could he have been one.

Miniver cursed the commonplace
  And eyed a khaki suit with loathing;
He missed the medieval grace
  Of iron clothing.

Miniver scorned the gold he sought,
  But sore annoyed was he without it;
Miniver thought, and thought, and thought,
  And thought about it.

Miniver Cheevy, born too late,
  Scratched his head and kept on thinking;
Miniver coughed, and called it fate,
  And kept on drinking.

In the following poem, Robinson pictures with tenderness
and rare humor an ancient derelict who, with his compan-
ionable jug, faces a future knowing "There was not much
that was ahead of him." This monologue is a challenge to the
reader to interpret age, weariness, and resignation while re-
taining that patina of wit that keeps the listener chuckling
through tears.

MR. FLOOD'S PARTY
Edwin Arlington Robinson

Old Eben Flood, climbing alone one night
Over the hill between the town below
And the forsaken upland hermitage
That held as much as he should ever know
On earth again of home, paused warily.
The road was his with not a native near;
And Eben, having leisure, said aloud,
For no man else in Tilbury Town to hear:

"Well, Mr. Flood, we have the harvest moon
Again, and we may not have many more;
The bird is on the wing, the poet says,
And you and I have said it here before.
Drink to the bird." He raised up to the light
The jug that he had gone so far to fill,
And answered huskily: "Well, Mr. Flood
Since you propose it, I believe I will."

Alone, as if enduring to the end
A valiant armor of scarred hopes outworn,
He stood there in the middle of the road
Like Roland's ghost winding a silent horn.
Below him, in the town among the trees,
Where friends of other days had honored him,
A phantom salutation of the dead
Rang thinly till old Eben's eyes were dim.

Then, as a mother lays her sleeping child
Down tenderly, fearing it may awake,
He set the jug down slowly at his feet
With trembling care, knowing that most things break;
And only when assured that on firm earth
It stood, as the uncertain lives of men
Assuredly did not, he paced away,
And with his hand extended paused again:

"Well, Mr. Flood, we have not met like this
In a long time; and many a change has come
To both of us, I fear, since last it was
We had a drop together. Welcome home!"
Convivially returning with himself,
Again he raised the jug up to the light;
And with an acquiescent quaver said:
"Well, Mr. Flood, if you insist, I might.

"Only a very little, Mr. Flood —
For auld lang syne. No more, sir; that will do."
So, for the time, apparently it did,
And Eben evidently thought so too;
For soon amid the silver loneliness
Of night he lifted up his voice and sang,
Secure, with only two moons listening,
Until the whole harmonious landscape rang —

"For auld lang syne." The weary throat gave out,
The last word wavered; and the song being done,
He raised again the jug regretfully
And shook his head, and was again alone.
There was not much that was ahead of him,
And there was nothing in the town below —
Where strangers would have shut the many doors
That many friends had opened long ago.

BIRCHES by Robert Frost is a popular program selection which may be read by interpreters of all ages; even young teen-agers. Done in a conversational tone, thoughtfully and with wit, it has great appeal and charm.

BIRCHES

Robert Frost
(1875-1963)

When I see birches bend to left and right
Across the line of straighter darker trees,
I like to think some boy's been swinging them.
But swinging doesn't bend them down to stay.
Ice-storms do that. Often you must have seen them
Loaded wtih ice a sunny winter morning
After a rain. They click upon themselves
As the breeze rises, and turn many-colored
As the stir cracks and crazes their enamel.
Soon the sun's warmth makes them shed crystal shells
Shattering and avalanching on the snow-crust —
Such heaps of broken glass to sweep away
You'd think the inner dome of heaven had fallen.
They are dragged to the withered bracken by the load,
And they seem not to break; though once they are bowed
So low for long, they never right themselves:
You may see their trunks arching in the woods
Years afterwards, trailing their leaves on the ground
Like girls on hands and knees that throw their hair
Before them over their heads to dry in the sun.
But I was going to say when Truth broke in
With all her matter-of-fact about the ice-storm
I should prefer to have some boy bend them
As he went out and in to fetch the cows —

Some boy too far from town to learn baseball,
Whose only play was what he found himself,
Summer or winter, and could play alone.
One by one he subdued his father's trees
By riding them down over and over again
Until he took the stiffness out of them,
And not one but hung limp, not one was left
For him to conquer. He learned all there was
To learn about not launching out too soon
And so not carrying the tree away
Clear to the ground. He always kept his poise
To the top branches, climbing carefully
With the same pains you use to fill a cup
Up to the brim, and even above the brim.
Then he flung outward, feet first, with a swish,
Kicking his way down through the air to the ground.
So was I once myself a swinger of birches;
And so I dream of going back to be.
It's when I'm weary of considerations,
And life is too much like a pathless wood
Where your face burns and tickles with the cobwebs
Broken across it, and one eye is weeping
From a twig's having lashed across it open.
I'd like to get away from earth awhile
And then come back to it and begin over.
May no fate willfully misunderstand me
And half grant what I wish and snatch me away
Not to return. Earth's the right place for love:
I don't know where it's likely to go better.
I'd like to go by climbing a birch tree,
And climb black branches up a snow-white trunk
Toward heaven, till the tree could bear no more,
But dipped its top and set me down again.
That would be good both going and coming back.
One could do worse than be a swinger of birches.

programming creatively

*Two roads diverged in a wood, and I
I took the one less traveled by,
And that has made all the
    difference.*
    Robert Frost, from
    The Road Not Taken

*Creativity always has the stamp of the individual upon its
product, but the product is not the individual, nor his materials, but partakes of the relationship between the two.*
    Carl R. Rogers

We have arrived at the point in our study of interpretation
where we may choose between obvious roads or one "less traveled by." To
those more creative and venturesome souls among us, the possibility of putting our knowledges and skills of interpretation to use in unique ways is now
at hand.

Education, as Carl Rogers and others have pointed out, tends to encourage conformism, the stereotype, and regimentation. In this class, however, we hope your learning in the field of interpretation will motivate you
to applications which bear your own individual stamp. In the programming
of material there is infinite opportunity for creativity.

Perhaps you already have been discovering areas in which to use your interpretative skills. Are you consciously interpreting yourself as a more positive, interesting, and unusual person? Are you constantly searching with new perceptions for writings which you may adapt for program use? Are you discovering ways in which to use your interpretative powers in other classes, at church, in social contacts, in your home? These are all opportunities for creative use of what you have learned. As we get to the actual planning of programs and presentation of material before groups, there are all sorts of challenges to the creative individual.

program formats

There are, of course, rather obvious steps to be taken in programming well for any group. Whether we are asked to give a short inspirational message, a reading of one or two poems, or a lecture-recital, we need to know the following things:

1. General characteristics of the group — size, age level, cultural and educational background.
2. General information about the occasion — formal, informal, purpose, place, microphone or not.
3. What is expected — short entertainment, inspirational message, full program.

If the thing you are expected to do is give a whole program of readings, usually it is safe to rely on another obvious lesson from experienced readers and that concerns the format of a program. It is generally felt that a good all-purpose program of readings will have four sections: an opening section of rather humorous or entertaining nature (this could be a group of several short readings); a transitional section which could set the stage for the *pièce de résistance* or principal work to be read; the actual highlight of the program, probably a work of some substantial nature, longer, and with sustained interest and emotional intensity (perhaps a cutting from a play or a monologue, or even a well written story); and, finally, the concluding section, which may again feature some humor or material of light or inspirational nature.

The skeleton form for programming might be reduced to the following:

SECTION	PURPOSE	LENGTH	MATERIAL
A	Get interest	5-6 min.	Light verse, impromptu humor, light prose
B	Bridge to main reading	2-3 min.	Usually extemporaneous mood-changing remarks
C	Main reading	30-40 min.	Dramatic cutting, monologue, or a group of serious selections
D	Conclude with summary, unifying program, leave audience satisfied	5 min.	Short selection of prose or poetry, lighter in nature

The over-all length of such a program should be held to about one hour, seldom over one hour and a quarter. Most audiences become restless if any more time is taken up, and are especially apt to be nervous if they have already been sitting for some time before the entertainer arrives. If you have the misfortune of being introduced to an audience which has already been seated for well over an hour, it is wise to give them an opportunity to stand and stretch or shift their chairs about (if they are seated at a dinner table) before you start with your program. It may be a bit awkward to start this way, but you will be rewarded by improved attention once you begin.

Thinking within the skeleton form of a program, let us examine the sections to see how we can deal with them creatively.

(Section A) *Introduction*

There are many ways to get your program off to a successful start. Sometimes just the choice of title will go far toward setting the program on a delightful course. HOW NOT TO READ POETRY was chosen as the subject of a talk on interpretation which proved to be very interesting to a large group of women with no special background in oral reading. Another title to that talk could have encouraged at least half the audience to stay home.

Getting the attention of your group can be accomplished in many creative ways. One interpreter spent an hour or two in the morning going from business to business in the community where he was to meet a group of businessmen at a luncheon. He surprised them by having already "become acquainted" with many in their places of business. They were intrigued by his opening comments on his reception in town.

A college boy I knew, who had a particularly effective train whistle in his repertoire of imitations, once started by whistling and then saying:

> There was a man who thought
> That by going good and fast
> He could get across the railroad tracks
> Before the train came past.

> (Whistle — whistle)

> He could make the trainman whistle
> He could make the engine roar.
> (Pause — and faint whistle)
> There was a man who thought this.

> (Long pause)

> But there isn't any more.

It took him about one minute to get complete attention and an audience who expected a wonderfully humorous hour.

(Section B) *Bridge*

The main thing about a transitional bridge is that it must be strong and go quickly from one thing to another. The bridge itself may use more humor (if the introduction has) or it may settle down to the serious business of introducing the audience to the main body of the program. There is a great danger, however, that on arriving at the bridge an interpreter will "let down" and lose the attention he has gained in the introduction. It is a real challenge to your creative powers to plan a bridge that will function, will take your listeners from the introductory moments of fun to the more serious, but even more interesting, moments of reading ahead.

A bridge must change audience mood gradually. It takes careful planning to create a bridge that does not sway, "dump" your audience, or leave them feeling that they have been moved too abruptly from one section of your program to another.

You may encounter several other places within your program which call for a short bridge. Within the main body of the program, if you are using a group of readings rather than just one longer selection, brief transitions will be necessary. It takes creative organization to keep the program moving and have it progress smoothly between selections.

(Section C) *Pièce de Résistance; Main Body*

Just as the main course in a good meal comes after preliminary courses of soup or salad, so the main body of the program usually comes after the attention-getting section. This section may consist of one or several selections of greater difficulty and deeper emotional impact than those encountered in the beginning or concluding sections of the program. It may be a scene from a play, a story, a dramatic monologue. Vincent Price has developed a marvelously interesting program of readings built around the letters of Vincent Van Gogh to his brother, Theo, which he calls *Dear Theo*. The letters themselves, skillfully cut and arranged, with very little bridge material, comprise the main body of this lecture-recital.

The important thing in planning the main body of a program is to keep each moment alive. This does not mean it is necessary to maintain a high emotional peak for thirty minutes or more — it is quite as important to allow your audience moments of rest and relaxation. But those moments must be under control, and extraneous material not absolutely relevant to the organization of the program has a tendency to lose listeners. A creative interpreter will discover and invent ways to sustain interest in a longer selection by careful cutting, skillful bridges, and attention to the ebb and flow of emotional strain.

(Section D) *Conclusion*

Your audience must be brought back to the world of reality with a sense of satisfaction for what you have presented, and be left wishing for more. It is always well to end before anyone wants you to. At the same time, it is a skillful and creative interpreter who can plan just the right concluding material to summarize the program and give it a sense of finish. Another short reading may be appropriate in this section, or a few concluding remarks may be all that is called for. The very last sentence should be memorable in some way, giving your program that dash of individuality that marks it as your creation.

programming for special occasions and groups

At times we are fortunate in being invited to give a program for a special occasion or before a special group. Here is an opportunity for creativity. It is fun to try to chart a program which will not only include the expected but delight your audience with some surprises.

If you can decide on the title, start enlisting interest and curiosity there. Your title will be suggested by a theme, perhaps. Themes often help in keeping a program unified and in giving an audience a means of recalling selections you have presented.

In deciding on the readings to be included, remember your four program sections. Try to get a nice balance between poetry and prose. Many interpreters overdo the reading of poetry, and it can become tiresome to an audience. Don't overlook the charm of the essay and the human interest of the short story. Both of these may be excellent to use in the main part of your program. Light verse is enjoyable during the introduction, sometimes in the conclusion, and occasionally a bit of it will help in a bridge or transition.

summary

Programming, even within the framework of a format which generally proves pleasing to audiences, offers infinite opportunity for creativity. In the *Introduction,* creativity can be used in enlisting the attention of the audience through unique and different approaches; in the *Bridge* sections, the interpreter faces a real challenge to maintain audience interest; in the *Main Body* of a program it takes imagination to keep each moment alive, at the same time allowing for audience rest and relaxation; and finally, in the *Conclusion* the creative interpreter will seek ways to tie up his whole package and leave it as a memorable gift in the minds of his listeners.

In planning programs for special occasions or groups, an unusual title and underlying theme often give a program the stamp of a creative interpreter.

applications: _____

1. Collect as many helpful definitions of *creative thinking* as you can find. John Ciardi, for example, in "What Every Writer Must Learn," *Saturday Review,* December 15, 1956, p. 7, says that creativity is "the imaginatively gifted recombination of known elements into something new."
2. Apply these definitions to the problem of creative program planning by writing out in your own words, referring to your definitions for support, a readable essay on the subject: *How to Program Creatively.* Be prepared to read it aloud to the class.
3. Plan a program to be given before any of the following:
   A women's luncheon group (age, approximately 25-60; 200 in attendance; near Valentine's Day)

A Rotary Club meeting (men of all ages; 75 attending; near Thanksgiving)

A children's library hour (children of ages 6-10; Saturday afternoon from 2:00-3:00 P.M.; near Christmas)

4. Plan a program of your own choice readings, the ones you particularly love and enjoy. Choose the title and theme with care.

preview of chapter 10:

USING THE VOICE EFFECTIVELY

The voice is accepted by most people as a key to personality, character, and culture. It is possible to improve most voices; few have physical problems beyond normal control. In the consideration of the voice, we will be discussing psychological influences as well as physical aspects. We will see how the self-image controls in great measure the beauty of the voice, and we will consider methods for improving physiological processes that affect voice production. Finally, we will talk about speech patterns as they relate to desirable communication.

selections for study and interpretation

Included in this section of reading suggestions are selections ranging from light verse to inspirational excerpts. They are representative of the type of thing most interpreters collect for their personal anthologies to use in program planning. Some are just for fun and help in introductions and bridges. Some provide an inspirational note which is often demanded in programs. Others suggest the type of material which is useful in planning programs for particular occasions and groups. Have you been successful in discovering some real treasures for your anthology?

A leading contemporary feminine poet in the field of light verse is Phyllis McGinley. Her highly amusing and original verse is a guaranteed "ice breaker" on a program.

LINES SCRIBBLED ON A PROGRAM
AND DISCOVERED BY A WAITER SWEEPING UP
AFTER A LITERARY DINNER

Phyllis McGinley
(1905-   )

Whenever public speakers rise
   To dazzle hearers and beholders,
A film comes over both my eyes.
   Inevitably, toward my shoulders
I feel my head begin to sink.
It is an allergy, I think.

No matter what the time or place,
   No matter how adroit the speaker
Or rich the tone or famed the face,
   I feel my life force ebbing weaker.
Even the chairman, lauding him,
Can make the room about me swim.

The room swims. And my palms are wet.
   Languor and lassitude undo me.
I fumble with a cigarette
   For ashtrays never handy to me,
Lift chin, grit teeth, shift in my chair,
But nothing helps — not even prayer.

From all who Talk, I dream away —
From statesmen heavy with their travels,
From presidents of P.T.A.
Exchanging honorary gavels;
From prelate, pedant, wit, and clown,
Club treasurer, John Mason Brown;

From lecturers on the ductless gland,
Ex-Communists, ex-dukes, exhorters,
Poets with poems done by hand,
Political ladies, lady reporters,
Professors armed with bell and book,
Mimes, magnates, mayors, Alistair Cooke.

The hot, the fluent, and the wise,
The dull, the quick-upon-the trigger —
Alike, alike they close my eyes.
Alike they rob me of my vigor.
For me Demosthenes, with pain,
Had mouthed his Attic stones in vain.

The aforementioned being clear
Concerning speech, concerning speaker,
Alas, what am I doing here,
Facing my empty plate and beaker,
And watching with a wild unrest
The rising of the evening's Guest?
Ah, was it mine, this monstrous choice?
Whose accents these? And whose the voice
That wakes in me a pang well known?

Good God, it is my own, my own!

Richard Armour, college professor, lecturer, critic, and essayist, is an outstanding contemporary in the light verse field. He has numerous volumes of verse highly appropriate to the oral interpreter's use.

DISCLOSURE

Richard Armour
(1906-   )

(How can I know what I think till I see what I say? W. H. Auden, in POETS AT WORK)

How could the poet
possibly know
till the very last word
in the very last row?

For a poem's a word
plus a word plus a word,
added, subtracted,
and thoroughly stirred.

And thought makes the word
and the word makes thought,
and some things come
that were never sought.

At what he has said
when the say is done,
the poet's surprised
as anyone.

MY MATTRESS AND I

Richard Armour

Night after night, for years on end,
My mattress has been my closest friend.

My mattress and I are cozy and pally;
There are hills on the sides — I sleep in the valley.

It clearly reveals the shape I'm in:
Where I'm thin it's thick where it's thick I'm thin.

Its contours reflect the first and the last of me.
It's very nearly a plaster cast of me.

I miss my mattress when I am gone;
It's one thing I've made an impression on.

Few have equaled Dorothy Parker's skill in caustic, sardonic
light verse. It is elegantly succinct.

RÉSUMÉ
Dorothy Parker
(1893-   )

> Razors pain you;
> Rivers are damp;
> Acids stain you;
> And drugs cause cramp.
> Guns aren't lawful;
> Nooses give;
> Gas smells awful;
> You might as well live.

PHILOSOPHY
Dorothy Parker

> If I should labor through daylight and dark,
>   Consecrate, valorous, serious, true,
> Then on the world I may blazon my mark;
>   And what if I don't, and what if I do?

A CONSERVATIVE
Charlotte Perkins Stetson Gilman
(1860-1935)

> The garden beds I wandered by
>   One bright and cheerful morn,
> When I found a new-fledged butterfly,
>   A-sitting on a thorn,
> A black and crimson butterfly
>   All doleful and forlorn.
>
> I thought that life could have no sting
>   To infant butterflies,
> So I gazed on this unhappy thing
>   With wonder and surprise,
> While sadly with his waving wing
>   He wiped his weeping eyes.
>
> Said I, "What can the matter be?
>   Why weepest thou so sore?
> With garden fair and sunlight free
>   And flowers in goodly store;" —
> But he only turned away from me
>   And burst into a roar.

Cried he, "My legs are thin and few
  Where once I had a swarm!
Soft fuzzy fur — a joy to view —
  Once kept my body warm,
Before these flapping wing-things grew,
  To hamper and deform!"

At that outrageous bug I shot
  The fury of mine eye;
Said I, in scorn all burning hot,
  In rage and anger high,
"You ignominious idiot!
  Those wings were made to fly!"

"I do not want to fly," said he,
  "I only want to squirm!"
And he drooped his wings dejectedly,
  But still his voice was firm!
"I do not want to be a fly!
  I want to be a worm!"

O yesterday of unknown lack!
  To-day of unknown bliss!
I left my fool in red and black,
  The last I saw was this, —
The creature madly climbing back
  Into his chrysalis.

Rebecca McCann in her lifetime did many clever quatrains
like the following examples.

CHASE

Rebecca McCann
(1897-1927)

I long for a life of more leisure.
I rush through the day, till it feels
As if I am chasing tomorrow
While yesterday snaps at my heels.

COMMON SENSE

Rebecca McCann

> Common sense is good to have
> But never let it master you —
> For then it might deprive you of
> The foolish things it's fun to do.

DOUBLE MEANING

Rebecca McCann

> Though words may seem to be direct
> Their meaning often is twofold —
> When people say, "How young you look!"
> I realize I'm getting old.

TACT

Rebecca McCann

> When you've made an awful blunder
> Don't bewail your brainless act —
> Think of all your past successes,
> Show yourself a little tact.

JUST A GIRL

Anonymous

> Many a throne has had to fall
>   For a girl, just a girl
> Many a king has had to crawl
>   For a girl, just a girl
>
> When a hero goes to war
> He may go to fight for his country
> But 'tis likelier far
> That he sallies forth to battle
>   For a girl, just a girl.

When the doctor turns to say,
    "It's a girl, just a girl,"
Papa murmurs with dismay,
    "What! A girl, just a girl?"
But oh why the bitterness there?
Why the sadness displayed?
Some day some strong man will swear
That the great round world was made
    For that girl, just that girl.

Why was Troy swept out of sight?
    For a girl, just a girl.
Why did Adam take that bite?
    For a girl, just a girl.
But would heaven be so bright
And would any good man care to achieve it
If he might not there claim forever
    Just a girl, a glorious girl?

ADVICE TO THE MARRIED WOMAN

Anonymous

When you marry him, love him.
After you marry him, study him.
If he is honest, honor him.
If he is generous, appreciate him
When he is sad, cheer him.
When he is talkative, listen to him.
When he is quarrelsome, favor him with a moderate
    amount of hostility.
If he is slothful, spur him.
If he is insecure, encourage him.
If he is noble, praise him.
If he is secretive, trust him.
If he is jealous, cure him.
If he cares nought for pleasure, coax him.
If he favors society, accompany him.
When he deserves it, kiss him.
Let him think how well you understand him; but
    never let him know that you manage him.

If you were asked to read a selection at a Lincoln's Birthday program, you might choose to give Walt Whitman's moving tribute. If the audience were more sophisticated, the Vachel Lindsay reading, ABRAHAM LINCOLN WALKS AT MIDNIGHT, might be more appropriate.

OH CAPTAIN! MY CAPTAIN!

Walt Whitman
(1819-1892)

O Captain! my Captain! our fearful trip is done,
The ship has weathered every rack, the prize we sought is won.
The port is near, the bells I hear, the people all exulting,
While follow eyes the steady keel, the vessel grim and daring;

But O heart! heart! heart!
O the bleeding drops of red,
Where on the deck my Captain lies,
Fallen cold and dead.

O Captain! my Captain! rise up and hear the bells;
Rise up — for you the flag is flung — for you the bugle trills,
For you bouquets and ribboned wreaths — for you the shores
a-crowding,
For you they call, the swaying mass, their eager faces turning;

Hear Captain! dear father!
This arm beneath your head!
It is some dream that on the deck,
You've fallen cold and dead.

My Captain does not answer, his lips are pale and still,
My father does not feel my arm, he has no pulse nor will,
The ship is anchored safe and sound, its voyage closed and done,
From fearful trip the victor ship comes in with object won;

Exult, O shores, and ring, O bells!
But I with mournful tread,
Walk the deck my Captain lies,
Fallen cold and dead.

ABRAHAM LINCOLN WALKS AT MIDNIGHT
In Springfield, Illinois

Vachel Lindsay
(1879-1931)

It is portentous, and a thing of state
That here at midnight, in our little town
A mourning figure walks, and will not rest,
Near the old court-house pacing up and down,

Or by his homestead, or in shadowed yards
He lingers where his children used to play,
Or through the market, on the well-worn stones
He stalks until the dawn-stars burn away.

A bronzed, lank man! His suit of ancient black,
A famous high top-hat and plain worn shawl
Make him the quaint great figure that men love,
The prairie-lawyer, master of us all.

He cannot sleep upon his hillside now.
He is among us: —as in times before!
And we who toss and lie awake for long,
Breathe deep, and start, to see him pass the door.

His head is bowed. He thinks of men and kings.
Yea, when the sick world cries, how can he sleep?
Too many peasants fight, they know not why;
Too many homesteads in black terror weep.

The sins of all the war-lords burn his heart.
He sees the dreadnaughts scouring every main.
He carries on his shawl-wrapped shoulders now
The bitterness, the folly and the pain.

He cannot rest until a spirit-dawn
Shall come; —the shining hope of Europe free:
A league of sober folk, the worker's earth,
Bringing long peace to Cornland, Alp and Sea.

It breaks his heart that kings must murder still,
That all his hours of travail here for men
Seem yet in vain. And who will bring white peace
That he may sleep upon his hill again?

Were you asked to entertain a group on St. Patrick's Day, what could be more delightful than WHAT IS IT TO BE IRISH? by Hal Boyle, the distinguished newspaper columnist.

WHAT IS IT TO BE IRISH?

Hal Boyle
(1911-   )

What is it to be Irish?

On 364 days of the year being Irish isn't visibly different from being Scotch, French, Italian, Jewish, Serbian, Dutch, or — yes — even English.

The Irishman pays his bills, complains against his taxes, does his work and listens to his wife like the man of any other race.

But on this one day of the year — holy St. Patrick's Day — the Irishman becomes an Irishman.

And on this day you have to be Irish to know what it is to be Irish.

The outer signs, of course, can be seen by all. The Irishman overnight grows a foot taller and stalks the earth a giant. All traffic lights turn green before him and if they don't he sees red.

But this air of majesty is only token evidence of interior change. The men of other races who envy the Irishman his bearing on St. Patrick's Day would envy him far more if they could look inside the Irishman's soul.

What is it to be Irish?

How can you put the wonder of it into words? If a psychiatrist stretched himself out on his own warm couch after his last customer had gone home and he dreamed of the man he himself would most like to be — well, he might be perfect, but he'd still be only half an Irishman on St. Patrick's Day.

What is it to be Irish?

It is to have an angel in your mouth, turning your prose to poetry.

It is to have the gift of tongues, to know the language of all living things.

Does an Irishman pause and turn an ear to a tree? It is because on this day he wants to hear what one sleepy bud says to another as it opens its pale green hands to the warm sun of Spring.

What is it to be Irish?

Oh, on this day it is music. Not just the cornet in the parading high school band, but the deep, deep music of living; the low, sad rhythm of eternity.

The Irishman hears the high song of the turning spheres, the dim lullaby of the worm in its cocoon.

All the world is in tune and he is in step with the tune, the tune only he can hear.

What is it to be Irish?

It is to live the whole history of his race between a dawn and a dawn — the long wrongs, the bird swift joys, the endless hurt of his ancestors since the morning of time in a forgotten forest, the knock at his heart which is part of his religion.

What is it to be Irish?

It isn't only the realization that he is descended from kings. It is the realization he is a king himself, an empire on two feet striding in power, a strolling continent of awe.

What is it to be Irish?

Why on St. Patrick's Day, to be Irish is to know more glory, adventure, magic, victory, exultation, gratitude and gladness than any other man can experience in a lifetime.

What is it to be Irish?

It is to walk in complete mystic understanding with God for 24 wonderful hours.

> There is a tendency among contemporary scholars and teachers to ignore or snub material such as Ingersoll's moving essay, AT THE TOMB OF NAPOLEON, or anything as emotional as William Jennings Bryan's eulogy, IMMORTALITY, which follows it, and yet both selections, and others of this nature, have their place and time in platform work. We should avoid becoming so sophisticated that we rule out inspirational and stirring words men have spoken and written.

AT THE TOMB OF NAPOLEON

Robert G. Ingersoll
(1833-1899)

A little while ago, I stood by the grave of the old Napoleon — a magnificent tomb of gilt and gold, fit almost for a dead deity — and gazed upon the sarcophagus of black Egyptian marble, where rest at last the ashes of that restless man. I leaned over the balustrade and thought about the career of the greatest soldier of the modern world.

I saw him walking upon the banks of the Seine, contemplating suicide. I saw him at Toulon — I saw him putting down the mob in the streets of Paris — I saw him at the head of the army of Italy — I saw him crossing the bridge of Lodi with the tricolor in his hand — I saw him in Egypt in the shadow of the Pyramids — I saw him conquer the Alps and mingle the eagles of France with the eagles of the crags. I saw him at Marengo — at Ulm and Austerlitz. I saw him in Russia, where the infantry of the snow and the cavalry of the wild blast scattered his legions like winter's withered leaves. I saw him at Leipsic in defeat and disaster

— driven by a million bayonets back upon Paris — clutched like a wild beast — banished to Elba. I saw him escape and retake an empire by the force of his genius. I saw him upon the frightful field of Waterloo, where Chance and Fate combined to wreck the fortunes of their former king. And I saw him at St. Helena, with his hands crossed behind him, gazing out upon the sad and solemn sea.

I thought of the orphans and widows he had made — of the tears that had been shed for his glory, and of the only woman who ever loved him, pushed from his heart by the cold hand of ambition. And I said I would rather have been a French peasant and worn wooden shoes. I would rather have lived in a hut with a vine growing over the door, and the grapes growing purple in the kisses of the autumn sun. I would rather have been that poor peasant with my loving wife by my side, knitting as the day died out of the sky — with my children upon my knees and their arms about me. I would rather have been that man and gone down to the tongueless silence of the dreamless dust than to have been that imperial impersonation of force and murder known as Napoleon the Great.

IMMORTALITY

William Jennings Bryan
(1860-1925)

> (*Excerpted from a eulogy of Mr. Bryan's given in memory of a friend and colleague before the Fifty-third Congress.*)

. . . If the Father deigns to touch with divine power the cold and pulseless heart of the buried acorn, and make it burst forth from its prison walls, will He leave neglected in the earth the soul of man, who was made in the image of his Creator? If He stoops to give the rose-bush, whose withered blossoms float upon the breeze, the sweet assurance of another springtime, will He withhold the words of hope from the sons of men when the frosts of winter come? If matter, mute and inanimate, though changed by the forces of nature into a multitude of forms, can never die, will the imperial spirit of man suffer annihilation after it has paid a brief visit, like a royal guest, to this tenement of clay?

Rather let us believe that He, who in His apparent prodigality, wastes not the rain drop, the blade of grass, or the evening's sighing zephyr, but makes them all to carry out His eternal plans, has given immortality to the mortal, and gathered to Himself the generous spirit of our friend.

Instead of mourning, let us look up and address him in the words of the poet:

> "Thy day has come, not gone;
> Thy sun has risen, not set;
> Thy life is now beyond
> The reach of death or change,
> Not ended — but begun.
> O, noble soul! O, gentle heart! Hail, and farewell."

This very human and charming selection first appeared as an editorial by the late Ben Hur Lampman in the PORT-LAND OREGONIAN as a response to a question by a subscriber to the ONTARIO ARGUS. It is reprinted through the courtesy of Mrs. Ben Hur Lampman of Portland, Oregon.

WHERE TO BURY A DOG

Ben Hur Lampman
(1886-1954)

"Where shall I bury my dog?"

We would say to the Ontario man that there are various places in which a dog may be buried. We are thinking now of a setter, whose coat was aflame in the sunshine, and who, so far as we are aware, never entertained a mean or unworthy thought. This setter is buried beneath a cherry tree, under four feet of garden loam, and at its proper season the cherry tree strews petals on the green lawn of his grave.

Beneath a cherry tree, or an apple, or any flowering shrub is an excellent place to bury a good dog. Beneath such trees, such shrubs, he slept on a drowsy summer, or gnawed at a flavorous bone, or lifted head to challenge some strange intruder. These are good places, in life or in death.

Yet it is a small matter. For if the dog be well remembered, if sometimes he leaps through your dreams actual as in life, eyes kindling, laughing, begging — it matters not at all where that dog sleeps; on a hill where the wind is unrebuked, and trees are roaring, or beside a stream he knew in puppyhood, or somwhere in the flatness of a pasture land where . . . cattle graze. It is all one to the dog, and all one to you, and nothing is gained, and nothing lost, if memory lives.

But there is one best place to bury a dog.

If you bury him in this spot, he will come to you when you call — come to you over the grim, dim frontiers of death, and down the well-remembered path, and to your side again. And though you call a dozen living dogs to heel they shall not growl at him, nor resent his coming, for he belongs there. People may scoff at you, who see no lightest blade of grass bent by his footfall, who hear no whimper, people who may never really have had a dog. Smile at them, for you shall know something that is hidden from them, and which is well worth the knowing. The one best place to bury a good dog is in the heart of his master.

THE POOR SCHOLAR'S SOLILOQUY first appeared in CHILDHOOD EDUCATION in 1944. It was written by Dr. Stephen M. Corey, now a Professor of Education,

Teacher's College, Columbia University, who, no doubt, had met in his earlier teaching days many a poor scholar with the problems and frustrations hinted at in this charming selection.

THE POOR SCHOLAR'S SOLILOQUY

Stephen M. Corey
(1904-   )

No, I'm not very good in school. This is my second year in the seventh grade and I'm bigger and taller than the other kids. They like me all right, though, even if I don't say much in the school room, because outside I can tell them how to do a lot of things. They tag me around and that sort of makes up for what goes on in school.

I don't know why the teachers don't like me. They never have very much. Seems like they don't think you know anything unless they can name the book it comes out of. I've got a lot of books in my own room at home — books like *Popular Science Mechanical Encyclopedia,* and the Sears' and Ward's catalogues, but I don't very often just sit down and read them through like they make us do in school. I use my books when I want to find something out, like whenever Mom buys anything second-hand I look it up in Sears' and Ward's first and tell her if she's getting stung or not. I can use the index in a hurry to find the things I want.

In school, though, we've got to learn whatever is in the book and I just can't memorize the stuff. Last year I stayed after school every night for two weeks trying to learn the names of the Presidents. Of course I knew some of them, like Washington and Jefferson and Lincoln, but there must have been thirty altogether, and I never did get them straight.

I'm not too sorry though because the kids who learned the Presidents had to turn right around and learn all the Vice Presidents. I am taking the seventh grade over but our teacher this year isn't so interested in the names of the Presidents. She has us trying to learn the names of all the great American inventors.

I guess I just can't remember names in history. Anyway, this year I've been trying to learn about trucks because my uncle owns three and he says I can drive one when I'm sixteen. I already know the horsepower and number of forward and backward speeds of twenty-six American trucks, some of them Diesels, and I can spot each make a long way off. It's funny how that Diesel works. I started to tell my teacher about it last Wednesday in science class when the pump we were using to make a vacuum in a bell jar got hot, but she said she didn't see what a Diesel engine had to do with our experiment of air pressure, so I just kept still. The kids semed interested though. I took four of them around to my uncle's garage after school and we saw the mechanic, Gus, tearing a big truck Diesel down. Boy, does he know his stuff!

programming creatively

I'm not very good in geography either. They call it economic geography this year. We've been studying the imports and exports of Chile all week, but I couldn't tell you what they are. Maybe the reason is I had to miss school yesterday because my uncle took me and his big trailer truck down state about two hundred miles and we brought almost ten tons of stock to the Chicago market.

He told me where we were going and I had to figure out the highways to take and also the mileage. He didn't do anything but drive and turn where I told him to. Was that fun! I sat with a map in my lap and told him to turn south or southeast or some other direction. We made seven stops and drove over five hundred miles round trip. I'm figuring now what his oil cost and also the wear and tear on the truck — he calls it depreciation — so we'll know how much we made.

I even write out all the bills and send letters to the farmers about what their pigs and beef cattle brought at the stockyards. I only made three mistakes in 17 letters last time, my aunt said — all commas. She's been through high school and reads them over. I wish I could write school themes that way. The last one I had to write was on, "What a Daffodil Thinks of Spring," and I just couldn't get going.

I don't do very well in school in arithmetic either, seems I just can't keep my mind on the problems. We had one the other day like this:

If a 57 foot telephone pole falls across a cement highway so that 17 3/6 feet extend from one side and 14 9/17 feet from the other, how wide is the highway?

That seemed to me like an awfully silly way to get the width of a highway. I didn't even try to answer it because it didn't even say whether the pole had fallen straight across or not.

Even in shop I don't get very good grades. All of us kids made a broom holder and a bookend this term and mine were sloppy. I just couldn't get interested. Mom doesn't use a broom much . . . and all our books are in a bookcase. . . . Anyway, I wanted to make an end gate for my uncle's trailer but the shop teacher said that meant using metal and wood both and I'd have to learn how to work with wood first. I didn't see why but I kept still and made a tie rack at school and the tail gate after school at my uncle's garage. He said I saved him $10.

Civics is hard for me, too. I've been staying after school trying to learn the "Articles of Confederation" for almost a week because the teacher said we couldn't be good citizens unless we did. I really tried, because I want to be a good citizen. I did hate to stay after school, though, because a bunch of us boys from the south end of town have been cleaning up the old lot across from Taylor's Machine Shop to make a playground out of it for the little kids from the Methodist home. I made the jungle gym from old pipe and the guys made me a Grand Mogul to keep the playground going. We raised enough money collecting scrap this month to build a wire fence clear around the lot.

Dad says I can quit school when I'm fifteen, and I'm sort of anxious to because there are a lot of things I want to learn how to do and as my uncle says, I'm not getting any younger.

BEN HUR: A Tale of the Christ was published in 1880. Highly popular throughout the years, it has been staged and twice made into a motion picture. Its author, Lew Wallace, was discussing the divinity of Christ with Ingersoll, the free thinker, one time when they were together on a train. Wallace decided to study the life of Jesus, and out of his research grew the tale. In BEN-HUR, one of the most beautiful Christmas readings available is to be found for the cutting.

Christ Is Born
BEN HUR, Chapter XI, Book
First, A Tale of the Christ

Lew Wallace
(1827-1905)

(*Cut for public performance by Baxter Geeting*)

A mile and a half, it may be two miles, southeast of Bethlehem, there is a plain separated from the town by an intervening swell of the mountain. . . .

At the side farthest from the town, close under a bluff, there was an extensive *marah*, or sheepcot, ages old. In some long-forgotten foray, the building had been unroofed and almost demolished. The enclosure attached to it remained intact, however, and that was of more importance to the shepherds who drove their charges thither than the house itself.

. . . .

[On this day] a number of shepherds, seeking fresh walks for their flocks led them up to this plain; and from early morning the groves had been made ring with calls . . . the bleating of sheep and goats, the tinkling of bells, the lowing of cattle, and the barking of dogs. When the sun went down, they led the way to the marah, and by nightfall had everything safe in the field; then they kindled a fire down by the gate, partook of their humble supper, and sat down to rest and talk, leaving one on watch.

There were six of these men, omitting the watchman; and afterwhile they assembled in a group near the fire, some sitting, some lying prone. . . . in appearance, rough and savage as the gaunt dogs sitting with them around the blaze.

. . . .

They rested and talked; and their talk was all about their flocks, a dull theme to the world, yet a theme which was all the world to them. . . .

Yet these men, rude and simple as they were, had a knowledge and a wisdom of their own. . . . In the verse of the Shema they found all the learning and all the law of their simple lives — that their Lord was One God, and that they must love him with all their souls. And they loved him, and such was their wisdom, surpassing that of kings.

While they talked, and before the first watch was over, one by one the shepherds went to sleep, each lying where he had sat.

The night, like most nights of the winter season in the hill country, was clear, crisp, and sparkling with stars. There was no wind. The atmosphere seemed never so pure, and the stillness was more than silence; it was a holy hush, a warning that heaven was stooping low to whisper good things to the listening earth.

By the gate, hugging his mantle close, the watchman walked; at times he stopped, attracted by a stir among the sleeping herds, or by a jackal's cry off on the mountain-side. The midnight was slow coming to him; but at last it came. His talk was done; now for the dreamless sleep with which labor blesses its wearied children! He moved toward the fire, but paused; a light was breaking around him, soft and white, like the moon's. He waited breathlessly. The light deepened; things before invisible came to view; he saw the whole field, and all it sheltered. A chill sharper than that of the frosty air — a chill of fear — smote him. He looked up; the stars were gone; the light was dropping as from a window in the sky; as he looked, it became a splendor; then, in terror he cried,

"Awake, awake!"

Up sprang the dogs, and, howling, ran away.

The herds rushed together bewildered.

The men clambered to their feet, weapons in hand.

"What is it?" they asked, in one voice.

"See!" cried the watchman, "the sky is on fire!"

Suddenly the light became intolerably bright, and they covered their eyes, and dropped upon their knees; then, as their souls shrank with fear, they fell upon their faces blind and fainting, and would have died had not a voice said to them,

"Fear not!"

And they listened.

"Fear not; for behold, I will bring you good tidings of great joy, which shall be to all people."

The voice, in sweetness and soothing more than human, and low and clear, penetrated all their being, and filled them with assurance. They rose upon their knees, and, looking worshipfully, beheld in the centre of a great glory the appearance of a man, clad in a robe intensely white; above its shoulders towered the tops of wings shining and folded; a star over its forehead glowed with steady lustre, brilliant as Hesperus; its hands were stretched towards them in blessing; its face was serene and divinely beautiful.

· · · · · · · · · · · · · · ·

Directly the angel continued:

"For unto you is born this day, in the city of David, a Saviour, which is Christ the Lord!"

· · · · · · · · · · · · · · ·

"And this shall be a sign unto you. . . . Ye shall find the babe, wrapped in swaddling-clothes, lying in a manger."

The herald spoke not again; his good tidings were told; yet he stayed awhile. Suddenly the light, of which he seemed the centre, turned roseate and began to tremble; then up, far as men could see, there was flashing of white wings, and coming and going of radiant forms, and voices as of a multitude chanting in unison.

"Glory to God in the highest, and on earth peace, good-will towards men!" Not once the praise, but many times.

Then the herald raised his eyes as seeking approval of one far off; his wings stirred, and spread slowly and majestically. . . . he rose lightly, and without effort, floated out of view, taking the light up with him. Long after he was gone, down from the sky fell the refrain in measure mellowed by distance, "Glory to God in the highest, and on earth peace, good-will towards men."

skills

using the voice effectively

Your attitudes toward yourself, toward the idea you are expressing, and toward your listeners are normally quite obvious in the quality of your voice. . . . The voice belies the words.

Aggertt and Bowen,
Communicative Reading

. . . it is the voice which is basic to oral communication. . . .

Charlotte Lee,
Oral Interpretation

When the telephone rings and you answer, the voice you hear invariably creates an immediate response. It makes you happy, angry, bored, perplexed, or maybe sad. If it is the voice of an unknown person, you create a mental image of that person. You form an opinion about his size, education, temperament, perhaps even his general interests. It is a common human reaction to judge a person by his voice.

Quite often, however, a voice is not an accurate picture of a person. You are often surprised at the sound of a friend's voice on the telephone. Haven't you said, more than once, "You don't sound like yourself"? Listening to poets reading their own poetry may be a disillusioning experience. The voice of the poet may be drab, shallow, and inflexible. Yet you know the poet's mental images are lively. Occasionally a poet comes along, Dylan Thomas for example, whose voice matches his poetry in richness and communicative quality.

Recognizing the power of the human voice to give a picture of ourselves and to carry meaning and emotion from the printed page to the listener, we need to discover how we can develop the communicative potential of the voice. "Golden-voiced" and "silver-tongued" interpreters are not always possessed of naturally beautiful voices. Good voices can be built. Limitations to what can be done with a voice are not so great as we may believe. It is possible for practically all of us to have voices of sufficient beauty and strength to interpret just about anything we might aspire to read. Very rarely are there elements we cannot control, such as glandular conditions which require medical aid. (Thyroid deficiency may cause a voice to be unpleasantly low.) The average person has the physical equipment to work with. Let us begin!

self-concepts and the voice

Let us begin by realizing there are two general ways to improve the voice. We must use both to be fully effective. The first of these is psychological, having to do with understandings about ourselves and our voices. The second is physiological, having to do with understandings about the voice itself, how it is produced, and how it can be improved for the purposes of oral interpretation.

Most of us have a "mind set" about our own voice. We have an attitude toward it — we like it or we don't, or perhaps we are just indifferent about it. We think of it as weak, strong, raspy, pleasant, dull, or exciting. We tell ourselves we have an unpleasant voice or an attractive one, or perhaps we just think of it as medium-passable. What we tell ourselves may be true. A tape recording will help us know for sure. But we should realize also that what is true about the voice now need not be true even tomorrow, a week from today, certainly not next month. There are ways to improve on what we hear now.

Self-concepts have much to do with the shaping of voices. If one views himself as efficient and dynamic, chances are his voice reflects this by being of good quality and distinct. If he has felt a lack of poise and security, his voice probably sounds hesitant, flat, and thin.

The most important step toward voice improvement is that first step — motivation. We need a reason, a really good reason, for wanting to sound better. If we are seeking to become teachers, actors, speakers, or more attractive people, we have motivation. Nothing is more important to any of these than a fine voice.

Nothing is more basic than (and nothing will replace) a healthy self-respect in attaining an effective voice. All voice improvement rests on psychological conditioning. It is a simple truth overlooked or left unmentioned by most speech experts because of its elementary nature, but nothing is basically more vital than to establish the belief that you are a valuable person and have good vocal equipment which you want very much to improve, and can.

health and the voice

Fundamental to a vibrant, flexible voice is good physical health. We may understand the mechanical aspects of voice production (the way we breathe, produce tone, articulate meaningful sounds) and practice exercises faithfully toward the end of achieving better quality, but we must also attend to our general health. Adequate rest, good food, exercise, and correct posture all assist in the building of a desirable voice. The voice is a fine and sensitive instrument. Just as the musician protects and cares for his violin or clarinet, so must we protect and care for our voices. Physical abuse in the nature of inadequate rest, too much smoking, excessive yelling or vocal strain of any type, will damage the instrument.

voice production

Your voice is the result of the way you breathe, subsequent reactions in your nose, mouth, and throat cavities and passages, and the way you break up sound into verbal symbols. These three processes have been given the following labels by most teachers of speech:

1. Respiration (breathing)
2. Phonation (sound vibrating and resonating)
3. Articulation (sound breaking up into speech)

Respiration

Normal breathing and breathing while you are speaking do differ. There is a reason to know how to breathe while you are speaking. By understanding the process you will be able to improve the strength, resonance, and clarity of your voice.

The chest cavity contains the lungs, two masses of spongy, elastic tissue, which are connected by the bronchial tubes to the windpipe, leading up to the throat. At the bottom of the chest cavity is the diaphragm, dividing the body trunk in two parts, extending across the body almost blanketlike. The diaphragm is attached to the breastbone in front, to the spinal column in back, and is moored to the lower ribs at the sides. It is the principal muscle of inhalation.

Air comes into the lungs because of the enlargement of the chest cavity when the diaphragm (or blanket-like floor of the cavity) straightens out and the rib cage rises. When the interior area is enlarged, a vacuum is created. Air rushes in to fill the added space — rushes into the lungs, which expand. Atmospheric pressure outside the body is balanced by this influx of air. This is what happens when we breathe in.

When we exhale or breathe out, another set of muscles reduces the size of the chest cavity. The diaphragm is forced up into a relaxed position, and the rib cage is lowered.

It is possible in normal breathing to have this intake and expulsion of air without active use of the diaphragm. Chest breathing will sustain life. Most speech experts believe, however, that diaphragmatic breathing gives a larger, stronger column of air (exhaling) upon which we depend for speech. We speak while we exhale. In speaking, the exhalation process takes longer than inhalation. Shortness of breath will result in thin tone, poor quality, and choppy phrasing.

HOW CAN WE PRACTICE TO IMPROVE BREATHING? First, expel all air. Force it out. Then wait. Suddenly relax and notice how air rushes in to fill your lungs. Now, this time, as you exhale, try to project a steady, clear "OOOOOOOOOOOOOOOOOOOOOOO" stretching it as long as you can, maintaining even tone quality.

Repeat this process. Each time, raise the pitch of your "OOOOO" until it goes to the limit of your comfortable range. Then start down the scale and do the same.

Now, as you expel your column of air, try for variety in pitch but be careful to sustain the tone quality as you read:

```
                              thrush
There's
          a          brown
              merry,                              up in the tree.
                                      sitting
```

```
He's                            He's
        singing                        singing
                 to me                              to me.
```

```
And                       say,
        what does he                          boy?
                              little girl, little
```

```
            0                         running  o- ver with J
       0        0                                            o
     0              0      the world's                        y!
   0                      0
```

Were you able to do it in one breath? Good! Now, take any poem you may particularly enjoy and which lends itself to simple phrasing and tonal variety. Read at least a verse on one column of air. Keep the tone flexible in pitch but steady in quality. It isn't easy, but practice will bring fast improvement. You will soon notice how much better your voice sounds and you will clear up some problems you may have had in projection. If you have no poem to practice on, we offer the following pretty verse:

> Fair daffodils, we weep to see
>   You haste away so soon:
> As yet the early rising-sun
>   Has not attained his noon.
>   Stay, stay,
>   Until the hasting day
>   Has run
>   But to the even-song;
> And, having prayed together, we
>   Will go with you along.
>   From "To Daffodils," *Robert Herrick*

Finally, take a longer poem and practice breath control as you read, taking your air quickly and unobtrusively, then supporting your phrasing with that column of air until you come to the next natural pause. Try to take in enough air to support a sustained, clear tone that slides easily up and down the scale giving life and vibrancy to your voice. (Selections for practice are included at the end of this Chapter.)

Phonation

The sound-producing mechanism of the body is involved in a rather complicated process known as phonation. Simply stated, it is the vibration and resonance of sound.

Let us recall the column of air described in the breathing process. Watch the column of air as it proceeds upward through the voice box (larynx) located in the throat. The voice box has a pair of lips (glottis, or vocal bands, or vocal chords) which start vibrating as the air passes through them. To get a sketchy idea of this process, think of times when you have stretched the neck of an inflated balloon and, as the air escaped through the rubber mouth, there was a squeak. If you became expert, you could even make a tune come out. Or, maybe you have blown through the mouthpiece of a trumpet. The mouthpiece alone emits a sound, though of pretty poor quality. Your voice would sound about as bad if you didn't have resonators to finish the job.

Now, let us follow the air column being forced out the lips of the voice box. It goes to the passages and cavities (resonators) in your mouth, throat (pharynx), and upper part of your voice box as well as your nose. Instead of squeaks and squawks, sound waves are set up which give your voice amplification and quality. It is as if you had attached the mouthpiece to the tubing of the trumpet and the sound had come out rich and vibrant.

In this process it is quite possible to impair the voice quality by tightening or tensing the throat and voice box, giving a high-pitched, strident tone. If you are seeking to sound like a very old person, you may actually tighten your throat to get this tone. A relaxed vocal mechanism will give you a deeper, better pitched, more forceful sound. Tension in the resonating chambers also gives you poor tone quality and insufficient power.

HOW CAN WE PRACTICE TO IMPROVE PHONATION? First, relax the whole body. Stretch, flop over touching the floor and sway your body from side to side, your arms swinging loosely. Now stand up easily, rotate your head several times and drop it forward on your chest. Yawn. Breathe in several long, relaxed breaths. Now, start vocalizing the vowels: A, E, I, O, U. Say them all on one long column of air, maintaining that steady, relaxed tone.

Now try any bit of poetry you wish, thinking not at this time of syllabication so much as of tone quality — that well-rounded vowel quality. Keep it relaxed and easy. A favorite of speech teachers throughout the years has been "Thou too, sail on, O Ship of State!/ Sail on, O Union, strong and great!/ Humanity with all its fears,/ With all the hopes of future years,/ Is hanging breathless on thy fate!" Longfellow is full of wonderful bits to practice while relaxing: "And the night shall be filled with music,/ And the cares, that infest the day,/ Shall fold their tents, like the Arabs,/ And as silently steal away." He has many others.

Now, for resonance, take a dee-e-e-e-e-ep breath and as you exhale say, "ME — ME — ME — ME — ME." Try the same with "NO — NO — NO — NO — NO — NO." Then "YANG — YANG — YANG — YANG — YANG." These are the only nasal sounds properly sounded THROUGH the nose. There are just these three — M, N, and NG. Find your optimum pitch (that pitch at which you read with greatest comfort and relaxation) and experiment with:

> Over the hill, over the hill,
>   The dews are wet and the shadows long;
> Twilight lingers and all is still
>   Save for the call of a faery-song.
>
> Calling, calling out of the west,
>   Over the hill in the dusk of day,
> Over the hill to a land of rest,
>   A land of peace with the world away.
>
> Never again where grasses sweep,
>   And lights are low, and the cool brakes still —
> Never a song, but a dreamless sleep,
>   Over the hill . . . over the hill.
>   "May-Eve," Thomas S. Jones, Jr.

Articulation

Intelligible speech depends on articulation, which means breaking up sound into understandable words and phrases. Articulation transforms sound into language.

We accomplish articulation with the lips, tongue, jaw, teeth, and the hard and soft palates. The hard palate is another name for the roof of the mouth, and the soft palate is the fleshy extension of that roof, toward the back of the mouth. The manner in which these articulators work in producing language is somewhat too complicated for us to consider in detail. It is enough for us to understand that speech very often fails to communicate as a result of laziness or faulty use of one of the articulators. For example, we say someone has "frozen lips," meaning we wish he would make his lips more mobile and thereby make the words more distinct. Another person may have a "thick tongue," giving a "slobbish" quality to his speech. Some men clamp pipes between their jaws and their articulation sounds sluggish. Even without pipes some of us have tight jaws. Good articulation calls for active jaws, lips, and tongue.

HOW CAN WE PRACTICE TO IMPROVE ARTICULATION? We can begin by consciously activating the articulators if they are not performing properly now. Indistinctness arises mainly from lethargy in enunciating consonants. Consonants really control enunciation. Vowels make speech musical. But both consonants and vowels are improved with active articulators.

Practice the vowel sounds first. Say "ee" as in beef; "ah" as in father; "oh" as in float; and "oo" as in root. Are your articulators active?

Take next the consonant sounds. There are general categories of consonants upon which you might concentrate. First there are the plosives — p, b, t, d, k, and g — in which a short explosion of air makes the sound. You just can't speak clearly without positive plosives. Practice anything which exercises these sounds, from "the big black bear bit the big black bug" to "Peter Piper picked a peck of pickled peppers." Find or make up some exercises for the rest of the plosives and be sure your articulators are active in repeating them.

Next, put some practice time on the fricatives — f, v, s, and z — in which sound is made by forcing air through the articulators. (Fricatives also include th, sh, and zh [decision] and h [hot].) Discover some practice sentences such as "I fell very fast through a short space." Perhaps the most difficult sound to pronounce pleasantly among the fricatives is s and sometimes z. It is necessary to avoid a hiss and still not sound as if you had a lisp. Here is an excellent old nursery rhyme on which to get that s just right:

> Sing a song of sixpence
> A pocket full of rye,
> Four and twenty blackbirds
> Baked in a pie.
>
> When the pie was opened,
> The birds began to sing.
> Wasn't that a dainty dish
> To set before the King?

In addition to the plosives and the fricatives, there are the affricates, which combine the elements of plosive and fricative sound. Can you properly pronounce ch as in charity? How about j as in judge? Practice "judge not, lest ye be judged" and "faith, hope, and charity . . . but the greatest of these is charity."

Also check to see if you are articulating the semivowels wh as in when, w as in win, l as in light, r as in rope, and y as in yellow. Compose a practice exercise of your own.

We have mentioned before that there are ONLY THREE sounds properly nasal in production — m, n, and ng. Yet many people have the serious fault of nasalizing other sounds, which we call "talking through the nose." Nasality results at times from enlarged tonsils, nervousness, or a psychological disposition to be complaining and whiny. To test yourself for the improper nasalizing of tones, hold a small mirror under your nose and read the following. If any mist forms on the mirror, you are in trouble, for there are no nasal sounds in these sentences:

1. "Style is the dress of thoughts." (Philip Dommer Stanhope.)
2. "He said little but to the purpose." (Lord Byron.)

Now that we have discussed the importance of conscious application to activating the articulators and have considered specific ways in which we can do so as we approach the vowel and consonant sounds, let us not overlook another important part of articulation. That is pronunciation. In the final analysis, some persons are articulating badly simply because they are mispronouncing words. They may err in two ways: by leaving out syllables or by adding them. For example, there is the person who says "po-try," leaving out the e altogether. Properly pronounced, of course it is po-e-try. Then there is the person who says "athalete" instead of athlete. He has inserted an a which does not belong in this word.

Suppose you test yourself as you pronounce these words:

> diamond, duel, poem, often, interpretative, intensity, power, our, mountain, pretty, sculpture, picture, and interesting.

Did you add or omit any syllables? Did you pronounce "often" with a t? You should pronounce it without a t — "off-en" is correct. Study words carefully in your selections for interpretation and be sure you are giving them the proper pronunciation.

Speech Patterns

Certain problems arise outside the realms of voice production which we have discussed. These may be considered as faults in speech patterns. A desirable speech pattern is one which strikes most listeners as being agreeable and suitable to the material being read. But some people suffer from patterns of speech which (1) sound monotonous, (2) are too slow or too fast, or (3) are so suffused with regional dialect that communication is interrupted. There are other faulty speech patterns, but most of the problems fall into one of these three categories.

Let us consider first the monotone, the person who seems unable to lift or lower his voice often enough to get it out of the realm of a very limited pitch. He makes you want to deafen your ears. Vocal monotony, in most cases, is a pattern which has developed from habit. It may stem from laziness, from a tendency to be too deliberate and laborious in one's thinking, or it may result from an effort to "hold the floor" once one is launched on a discussion. In most cases it is a habit which can be broken by conscious effort. Voices need variety in pitch to communicate meaning and emotion and to hold attention. This part of speech has been called a "melody pattern." Your melody pattern distinguishes your manner of speaking from that of others. It tells others whether you are interesting, deliberate, boring, or exuberant. Sometimes whole nations are characterized by their melody patterns. The Welsh are thought of as poetic because their dialect falls so poetically on the ear. Strive in your melody pattern for flexibility and the variety which will make your voice attractive to the listener.

Next, the problem of faulty speech patterns has probably occurred to you as you have heard persons who "word jam," or who speak so rapidly or so slowly that you have trouble getting the meaning. "Word jam" refers to the habit of lumping several words together — "Ican 'nunerstanwhayousay." After jamming a group of words together, this person may pause and prepare for another bunch of words. He talks in fits and starts. Too rapid speaking is really seldom heard. Too slow speaking occurs more frequently. If you suffer from any of these problems, try to establish a steady, communicative speed at which listeners can perform their listening function most comfortably.

The problem of regional dialect requires individual help at times. It is not necessary, however, and not even desirable always to overcome all regional touches. An exception may be when one expects to become a professional speaker or actor. Then it is important to clear the speech pattern of regional inflections.

The United States hears three principal dialects: the Eastern (we sometimes call it "Bostonian"), the Southern, and the General American. There are a great many smaller regional dialects of more intense nature. There is the "Bronx," for example, found in New York. There is also the "mountaineer" speech of the Appalachians. Perhaps the General American is most acceptable if you are planning on a career in radio or television. For professional speech or acting, the speech pattern needs a little more polishing with some of the refinements of standard diction. But a poor surface polish that sounds, and is, superficial may be most distressing to listeners.

If you have a very strong dialect in your speech pattern, it is your responsibility to bring your speech into conformity with those around you, at least to the extent that it does not interfere with easy communication. If you are able to use a regional dialect with ease, it may be a real advantage in interpretation. Select some readings to bring your talents into play. If you attempt to interpret a selection with much regional dialect that does not come naturally to you, however, it would be an error to try to read with great attention to exact pronunciation. It would be better to read the selection with just a hint of dialect. If it is a French dialect, accent the last syllables of words. If it is a Scotch dialect, roll you "r's." That is enough. To do more might interfere with communication of the total meaning.

In general, there is no better way to improve your own speech pattern than to listen to those around you and to the many wonderful performers available to us on radio and television. Try to analyze what it is about their speech pattern that is clear, natural, and simple, and then strive to bring your own speech pattern into balance.

summary

People are frequently judged by their voices. A pleasing, well pitched, clear voice seems to fit a well educated, cultured person. It behooves us to develop voices which give others evidence of our ability as people. It is possible to improve most voices; few are limited by physical conditions beyond control.

Psychological attitudes toward oneself influence the voice; belief in oneself as a person is basic to voice improvement. Motivation is imperative to an effective program of voice development. Fundamental also to voice improvement is a program encouraging good health.

The voice is a result of respiration (breathing), phonation (sound vibrating and resonating), and articulation (sound breaking up into speech). Understanding the physiological processes involved in each helps us to appreciate and use certain exercises for vocal improvement. Speech patterns distinguish individual voices. Common faults noted in certain speech patterns include monotony; speed or rate of speaking which is too slow, too fast, or too spasmodic; and the presence of excessive regional dialect. In general, the problems connected with speech patterns can be corrected by listening to those around you who have attractive voices and by practicing to incorporate their enviable qualities in your own speech. Given a reasonably normal vocal instrument, you can make of it a tool of communication and interpretation which will give you pride and satisfaction.

applications: _____

1. Keep a note pad by the telephone and make a notation on each of the next five voices you hear. Describe the voice and try to select its strong and weak qualities. Analyze it. If you were to prescribe exercises for its improvement, what would they be?
2. Tape your own voice. listen to it carefully and endeavor to determine how it could be improved. Work with someone else, if possible, and try honestly to appraise each other's voice. Outline a course of improvement of each voice — your own and that of your friend.
3. Think about your present self-concept. Is it conducive to voice improvement? If not, think about what you can do to upgrade your confidence, and outline a plan for improving your voice.
4. Of the people around you, or those you listen to on radio or television, which have the best speech patterns? List them. What clues can you take from them to help in improving your own speech pattern?
5. Search anthologies and other sources and find at least three appealing selections having to do with the voice. Select one of these for preparation for oral performance before the class.

preview of chapter 11:
USING THE BODY EFFECTIVELY

What we have to say is vastly influenced by how we look and handle ourselves when we say it. Many factors such as grooming, clothes, posture, movement, facial expression, and gesture combine to present a framework for verbal expression. We will be discussing all of these and finally relating them to the problem of handling that great bugaboo of performers, stage fright.

using the voice effectively

selections for study and interpretation

There is much opportunity for practice in using the voice to express emotion, suggest age, interpret all aspects and attitudes of silence in the following selection of Edgar Lee Masters.

SILENCE

Edgar Lee Masters
(1868-1950)

I have known the silence of the stars and of the sea,
And the silence of the city when it pauses,
And the silence of a man and a maid,
And the silence for which music alone finds the word,
And the silence of the woods before the winds of spring begin,
And the silence of the sick
When their eyes roam about the room.
And I ask: For the depths
Of what use is language?
A beast of the field moans a few times
When death takes its young.
And we are voiceless in the presence of realities —
We cannot speak.

A curious boy asks an old soldier
Sitting in front of the grocery store,
"How did you lose your leg?"
And the old soldier is struck with silence,
Or his mind flies away
Because he cannot concentrate it on Gettysburg.
It comes back jocosely
And he says, "A bear bit it off."
And the boy wonders, while the old soldier
Dumbly, feebly lives over
The flashes of guns, the thunder of cannon,
The shrieks of the slain,
And himself lying on the ground,
And the hospital surgeons, the knives,
And the long days in bed.
But if he could describe it all
He would be an artist.
But if he were an artist there would be deeper wounds
Which he could not describe.

There is the silence of a great hatred, /
And the silence of a great love, /
And the silence of a deep peace of mind, '
And the silence of an embittered friendship. (
There is the silence / of a spiritual crisis, (
Through which your soul, / exquisitely tortured, /
Comes with visions | not to be uttered
Into a realm of higher life. |
And the silence of the gods | who understand each other without
    speech. \
There is the silence of defeat. |
There is the silence of those / unjustly punished; /
And the silence of the dying | whose hand
Suddenly grips yours. |
There is the silence | between father and son, |
When the father | cannot explain his life, |
Even though he be misunderstood for it.

There is the silence that comes | between husband and wife. /
There is the silence of those | who have failed; \
And the vast silence | that covers
Broken nations | and vanquished leaders. |
There is the silence of Lincoln, |
Thinking of the poverty of his youth. \
And the silence of Napoleon \
After Waterloo. |
(And the silence of Jeanne d'Arc
Saying amid the flames, "Blessed Jesus" —
Revealing in two words all sorrow, all hope)
There is the silence of age, \
Too full of wisdom | for the tongue to utter it
In words intelligible | to those who have not lived
The great range of life. \
And there is the silence of the dead. \
If we who are in life | cannot speak
Of profound experiences, \
Why do you marvel | that the dead
Do not tell you of death? |
Their silence shall be interpreted |
As we approach them. |

Almost in direct contrast to Masters' SILENCE, this poem
of Walt Whitman's demands full, rich voice. Think of your
voice as an instrument, playing each character mentioned
in a way that suggests the quality of that person.

I HEAR AMERICA SINGING

Walt Whitman
(1819-1892)

I hear America singing, the varied carols I hear,
Those mechanics, each one singing his at it should be blithe
    and strong,
The carpenter singing his as he measures his plank or beam,
The mason singing his as he makes ready for work, or leaves
    off work,
The boatman singing what belongs to him in his boat, the
    deckhand singing on the steamboat deck,
The shoemaker singing as he sits on his bench, the hatter
    singing as he stands,
The wood-cutter's song, the plowboy's on his way in the
    morning, or at noon intermission or at sundown,
The delicious singing of the mother, or of the young wife
    at work, or of the girl sewing or washing,
Each singing what belongs to him or her and to none else,
The day what belongs to the day — at night the party of young
    fellows, robust, friendly,
Singing with open mouths their strong melodious songs.

This very beautiful poem demands precise diction, a most
thoughtful and considered interpretation. Sympathetically
done, it can prove a spellbinder!

A BALLAD OF TREES AND THE MASTER

Sidney Lanier
(1842-1881)

Into the woods my Master went,
Clean forspent, forspent,
Into the woods my Master came,
Forspent with love and shame.
But the olives they were not blind to Him;
The little gray leaves were kind to Him;
The thorn-tree had a mind to Him
When into the woods He came.

Out of the woods my Master went,
And He was well content.
Out of the woods my Master came,
Content with death and shame.
When Death and Shame would woo Him last,
From under the trees they drew Him last:
'Twas on a tree they slew Him — last
When out of the woods He came.

Have lots of fun with the following poem by Ralph Pomeroy.

GAPS, BARRIERS AND A BRIDGE

Ralph S. Pomeroy
(1926-   )

My mother, born in Northumberland,
always spoke with a slur (not burr).

To her last days she kept an after-murmur:
a slight catch in the consonants.

My aunt, her older sister, spoke with
the same slur
but resisted our insistence she had it.

She knew better: we were mistaken.

So we'd gather round and tease
Aunt Min once more into trying to say:

Round and round the rugged road
the ragged rascals ran.

Aunt Min once more would scowl, close her eyes,
sigh and begin: Wound and wound the wugged
woad — at which we roared.

Childwen, she'd say, don't stawt laughing;
Pawt of what I'm saying is the
way I am and have to say it.

Now, more than two decades later,
having travelled, heard some talk and done some,
tried and been tried with a length of language,

I've grown to grant Aunt Min knew better.

A neutral-toned semantic's hardly human:
In Northumberland the r's need muffling.

There, if anywhere, the woads are wugged
and everywhere the wagged wascals wun.

A former professor of English at the University of California, Sill left us considerable poetry. The favorites of interpreters have been THE FOOL'S PRAYER and the following, THE ORGAN. Interesting things can be done with the voice in giving this poem a rich interpretation.

THE ORGAN

Roland Sill
(1841-1887)

It is no harmony of human making
    Though men have built the pipes of burnished gold;
Their music, out of Nature's heart awaking
    Forever new, forever is of old.

Man makes not — only finds — all earthly beauty,
    Catching a thread of sunshine here and there,
Some shining pebble in the path of duty,
    Some echo of songs that flood the air.

That prelude is a wind among the willows,
    Rising until it meets the torrent's roar;
Now a wild ocean, beating his great billows
    Among the hollow caverns of the shore.

It is the voice of some vast people, pleading
    For justice from an ancient shame and wrong. —
The tramp of God's avenging armies, treading
    With shouted thunders of triumphant song.

O soul, that sittest singing dreary dirges,
　　Couldst thou but rise on some divine desire,
As those deep chords upon their swelling surges
　　Bear up the wavering voices of the choir!

But ever lurking in the heart, there lingers
　　The trouble of a false and jarring tone,
As some great Organ which unskilled fingers
　　Vex into discords when the Master's gone.

What a challenge this short poem can be to the full range of vocal possibilities!

OZYMANDIAS

Percy Bysshe Shelley
(1792-1822)

I met a traveller from an antique land
Who said: "Two vast and trunkless legs of stone
Stand in the desert. Near them, on the sand,
Half sunk, a shattered visage lies, whose frown,
And wrinkled lip, and sneer of cold command,
Tell that its sculptor well those passions read
Which yet survive, stamped on these lifeless things,
The hand that mocked them, and the heart that fed:
And on the pedestal these words appear:
'My name is Ozymandias, king of kings:
Look on my works, ye Mighty, and despair!'
Nothing beside remains. Round the decay
Of that colossal wreck, boundless and bare
The lone and level sands stretch far away."

Davies, born in a public house, self-educated, at times a panhandler, peddler, and beggar, started writing poetry when he was 35. He took infinite delight in simple things. When he died at 70 he had completed 25 volumes and had written more than 600 poems.

LEISURE

W. H. Davies
(1870-1940)

What is this life if, full of care,
We have no time to stand and stare.

No time to stand beneath the boughs
And stare as long as sheep or cows.

No time to see, when woods we pass,
Where squirrels hide their nuts in grass.

No time to see, in broad daylight,
Streams full of stars, like skies at night.

No time to turn at Beauty's glance,
And watch her feet, how they can dance.

No time to wait till her mouth can
Enrich that smile her eyes began.

A poor life this if, full of care,
We have no time to stand and stare.

using the body
effectively

A fair exterior is a silent recommendation.
    Maxim 267, Publilius Syrus

His look
Drew audience and attention. . . .
    John Milton

What you are speaks so loudly, I cannot hear what you say.
    Ralph Waldo Emerson

We have a hangover from tradition which says it makes little difference how a person looks — what matters is what he IS. On the other hand, television commercials would convince us nothing surpasses appearance in today's society. If we have white teeth (with fewer cavities), glossy hair, slender lines, and long lashes, we have it made! Naturally, rational attitudes toward the importance of appearance lie somewhere between these extremes. We must accept the fact that although not all people will judge us by what they see, most of them will; and what we have to say is vastly colored by how we look when we say it, or even before we open our mouths to speak.

Many factors focus on the effective use of the body in oral interpretation: dress and make-up, posture, and movement and gesture. The main purpose of considering these items is to improve communication through the creation of an attractive, poised, and yet dynamic person. Such a person will have much better listener response than one who appears to be suffering from nervousness, lack of confidence, or apathy.

Let us consider the main areas in which we can bring about effective use and control of the body for the purposes of oral interpretation.

grooming and make-up

A once-over by your audience or listeners will give them an impression of you as a person and of your capabilities as a performer. Clothes and grooming make this impression favorable or unfavorable. "Dressing up" is seldom the answer. Dress to suit the occasion. Clothes should always fit well, be simply designed and seldom so unusual that they attract attention. There are exceptions to these general rules, of course.

Clothes are important because they tend to lay foundations for lasting impressions. If you are sloppily attired, you will have an uphill struggle to convince your listeners that your mind and preparation are not similarly sloppy. Perhaps you can create the impression, despite wrinkled clothes, that you are serene and thoughtful, but it will take much more persuasion than it would have if, in the first impression, you presented the picture of a poised performer.

Most attractive people become attractive through a learned manner of dressing which distinguishes them, which gives them individuality, and which helps them to communicate with others.

Make-up for women is a touchy subject. Fashion constantly dictates excesses. For stage use, it frequently is necessary to use considerable make-up in order to appear healthy, normal, and expressive. But for average situations, too much make-up indicates egotism, superficiality, lack of taste, and even lack of self-assurance. Properly applied, however, make-up can contribute greatly to a woman's facial expression, attractive appearance, and poise.

perfecting posture

Almost more important than grooming and proper clothes is posture. Posture indicates, more than anything else physical about you, what you think of yourself. If you feel adequate, sure, confident, you undoubtedly have a pretty good posture already. If you feel insecure, fearful, unhappy, the evidence is probably clearly pictured in the way you hold yourself. Children usually have good posture, at least until others begin to raise doubts in their minds about their adequacies as human beings.

It may be that poor posture is, in some, an affectation. Some so-called intelligentsia affect poor posture to show their disregard for the body and their reverence for the world of thought. Beatniks may affect poor posture to suggest contempt for social structure. If you are temporarily enamored of such attitudes of mind, it would be folly to try to change you. About all that can be said is that — other things being equal — the well groomed person with a good posture has at least two things working for him when he meets a listener, two things which influence effective communication. Also, these two things, so much a part of the first impression, are very apt to determine the course of the lasting impression.

meaningful movement

Much is revealed about a person in his walk. Epictetus, sixty years before Christ, spoke of a person who walked as if he "had swallowed a ramrod." In the early seventeenth century, Robert Burton spoke of someone walking "as if he trod upon eggs." John Greenleaf Whittier characterized a whole age as being "dull and mean. Men creep, Not walk." It is true that in a walk we may read the thinking of a man. In the general manner of walk of a society we may discern the attitudes of a civilization.

What does your walk reveal about you?

It is sad that many girls nowadays are "trained to walk" by methods dear to charm schools, methods which promote a graceful but superficial movement from place to place. It is a style and pace which says to the on-looker: "Look at me. Am I not poised, beautiful, and elegant?" We are not in sympathy with such methods. They are a false approach to affecting grace, poise, and self-control.

A graceful walk is a purposeful one — a confident walk which says that you know where you are going and are moving there in an efficient manner. Shuffling, dragging the feet, clicking the heels, excessive hurry, or too much hesitation — all are disagreeable methods of walking.

Walking attracts favorable, unfavorable, or *no* attention, depending on how you do it. It is important to evaluate all walking movement in terms of what it is doing to establish rapport with your listeners.

Among the reasons for movement are these: to get somewhere, naturally; to gain attention; to keep attention; to make a point; to relax; to denote a transition in ideas; to rest your listeners. When it is random movement, meaningless pacing back and forth, it becomes an interruption of communication. Since walking or movement attracts attention, it must always be accomplished with a sense of purpose and control.

facial expression

Too often nowadays teachers of oral interpretation ignore the important role of the face. It is considered a bit old-fashioned to remind students of "facial expression." Yet, as we watch more and more television, we realize the vast importance of mobilizing the facial muscles.

Emotion is registered in the face. Without a look of joy, horror, peace, or excitement, as the situation may demand, the voice alone can not do a proper job of expressing emotion. The face is a frame for the voice, amplifying and extending its inferences.

visual contact

In facial contacts, we focus on the eyes most of the time. We have heard of the capacity of the eyes to express emotion. We say he has "an envious eye," "a shifty eye," "an angry eye." It is with our eyes that we often obtain, and certainly hold, listener interest. It is through our eyes that we reflect understanding in the communication process.

In meeting an audience, it is a good idea to look over the group, from front to back and side to side, giving the impression that you have taken each one into the orbit of your vision. To ignore eye contact is to disregard one of the most powerful tools you have for two-way communication.

During the reading of a selection, the interpreter must be skillful in frequently looking out at his listeners. He must learn to encompass quickly large segments of print (adequate preparation, almost memorization, is the only means of doing this) and then look at his audience while delivering most of the printed material.

Occasionally a selection will be of intimate nature or so full of emotion that continued direct eye contact would prove embarrassing or distasteful. Then, the interpreter will have to judge how to use his eyes. Looking down for any length of time is not good. Probably the better way would be to look a bit above and beyond the audience, occasionally dipping back down to them briefly to take them up with you in thought. Love poems and sonnets, passages of great tenderness, moments of lofty thought, call, at times, for a relaxation of direct eye contact. But usually the eye-to-eye contact with the audience is recommended to keep communication lines open.

gesture — sign language

Most people gesture naturally; that is, they move their shoulders, arms, and hands, bend their heads, and turn their bodies to indicate feelings or reactions, to help explain meanings. Only when they come to a platform to read or to speak to an audience do they become self-conscious about gesturing. It takes on an awful unnaturalness that poses the problem of how much, when, and how. All of these problems lack precise answers, of course. Handling gesture effectively depends on many factors: on the audience situation, on the reading itself, on the reader's degree of poise and experience.

Probably most beginners make a mistake in using too little gesture, particularly in a classroom situation where there is opportunity for experimentation and practice. Gestures have been discouraged by teachers who fear (often justifiably) their eventual overuse. Practicing exaggerated gestures at first may help you find and free yourself in this area of communication, however, and it is worth a try. Instead of measly little gestures, try for broad, sweeping gestures. Keep the arm rounded, not stiff or angular. Keep the hands palm up most of the time, and avoid spreading the fingers. Experiment and see if you like the effect. Don't use too many gestures but, when you do, keep them broad at first. Experience will soon dictate the type and extent of gestures which complement your performance.

Things to avoid in gesture are vagueness, poor timing, and monotony. Gestures should always be positive, direct, and meaningful. They need to be brought into play at the precise moment when they can help get the message across, usually just a fraction of a second before you state it. Gestures need to be varied. Monotonous gestures are worse than none.

Think of gesture as sign language, as an aid to complete communication. Do not think of gestures as something to do with your hands. Your hands can always be allowed to rest at ease at your sides, or they may be put in your pockets (a cowardly device!) The look of the professional comes when you can bring your hands and arms into play now and then to reinforce, to describe, or to suggest a point you want to make.

handling stage fright

One of the greatest rewards of practicing the suggestions for effective use of the body is that of minimizing stage fright. Scientific studies of stage fright assure us it is no different from fright of any other type so far as our bodies are concerned. Loud and unexpected noises, falls, and weird sights set up a reaction of fright which contracts our throats, tenses our muscles, makes us breathe faster. To all intents and purposes, we are suffering the same as we do when we walk out on a platform and face an audience.

In performance we have quite an advantage. We may anticipate our situation and prepare to handle our fright. Skill in using the body effectively, in walking with poise, in establishing and holding visual contact with listeners, in smiling and bringing the face into expressive attitudes, and in gesturing with ease — all of these help in overcoming, or at least in handling, stage fright. (There is only one other thing which may be of equal value, and that is adequate preparation, which is discussed in Chapter 8.)

The inexperienced body is apt to "freeze," just as the unprepared mind is apt to become confused and black out.

If, after creating the conditions for handling stage fright effectively by mastering the bodily skills, you still suffer from a measure of this miserable condition, think of it as an asset. Reasonable amounts of stage fright can be put to good use. It is of value in alerting your attention, in clearing your head, in focussing your thoughts, in stimulating your responses. The appearance of poise may at first be a mask covering a degree of inner turmoil. But repeated performance will tend to diminish that turmoil and in time you will have gained sufficient control to enjoy maximum performance.

Panaceas for stamping out stage fright are about as numerous (and helpful) as remedies for colds and hiccoughs. Like both of these, stage fright usually has to run its course, and gradually you find your way of dealing with it or build up an immunity. Wise counselors have given some steps to overcome stage fright which may be summarized as follows: breathe deeply and slowly; picture yourself as calm and collected; look over your audience before beginning, establishing eye contact with some friendly faces; become intensely interested in the audience and forget yourself; pause and shift position if your voice quivers or your knees shake; take solace in the fact that everyone else has stage fright too. You can try these remedies. Perhaps they will work as aspirin for your cold or sips of water for your hiccoughs, and tide you over until you have mastered the whole impulse to panic.

One student who met his stage fright in an effective way began his performance by saying that he would like to speak to the class as a friend — "with the same friendly attitude my knees have as they say to one another, 'Shake, old pal.' "

Franklin Delano Roosevelt will always be remembered for his statement that we have "nothing to fear but fear itself." And Barney Fife will probably be almost as famous for his comment that that was what he had — "fear itself." If you have it too — "fear itself" — take heart in the knowledge that you can at least conquer excessive fear by mastering the skills of interpretation, particularly those pertaining to the effective use of the body, thereby assuring yourself of a healthy mental attitude in relation to your listeners.

summary

Appearance and the manner of handling the body greatly influence our effect on others. Among the factors which focus attention on the body are dress and make-up, which should be appropriate always and in good taste; posture, an indication of one's self-concept; and movement and gesture, which are useful particularly in gaining and holding attention. Facial expression, in this day of increasing importance of television, is an area deserving more attention than it is given in most classes of interpretation. Skillful use of the eyes also becomes of paramount importance in two-way communication.

With the mastering of body movement and gesture comes increased poise and minimizing of stage fright. What residue of this unhappy condition remains after all measures have been taken to overcome it can be valued for its tendency to alert attention, clear the head, focus thought, and stimulate responses. Excessive fear seldom persists as reading experiences multiply.

applications: ─────────────────────

1. Have a friend take three or four candid camera snapshots of you (a Polaroid is fine for this). Honestly evaluate the way you look. Divide a paper with a line down the middle. Place "Assets" at the top of the left column and "Improvements Needed" at the top of the right column. Now list what in your opinion you have in your favor (for example, good posture, neat hair style, etc.) and what you need help on (for example, baggy pants, crooked hemline, etc.). Decide you will make the improvements noted.
2. Next time you walk to the front of the class to perform, think of the effectiveness of your walk. Try to move with purpose and grace. As you walk about the campus, keep thinking "my walk advertises what I am."
3. In all contacts from now on, informal or formal, try to heighten your facial expression and eye contact a bit if you are not a particularly communicative person. Try smiling more often and more generously.

Listen attentively. Show in your face and with your eyes that you appreciate and understand what others are saying.

4. Experiment on your next reading with gesture. Even if it seems a bit difficult, USE a few broad gestures to punctuate meaning. Keep them few, but make them strong gestures. Do not be afraid to TRY THEM OUT. Only by experimentation can you judge how much gesture to use.

preview of chapter 12:

INDIVIDUAL PERFORMANCE

Beginning our discussion of the section on APPLICATIONS is Chapter 12, which concerns individual performance. We will be considering informal performances — times when we read in casual family, small meeting, or friendly group situations. We will discuss the particular value of practicing before groups of children. We will also study types of formal performance, essential elements of preparation, and how to establish and keep audience contact. We will have something to say about the special art of book reviewing; about opportunities for individual performances; and, finally, about the ethics of procuring and using an agent.

using the body effectively

selections for study and interpretation

Cicero was unrivaled in eloquence, and yet he, too, suffered from stage fright if we are to believe what he had one of his characters say in his *Dialogue on Oratory*. The host, L. Crassus, and chief speaker, undoubtedly voices Cicero's own experiences when he says at one point:

Excerpt from
DIALOGUE ON ORATORY

Marcus Tullius Cicero
(106-43 B.C.)

. . . "If you would know what I myself think, I will express to you, my intimate friends, what I have hitherto never mentioned, and thought that I never should mention. . . . the better qualified a man is to speak, the more he fears the difficulties of speaking, the uncertain success of a speech, and the expectation of the audience. . . . Indeed, what I often observe in you I very frequently experience in myself; that I turn pale in the outset of my speech, and feel a tremor through my whole thoughts, as it were, and limbs. When I was a young man, I was on one occasion so timid in commencing an accusation, that I owe to Q. Maximus the greatest of obligations for immediately dismissing the assembly as soon as he saw me absolutely disheartened and incapacitated through fear."

A few years ago, the late J. Christopher Herold won much acclaim for *Mistress to an Age: A Life of Madame De Staël*, which was translated into seven languages. The subject of his book was an intellectual leader far ahead of her time. Her cousin, who somehow realized her genius, said, "The works of Madame de Staël seem to belong to the future," and she continued by describing Madame de Staël's writings as belonging to a literature "more spoken than written." In reading from her writings we feel the liberal tone of her thought and kinship with our time. Her life was dedicated to a desire to serve the interests of humanity; for this she was exiled from Paris. She wrote all her life, at times surrounded by many guests, and even while traveling. Sainte Beuve said, "Her words constantly need that [the illumination of her look, of her expression, of her accent] to fill them out; her pen did not complete them; there lacks almost always to her written phrase some indescribable accompaniment. This is perhaps an added reason for the refined reader to delight in . . . imaginatively conceiving the appropriate gesture and accent."

INFLUENCE OF THE PASSIONS

part of the introduction to the
treatise on the above, by Madame de Staël
(1766-1817)

Whatever may be thought of my plan, it is certain that my only object has been to combat unhappiness in all its forms; to study the thoughts, the sentiments, the institutions, that cause suffering to men; to seek what form of reflection, action, combination, can somewhat diminish the intensity of the troubles of the soul. The image of misfortune, under whatever aspect it presents itself, pursues and overwhelms me. Alas! I have so fully experienced what it is to suffer, that an inexpressible emotion, a sad uneasiness, takes possession of me at the thought of the sorrows of all men, and of every man: the thought of their inevitable misfortunes, and of the torments of the imagination; of the reverses of the good man, and even of the remorse of the guilty; of the wounds of the heart, — the most grievous of all, — and of the regrets that are felt none the less because they are felt with shame: in short, of all which is the source of tears; tears that the ancients preserved in a consecrated vase, so august in their eyes was human grief. Ah, it is not enough to have vowed that in the precincts of one's own existence — whatever injustice, whatever wrong, we may be the object of, — we will never voluntarily cause a moment's pain, we will never voluntarily relinquish the possibility of comforting a sorrow; the further effort must be made to strive by some ray of talent, by some power of mediation, to find the touching language that gently opens the heart, and to help in discovering the philosophic height where the weapons that wound cannot reach us.

In the following two poems, you can reach the heights of oral interpretation. Kipling and Rupert Brooke have written idealistically, emotionally, and dramatically. See if you can "let out the stops" without losing control. Use the skills of voice and body you have practiced. Be relaxed — expansive!

WHEN EARTH'S LAST PICTURE IS PAINTED

Rudyard Kipling
(1865-1936)

When Earth's last picture is painted and the tubes are
                              twisted and dried,
When the oldest colours have faded, and the youngest critic
                              has died,
We shall rest, and, faith, we shall need it — lie down for an
                              aeon or two,
Till the Master of All Good Workmen shall put us to work anew.
And those that were good shall be happy: they shall sit in a
                              golden chair;
They shall splash at a ten-league canvas with brushes of
                              comets' hair;
They shall find real saints to draw from — Magdalene, Peter,
                              and Paul;
They shall work for an age at a sitting and never be tired at
                              all!
And only the Master shall praise us, and only the Master
                              shall blame;
And no one shall work for money, and no one shall work for
                              fame,
But each for the joy of working, and each, in his separate
                              star,
Shall draw the Thing as he sees It for the God of Things as
                              They are.

THE GREAT LOVER

Rupert Brooke
(1887-1915)

I have been so great a lover: filled my days
So proudly with the splendor of Love's praise,
The pain, the calm, and the astonishment,
Desire illimitable, and still content,
And all dear names men use, to cheat despair,
For the perplexed and viewless streams that bear
Our hearts at random down the dark of life.
Now, ere the unthinking silence on that strife
Steals down, I would cheat drowsy Death so far,
My night shall be remembered for a star

That outshone all the suns of all men's days.
Shall I not crown them with immortal praise
Whom I have loved, who have given me, dared with me
High secrets, and in darkness knelt to see
The inenarrable godhead of delight?
Love is a flame: — we have beaconed the world's night.
A city: — and we have built it, these and I.
An emperor: — we have taught the world to die.
So, for their sakes I loved, ere I go hence,
And the high cause of Love's magnificence,
And to keep loyalties young, I'll write those names
Golden for ever, eagles, crying flames,
And set them as a banner, that men may know,
To dare the generations, burn, and blow
Out on the wind of Time, shining and streaming. . . .

These I have loved:
       White plates and cups, clean-gleaming,
Ringed with blue lines; and feathery, faëry dust;
Wet roofs, beneath the lamp-light; the strong crust
Of friendly bread; and many-tasting food;
Rainbows; and the blue bitter smoke of wood;
And radiant raindrops couching in cool flowers;
And flowers themselves, that sway through sunny hours,
Dreaming of moths that drink them under the moon;
Then, the cool kindliness of sheets, that soon
Smooth away trouble; and the rough male kiss
Of blankets; grainy wood; live hair that is
Shining and free; blue-massing clouds; the keen
Unpassioned beauty of a great machine;
The benison of hot water; furs to touch;
The good smell of old clothes; and other such —
The comfortable smell of friendly fingers,
Hair's fragrance, and the musty reek that lingers
About dead leaves and last year's ferns. . . .
                            Dear names,
And thousand others throng to me! Royal flames;
Sweet water's dimpling laugh from tap or spring;
Holes in the ground; and voices that do sing:
Voices in laughter, too; and body's pain,
Soon turned to peace; and the deep-panting train;
Firm sands; the little dulling edge of foam
That browns and dwindles as the wave goes home;
And washen stones, gay for an hour; the cold
Graveness of iron; moist black earthen mold;

Sleep; and high places; footprints in the dew;
And oaks; and brown horse-chestnuts, glossy-new;
And new-peeled sticks; and shining pools on grass; —
All these have been my loves. And these shall pass,
Whatever passes not, in the great hour,
Nor all my passion, all my prayers, have power
To hold them with me through the gate of Death.
They'll play deserter, turn with the traitor breath,
Break the high bond we made, and sell Love's trust
And sacramental covenant to the dust.
— Oh, never a doubt but, somewhere, I shall wake,
And give what's left of love again, and make
New friends now strangers. . . .
                              But the best I've known
Stays here, and changes, breaks, grows old, is blown
About the winds of the world, and fades from brains
Of living men, and dies.
                    Nothing remains.

O dear my loves, O faithless, once again
This one last gift I give: that after men
Shall know, and later lovers, far-removed
Praise you, "All these were lovely"; say, "He loved."

applications

communicating through
individual performance

To use the tools efficiently one must build new habits in one's nervous system. . . . Eventually the user reaches for these tools the way a carpenter reaches for his hammer.
Stuart Chase, *Power of Words*

For of course the true meaning of a term is to be found by observing what a man does with it, not by what he says about it.
P. W. Bridgman, quoted by S. I. Hayakawa in *Language in Action*

Now we come to a final section of this book, APPLICA-TIONS, in which we put all that we have learned to the real test — performance.

In the past three sections of the book, we have undertaken a natural progression of learning to interpret orally the words of others (and often our own). In Part I, ATTITUDES, we approached the total study through an evaluation of our feelings about ourselves and the possibility of becoming better interpreters. We emphasized the necessity for liberating ourselves from preconceived limiting and often damaging convictions. We undertook to relate ourselves to "the territory" of interpretation, to develop confidence in personal potential for mastery of improved knowledge and skills.

In Part II, MATERIALS, we surveyed the world of literature at our disposal — areas of prose, poetry, and drama — both past and contemporary. We discussed criteria of evaluation and methods of motivating the improvement and expansion of our own levels of appreciation. We considered problems involved in preparing and creatively programming these materials.

In Part III, we endeavored to focus on special SKILLS required for successful interpretation, skills relating primarily to the effective use of voice and body.

Now, in Part IV, we are in a position to experience the rewards of our carefully prepared attitudes, knowledges about materials, and skills, as we make applications of learning to performance. In this part of the book we hope to crystallize the use of our "tools" so that we will be able to reach for them "the way a carpenter reaches for his hammer." We will find these tools of great value in all situations in which we communicate orally — in casual, everyday situations, in platform situations as individual performers or members of a group, and in situations where we may find ourselves confronting the mass media. In this chapter we will be discussing individual communication.

informal performance

By now we realize that at all times we are performing. Even in our most casual moments we are giving some kind of a performance. Even when we pick up the telephone and say "hello!" it is a performance (not always one for which we would want to be remembered!).

If we have been practicing constructive attitudes, enriching our general levels of culture, and if we have been working for the improvemnt of voice, diction, gesture, and bodily grace, even the way we answer the telephone will have been changed. By now, we SHOULD be aware that in one "hello" we have given a picture of a person and an interpretation of a personality.

Casual Contacts

Unless we have been "turned off" in this class, we have built into our nervous systems some habits of speech which automatically assist us in making contacts with others more effective as acts of communication. We are certainly more positive, pleasant, vocally alive, attentive, responsive, and controlled. Whether we are talking with a friend, buying groceries, or discussing a parking ticket with the highway patrolman, new habits are bound to have influenced our performances!

There are many times when we will be in a situation to interpret informally from the printed page. For example, we want to read the family a few paragraphs from the paper, from a letter we have just received, or from a magazine or book we are reading. We may find ourselves elected to office in some organization. We have to read the minutes of a meeting, or proposals for action, or a message of inspiration. What a relief to ourselves and to others if we are able to make these moments stimulating rather than dreary experiences!

Reading to Children

Almost all of us will be called upon at some time to read to children. Perhaps now we are putting our interpretative powers to work on smaller brothers and sisters. Later, as parents, we will have much to do with instilling a love of reading in our children if we know how to make poems and stories come alive.

There is no better practice in interpreting "pictures," in making reading material visual, than to perform before a group of children, whose minds are much more pictorially oriented than are those of adults. With children, you can experiment less self-consciously with variations of tone quality and gesture. Children are attentive and empathic. Reading aloud to small, wide-eyed, interested spectators is an ego-building, fear-destroying practice. We heartily recommend finding yourself a junior audience.

. . . "A story never lives until it is told and heard by someone," it has been said, but some stories demand reading. Anyone can tell a story, but not all stories should be told. Some were written to be read exactly as they were written. . . . [For example] any story written by Dr. Seuss. The author's rare choice of words, his sense of timing and rhythm, are difficult to relate unless one reads the story.[1]

formal performance and platform behavior

The ultimate test of how effectively you can use your tools of interpretation will, of course, come in formal performance. This may be in the nature of reading before an audience a total program in which you are the sole performer, or perhaps a book review in which you interpret at times from the printed page. Can you, in the final test, deliver?

Essentials of Preliminary Preparation

All effective formal performance is dependent first on adequate preparation of material, which we have discussed previously but which cannot be overemphasized. Second, it is dependent on careful programming and a rather

---

[1]Henry A. Bamman, Mildred A. Dawson, and Robert J. Whitehead, *Oral Interpretation of Children's Literature* (Dubuque, Iowa: Wm. C. Brown Company Publishers, 1964), pp. 98-99. [Note: This reference has excellent suggestions on story telling, poetry reading, etc., for children.]

intimate knowledge of the audience. Third, you will have made sure you are appropriately dressed, that your clothes are pleasing but not overpowering. Fourth, you will have made sure, before you start, that a suitable stand is ready for any books or reading materials you have to use, and that the microphone (if you are using one, by all means insist on a good one!) is properly adjusted to the hall. You will have tested it before the audience arrives, found the proper level, and adjusted the speaker so that you will not have to touch it once you begin. (More on microphone technique in Chapter 14.)

Establishing Audience Contact

Now the time has come for you to walk on stage, or get up and go to the front of the audience, to perform. Place in your mind a picture of a relaxed, gracious person. Walk on with confidence. Refuse to be upset by noises, confusion, inadequate introductions, or any one of a hundred things which may happen, despite your careful preliminary preparations, to destroy your poise. If such occur, do the best you can with the situation — act the part of the experienced performer — rise to the occasion — take a deep breath — smile — graciously pause and wait for attention — *take command!*

Most of the time you need not worry about problem beginnings if the ground rules have been observed. You walk on stage, the audience is attentive, the microphone is perfect, and you see smiling, friendly faces throughout the group. Look at these warm people and enlist their attention with eye contact. Your first words are important. You are fortunate if you can somehow start very simply with an impromptu statement that puts you into the situation — a friendly remark about the pleasure you have in facing the audience, a gracious word of appreciation for the introduction. Your audience has confidence that you are NOT GOING TO BE TIED TO THE PRINTED PAGE, that you are able to communicate in your own right. If you can in some way bring in just a touch of humor, so much the better. Nothing is less effective, however, than twisting remarks to work in a too-familiar joke.

In your introductory remarks, maintain a spontaneous attitude. You may have almost memorized your introduction, but keep it sounding extemporaneous if possible. It is not unsuitable to bring yourself into the introduction if you do not overdo it.

Keeping Audience Contact

In maintaining audience contact once you have it, certain physical problems may threaten communication. Let us consider a few of these.

First, books, papers, and notes you may have to use should be perfectly organized so that you need do no shuffling and arranging once you are on stage. If you must use a number of sources, be sure they are properly arranged beforehand. Many excellent performances have been interrupted when readings have been out of order or improperly marked. If at all possible, place all of your readings in one folder, easily held in one hand, leaving the other hand free for gesture. If you are using a microphone and speaker's stand, be sure your readings are contained in something which will not rattle as pages are turned, fall off the stand, or prove in some way embarrassing to you. Sound will be amplified and what seems almost noiseless in rehearsal may sound like fire or thunder when placed close to a microphone. Be sure the pages are held together in such a way that they will turn quickly and easily and stay put, not flop back.

Second, whether or not you have memorized your selections, it is reassuring to your audience for you to have your manuscript in hand or on the speaker's stand. Few people nowadays endeavor to give a program from memory. If you are totally competent in memorization, are absolutely sure you will not stumble and hesitate for words, it is quite appropriate to leave your printed matter at home. There is nothing wrong in reading from memory, but you must be absolutely at ease in so doing. You will throw up a communication barrier between yourself and the audience at the first moment of hesitation UNLESS YOU HAVE YOUR BOOK IN HAND, in which case your listeners will remain relaxed, realizing that you have a ready means to remind yourself of what comes next.

In keeping your audience with you, it is necessary to remember what we had to say about audiences in Chapter 3 on listening — watch faces, listen for fatigue sounds, note any signs of restlessness. If necessary, cut your program to finish before your listeners tire. Seldom is it possible to predict with certainty the exact course of a program. Most experienced performers will vary their programs slightly to accommodate the needs and demands of individual audiences. Be prepared to offer an alternate poem if you can see that the one you had expected to read is just a bit too long. Be prepared to cut or expand your program slightly to suit the occasion. If, in the course of a reading, an unexpected thing happens — an airplane breaks the sound barrier, a truck rumbles by, the lights go off, or the microphone starts to whistle — react to it calmly and with humor, if possible. Do not try to go on undaunted, ignoring the obvious interruption. It is better to take a moment out to note it frankly, to show that it is not going to throw you off course. Then take the audience back to the point where you left off, regain everyone's attention, and proceed.

Leaving the Audience Graciously

It is always well to give the audience a bit of warning as you approach the close of your program. Plan to leave them just a little before they want you to. It is good to part company before they have had too much. Yet it is not good to leave an audience feeling cheated. Your program should not be too skimpy, your ending should not be too abrupt. Take time at the end to review what you have tried to do, and round out the program theme with a short, memorable statement. You need not thank the audience for its attention, but at times a bit of praise for excellent listening may be just the way in which to leave them with good feelings all around. Here again, the experienced performer will have to rely a bit on intuition, doing what the situation seems to demand. If he is prepared with alternative endings, he can draw on the one which seems just right or combine elements of several to bring the program to a perfect conclusion. As you finish your last words, pause and smile, pick up your book or books, and stay a moment or two to acknowledge audience applause graciously. Leave the stage or sit down before it ends, however. If there is continuing applause, you may reappear or rise briefly and bow slightly. Do not overdo the theatrics. Keep in mind the picture of the poised person who is grateful and pleased but not embarrassed by expressions of audience approval. Let your audience know you appreciate their applause.

the art of book review

In the course of our lives most of us will be asked to review books for selected audiences. Book reviewing has become a popular form of educational entertainment, and the person who has mastered the basic arts involved is in great demand.

A book review is not essentially a book criticism, Some so-called reviewers try to turn their programs into sessions of criticism, not always adverse criticism but frequently peppered with snide and unfavorable comments.

When you are asked to give a book review, you usually have been given the freedom to choose the book, and it is a constructive approach to select a book worthy of praise and interpretation. Your task, then, is to make that book appealing, interesting, and worth reading. A very good book review is usually based on a very good book.

There are many ways of reviewing a book. We can talk *about* it. We can describe in our own words what the author has to say. But the experienced interpreter is in a position to do better than that because he can *excerpt parts* of the manuscript and *give the main thought of the book in the author's own words*. Careful cutting and much preparation of excerpted material are ideal means of preparing for a book review. Of course, there is some danger of audience resistance to reading too much from the printed page. The amateur reviewer often loses his audience by overdoing the reading. A dullness creeps into his presentation when he looks down to read. Listeners drop by the wayside until he returns to his commenting. But the experienced interpreter knows how much to read and how to read it.

In every book review, of course, the commentator should make clear the title of the book and name of the author, mention and briefly comment on his or her other writings, and orient the audience to the author's place in the world of literature. The main body of the review should, however, get to the heart of the book under consideration, to the writing in it, to the story told or the points made. The flavor of the writing itself is very important and can be experienced only by successful interpretation. Finally, a reviewer is privileged to make a few comments concerning how the book affected him. Personal observations are always interesting to members of the audience. The experienced interpreter may depend much more than the unskilled reader on the book itself, on readings from it, bridging them with succinct and meaningful comment.

opportunities for personal performance

It is nothing to be ashamed of if you personally get a thrill out of performance. The world is in need of good performers. The opportunities for participating on a program are many and varied, but at first you may not know just how to find them.

If you would like to challenge yourself to growth through practice performances, we offer a few ideas:

1. Approach your local librarian with an offer to conduct a weekly story and poetry hour for small children. Sometimes you can get a PTA to sponsor you in a summer program at the library, for which you can charge a fee. You may want to divide the children into age groups and offer sessions on two or three levels.
2. Offer to participate in programs connected with your church, women's clubs, Young Republicans or Young Democrats, and men's service groups. Perhaps your minister would appreciate having you read Biblical selections some Sunday. An offer at church or synagogue is usually accepted in some way.
3. Offer to give an appropriate program for some organization to which you belong at school.

4. Call up the program chairman of a leading women's group and offer to review a book at section meetings. Most large organizations have "book sections" which would welcome you with open arms.
5. Discover whether there is in your community a senior citizens' group. Most communities have wonderful audience groups among their elderly who deeply appreciate good programs.

When you have had some successful performances you will find you have no problem finding more opportunities for performance. People begin to know you and call upon you. The problem, then, may be how to handle too many requests!

With considerable successful experience behind you, you may even start to charge a small fee, increasing it as your fame and popularity increase! (Requests will diminish.)

the use of an agent

If you finally achieve professional status, the thing to do is employ a good agent, who then seeks for you desirable audience situations and assures you of being rewarded with good pay for your work. The advantages to having an agent are many when you become a true professional, but it is important to select a reputable agent whose fees are not excessive. About 20 per cent of the amount you receive is average and fair for the agent's fee. Adequate compensation for a woman's club program may be in the range of $50.00 to $200, depending on the size of the audience and length of program desired. If the place is more than 15 or 20 miles from your home, expenses should be paid you or the fee increased to compensate for added basic costs.

It is possible in some larger areas to find a good local agent. You may have to go to a large city and arrange to try out before the agent's invited audience. If you succeed in pleasing them, the agent may take you on as his or her property, in which case you usually sign a contract stating that all of your future engagements will be handled through the agent. This eliminates opportunities for you to appear where you might want to at times (unless exceptions are noted in your contract which allow you some freedom in this matter). But it solves the problem of what to do when you are overwhelmed by requests for free programs! Referring all requests to your agent is then a welcome relief.

summary

All contacts with others, even the most casual, are opportunities for effective personal performance, for interpreting ourselves as we would have others know us. Informal situations at home, in meetings, and at school constantly present opportunities for us to read in a stimulating manner. Practicing before groups of children, who are responsive and attentive and more pictorially oriented than adults, will give us self-confidence and a chance to experiment with newly acquired skills of voice, body, and gesture.

Formal performance is the ultimate test of mastery of tools of interpretation. Essentials of preliminary preparation include knowledge of materials, creative programming, careful grooming and dress, and attention to physical arrangements of the meeting room. In establishing audience contact as you begin performance, it is necessary to remain poised no matter what may happen, to approach your task with spontaneity and enthusiasm and a touch of the impromptu. In keeping an audience with you, it is important to avoid distractions of all sorts, to have available your manuscript unless your memory is infallible, and to be attentive at all times to listener reactions. Parting from an audience graciously and before they tire is the final test of poise and skill as a performer.

A book review gives the able interpreter an excellent opportunity to program interestingly for a group within the framework of a currently popular selection. Book reviewing is a special art which is adaptable to many audience situations. With wide experience behind you, it may be you will want to seek an agent. It is important to discover one who is reputable and will treat you with honesty and consideration. An agent can be of great assistance to a professional performer.

applications: ─────────────

1. List the times during this semester when you have been expected to interpret something in an informal situation. How could your performance have been improved?

2. Make arrangements to give a story hour at your library for a group of children some Saturday soon. Plan what you will read for them and prepare a brief résumé of your program.

3. Plan a formal recital performance or book review for one of the following:

A church tea
An older citizens' group
A campus organization
A women's club

preview of chapter 13:
GROUP PERFORMANCE

We will be considering the various situations in which individuals may perform with a group in interpreting literary material. The verse-speaking choir is one of these. Reader's theatre is another. We will also review some of the materials available for group performance and consider special skills involved in artistic results.

communicating through individual performance

selections for study and interpretation

> Who could enumerate the many ways in which James Thurber enriched, humanized and brought delight to the American scene during his lifetime? As essayist, short-story writer, editor, and cartoonist he brought a certain inimitable flavor to bear on the follies of mankind. His fables are particularly wonderful for interpretation. THE WOLF WHO WENT PLACES seems appropriate to persons of college age. Do you agree?

THE WOLF WHO WENT PLACES[2]

James Thurber
(1894-1961)

A wealthy young wolf, who was oblivious of everything except himself, was tossed out of college for cutting classes and corners, and he decided to see if he could travel around the world in eighty minutes.

"That isn't possible," his grandmother told him, but he only grinned at her.

"The impossible is the most fun," he said.

She went with him to the door of the old Wolf place. "If you go that fast, you won't live to regret it," she warned him, but he grinned again, showing a tongue as long as a necktie.

"That's an old wolves' tale," he said, and went on his reckless way.

He bought a 1959 Blitzen Bearcat, a combination motorcar and airplane, with skyrocket getaway, cyclone speedrive, cannonball takeoff, blindall headlights, magical retractable monowings, and lightning pushbutton transformationizer. "How fast can this crate go without burning up?" he asked the Blitzen Bearcat salesman.

"I don't know," the salesman said, "but I have a feeling you'll find out."

The wealthy young wolf smashed all the ground records and air records and a lot of other things in his trip around the world, which took him only 78.5 minutes from the time he knocked down the Washington Monument on his takeoff to the time he landed where it had stood. In the crowd that welcomed him home, consisting of about eleven creatures, for all the others were hiding under beds, there was a speed-crazy young wolfess, with built-in instantaneous pickup ability, and in no time at all the wolf and his new-found mate were setting new records for driving upside down, backward, blindfolded, handcuffed, and cockeyed, doubled and redoubled.

2"*The Wolf Who Went Places*" from *Further Fables for Our Time* by James Thurber (Simon & Schuster, Inc., New York) is reprinted by permission of Mrs. James Thurber.

One day, they decided to see if they could turn in to Central Park from Fifth Avenue while traveling at a rate of 175 miles an hour, watching television, and holding hands. There was a tremendous shattering, crashing, splitting, roaring, blazing, cracking, and smashing, ending in a fiery display of wheels, stars, cornices, roofs, treetops, glass, steel, and people, and it seemed to those spectators who did not die of seizures as they watched that great red portals opened in the sky, swinging inward on mighty hinges, revealing an endless nowhere, and then closed behind the flying and flaming wolves with a clanking to end all clanking, as if those gates which we have been assured shall not prevail had, in fact, prevailed.

MORAL: *Where most of us end up there is no knowing, but the hellbent get where they are going.*

It is not easy to find short stories from contemporary writers that read aloud well. Margaret Craven has written many fine stories throughout the years which have appeared in THE SATURDAY EVENING POST and other periodicals. The following story seems to have been written with a definite knowledge of the problems that face many of our often maligned young people who are working almost beyond endurance to secure an education.

THE BOY WHO WORKED TOO HARD[3]

Margaret Craven

Rose, the middle-aged pantry girl, saw the boy wheel deftly into the lighted courtyard and slip his bike into the rack. She plucked a plate from the warming pile and assembled his dinner quickly, so he need not bolt his food to be finished when the washers carried out the soup-and-salad trays and it was time to do his twice-daily stint with the dishwater.

One of the pupils at Miss Oberly's select and expensive school for young ladies was pouting in her room and had sent down word she wished no dinner. Rose placed the girl's rare roast beef on the boy's plate in lieu of the hash which was the help's fare tonight. She put an extra pat of butter in his baked potato and poured a small pitcher of cream into his milk. She set the food on the table where he ate first and alone.

---

[3]THE BOY WHO WORKED TOO HARD by Margaret Craven, first published by The Saturday Evening Post. Copyright 1956 by The Curtis Publishing Company. Used with permission of the author.

She could hear him coming now through the service hall, and she wiped anxiety from her face.

He was a tall lad, no longer a boy and yet not quite a man, one of those lean youths slow to grow up to a big frame. He did not say "Hi, Rosie." He did not wait until she was busy ladling soup and untie her apron strings. He did not joke, or tease, or whistle some happy tune.

He said. "Hello, Rose," and sat down slowly, and she knew he wasn't hungry again, and her anxiety swelled to fear.

In the big dining room, the fortunate girls who were boarding pupils at Miss Oberly's bowed their fair heads for grace. Rose had to help serve the head table because a hasher was sick. She slipped through the door and bowed her head also. And because she was devout and had no son of her own, she said a prayer for this boy, Pete; and because she was a practical woman, her prayer was practical also. *Please make him eat his meat and drink his milk.*

Grace was over then and the dinner buzz began, muted tonight in respect for Miss Oberly's male guest.

As Rose set the soup at her place she could hear Miss Oberly's charming voice pouring on the honey. Yes, Miss Oberly was saying, most of her help came from the university. Such fine boys, and so dependable. And the guest said how nice that was. Nothing pleased him more than to see young men working their way through college. It developed such character.

For an instant Rose felt a dreadful impulse to pour the hot soup on his bald head. What boys like Pete Westcott needed was not more character. What they needed was thick steak, more fun, less worry, and enough financial backing so that next quarter's tuition did not loom perpetually over their heads.

When she returned to the kitchen the boy was washing dishes.

. . . .

"How are finals, Pete?" she asked.

"I've cracked them on the nose so far. One more to go. English Fifty-six tomorrow at nine. I haven't done the required reading. Have to get to the libe and do it." . . . Then he was done.

"Good night, Rose," he said. "You know something? If I get an A in English Fifty-six, I'll cop a Culbert scholarship. Pays three quarters' tuition," and he gave her a quick pat and was down the service hall and onto his bike, wheeling off into the night. . . . But he rode carefully. Two days ago he'd had a spill, picked himself up from the side of the road with a bloody knee. . . . Tomorow after the final he'd drop in at the university infirmary and have the knee painted and bandaged properly.

. . . .

He had written call cards for the books he wanted, and when the girl at the desk gave them to him he passed the reading rooms, climbed two flights of stairs to a small seminar room at the top of the building. It was empty, and he turned on the lights and spread the books on the table.

When he was set to begin, something strange happened. The words grew fuzzy. By no effort of the will could he concentrate on them. Sleep. That was what he needed. . . . He cradled his head in his arms.

When he awoke the buzzer was ringing, and the buzzer meant that in six minutes the building closed for the night. The call books could not be taken from the libe, and he had not read one word. . . . He turned in the books, and pedaled to his room adjoining Professor Tigby's garage.

In the morning when he opened his eyes, he remembered instantly. He did his breakfast stint with Miss Oberly's dishwasher, hurrying as fast as he could, saying nothing. He pedaled strenuously back to the campus to be on time for the nine-o'clock.

He was the last student to enter the room. Doctor Meredith, a woman of fifty and one of the bright brains of the university, was at her desk, checking the roll. On the arm of each chair waited the blue book, the examination paper tucked inside.

He opened his and withdrew the sheet. He held his breath as he read the questions. He must answer three out of four, and two he knew, and two were on the required reading which he had not read.

. . . .

He knocked off the first question in twenty-five minutes, and the second in thirty-one. Then he read the two questions he did not know.

IN HENRY JAMES' *TURN OF THE SCREW* WHOM DID MILES AND FLORA LOVE? DISCUSS.

There was no use trying to bluff that one. He read the second.

DID *THE GENTLEMAN FROM SAN FRANCISCO,* BY IVAN BUNIN, COMMIT SUICIDE? DISCUSS.

He considered the facts. The unknown gentleman from San Francisco was dead. Obviously he had not strung himself up by his own suspenders, because if he had done so, there would be no question as to his suicide. Ivan Bunin was a Russian, and the Russian writers like the great problems dusted with a touch of metaphysics.

Pete discussed. He discussed for fifty-seven minutes. He began with the psychological implications of suicide, the spiritual vacuum of today which led to it. He even hauled in poor old Doc Freud, but not too obviously. He swung boldly at modern materialism. When he had finished he was almost proud of himself. With any luck at all, he was sure it would take a divine providence to know he had not read Ivan Bunin's classic. . . .

. . . In the quadrangle, other students who had finished their last final were sitting on the low wall under the trees, the tension over. Pete sat down too. He had never felt so tired. His knee was hurting him again, and he remembered that he was going to the infirmary to have it dressed. . . .

When the doctor came in . . . the boy was asleep. . . . He looked at this boy now and he knew his kind well. Here was a kid from a family that had gone to college for generations, who wanted to be a lawyer, a doctor, an engineer —

anything at all which requires long, expensive training. And if something upset the family's budget, did he give it up? He did not. He put himself up against a lonely, desperate battle before he was grown to it, physically or emotionally. . . .

He woke the boy and dressed his knee.

"Take off your shirt," he ordered, and the anger showed in his voice.

He went over him carefully and questioned him. How many hours was he carrying? How many jobs was he holding down? How much sleep did he get each night? How long had it been since he'd had a real vacation? Then he gave it to him straight. . . .

"What do you think you're made of? Iron? What are you trying to do to yourself? You're leaving the university for at least three months. I want you to put on some weight. I want you outdoors. I want you to have at least nine hours' sleep every night. . . . Where do you live? . . . All right, you go there. You take this tablet and go to bed. I'll be over in the morning. . . ."

The boy walked to his room at Professor Tigby's, too stunned to think. He told Mrs. Tigby what had happened, and asked her to call Rose and tell her he wouldn't show up tonight for work. Then he went to bed.

. . . .

When he woke up it was evening, and Rose was there.

"Mrs. Tigby let me in. I've brought you some dinner, and don't tell me you're not hungry. I snitched the chicken breast off Miss Oberly's plate, and I won't have it wasted. Sit up now."

He sat up. "Rose," he said, "what am I going to do? I can't go home. Since Dad's death, Mother has just enough to take care of herself and my kid sisters. She'd worry so."

"Now don't talk. I'll do the talking. And stop sounding as if the world had ended. . . .

"What you need is a good sea trip," she said casually. "Nothing like salt air to put a man on his feet. The cook at Miss Oberly's has a brother who's a steward on a boat. He's in port, and tonight the cook's going to call him up and find out exactly how you go about getting a job."

A week later the boy went to San Francisco.

. . . .

He was lucky, but he didn't know it yet. He had a job on a good line on a well-run ship so popular with its crew that the turnover was small. . . .

His first task was to wash the windows on the promenade deck, and when he had been working a couple of hours, the second mate came along to see how he was going.

He was a good-looking man in his early thirties, with a strong, intelligent face, the fingers of one hand twisted by dengue fever.

"Do these three over," he ordered. "And these two. There's plenty of time at sea. The main thing is to do the job well."

"Yes sir-r-r-r."

He painted much of the way to Japan.

When he wasn't painting, he was polishing brass or washing down the decks. He bleached and he sanded them, and he ran the holystone, learning to let it slide with the ship's roll. When he was missing a fork at mess, he asked "Where's my gear?" And when a seaman called out, "Catch that lazy guy?" he no longer looked around to see which man was loafing on the job.

When the ship approached the first port in Japan, things took a more seaman-like turn. Pete was in the bow, mostly getting in the way, and when the bos'n had the heaving line ready, he said to him, "You think you're man enough to reach the dock with this?" and Pete said he didn't know, but he'd like to try. He gave the line everything he had, and it reached the dock, crossed the dock, and the monkey fist on the end went through a warehouse window with a splintering crash. No one spoke. But after this he had a name. They called him Slim.

The marvelous world unfolded before him, the lovely islands of Japan and the roadsteads of the East.

There was only one minor mishap on the whole voyage. The ship had to be pulled off a sandbar in the Philippines and went to the old Dewey dry dock at Olongapo in Subic Bay for repairs, and it was here that Pete became a bona-fide member of the crew in good standing.

On his day off, he and another ordinary went ashore. Olongapo was a lazy little place then, before the war, and they sauntered up the hot, dusty road and into the open market.

In one booth a group of Filipino women were squealing loudly because a rat was loose underfoot, and Pete seized a board and smacked the rat neatly on the nose. . . . Nobody believed it, but after this, Pete had two names. They called him Big Slim. . . .

Then the ship started back, making the same ports.

There was one time that stood out above the others. In the Inland Sea of Japan he stood watch alone in the bow, ringing the bell every half-hour to show he was awake, checking the running lights and calling out, "The lights are shining brightly, sir!" listening for the answering "Aye-aye!" all the magic of the night around him, and the ship slipping quietly through the sea.

The last two days they hit fog, the ship slowing, the boy's spirit slowing also, because he wanted to go back and he dreaded to go back. . . . And when the ship crept through the Gate and nosed to its berth, something peculiar to all sea voyages happened to Pete. There on the dock waited his problems. Even the forgotten, yet somehow macabre, Gentleman from San Francisco seemed to wait also in the fog.

It was early morning when he arrived, and summer now, two days before registration. He went to Professor Tigby's and Mrs. Tigby told him he could have his old room. Next he telephoned Miss Oberly's and found that, though the school staff would be reduced during the summer, he could have his old job in the soap suds.

Then he put air in the tires of his bike and went to the campus post office for his mail. . . . There was a letter from the university concerning his grades for the last quarter that he was in school — all A's except English 56, which was marked "Incomplete." (And) there was a note from Doctor Meredith. There seemed to be a slight uncertainty about Mr. Westcott's examination, she wrote. Would he call her, please, and come to her flat for a brief chat?

There was no use putting it off. No use at all. He checked to be sure she was in residence during the summer. She was. He telephoned and asked if he might come over that very afternoon about four? Doctor Meredith said she would be pleased to see him.

At two, Pete went to the libe, and he read very slowly and carefully every word of THE GENTLEMAN FROM SAN FRANCISCO. Had he committed suicide? Physically, no. Spiritually, yes. And when he had ascertained this, he knew he had yet a slim chance.

. . . .

When he reached the old white house where Doctor Meredith had her flat, he went up the steps slowly, his heart pounding as hard as when he walked the boom.

Doctor Meredith opened the door.

"How nice of you to come, Mr. Westcott," and she led him in. "One of my students told me you had been to sea. As a cadet, I suppose."

"As an ordinary seaman," Pete said.

She asked him to sit down. "If you'll excuse me for a moment, I'll bring us a cup of tea. I think the water's boiling."

It was not at all the kind of living room he would have expected Doctor Meredith to call her own. . . . It was a woman's room, and never had it occurred to him that Doctor Meredith was anything at all but a neuter and middle-aged body topped by brains.

She came in with the tea tray, and he took it from her and placed it on the table by the sofa. On the tray were Doctor Meredith's best teacups and a plate of chocolate cake with lush white frosting.

"Now," she said briskly, pouring the tea, "tell me about your experiences at sea," and, to his amazement, he found himself doing it. . . .

"When I was your age I hoped to take such a trip," Doctor Meredith said slowly. "Then my father died and left me with a mother to support, and somehow — well, it's been work, work, work."

There was a silence. The dreaded moment had come.

"Mr. Westcott, there's something I want to ask you."

"Really?" said Pete, exactly as if he didn't know what it was.

"Tell me, when you took the final examination in English Fifty-six had you read THE GENTLEMAN FROM SAN FRANCISCO?"

Now, three months at sea had left him very little bluff, but he gathered the few remaining smidgens and he gave them to her in one fine sentence.

"Why, Doctor Meredith," said Pete, "couldn't you tell from my examination?"

"Frankly, I could not. I gave your paper to three of my colleagues, and none of us could tell."

And so she had him. He had no recourse left him but the truth, which he could mitigate perhaps by telling her how badly he needed the scholarship, by telling her he had left college on the doctor's orders.

"When I took the examination I had not read THE GENTLEMAN FROM SAN FRANCISCO," he said. "I have read it since."

"I see," said Doctor Meredith. "Thank you. I shall hand in your grade to-morrow. I — I shall give you an A."

"Gee," he said, "I needed it," and he rose to go. She went with him to the door.

"I hope you're taking English Sixty-two with me this summer," she said.

"If it isn't an eight o'clock. You know something, Doctor Meredith? Those little twirps at Miss Oberly's school, where I wash dishes, eat too many eggs. It's the yolks between the fork tines that slow a man up."

"I see. Yes. I can understand that."

When he had reached the street, he looked back. She was still standing in the door, and on her face was the look of something deeply felt, consciously restrained. . . .

Then he pedaled his way down the familiar streets. He would go to Miss Oberly's early this night. He would take the kimono he had brought home to Rose, and he would tell Rose all about everything.

At the main intersection he had to stop for traffic. A group of tourists from a rubber-neck wagon were waiting at the curb, and one shrill feminine voice rose about the others.

"It's the most beautiful place . . . just like a country club."

Pete heard this without resentment, with tolerance, almost with amusement. Then he went on.

It would be nice to come here topside, he thought, but it did not bother him that he was not. It did not bother him because, after all, it was not the topside passengers who made the ship go. It was the crew. . . .

He pedaled easily, his hand in his pockets, and the boy was gone now.

The boy was back there somewhere in the Inland Sea of Japan, calling out, "The lights are shining brightly, sir!" and listening for the "Aye-aye!" to reach him in the night.

An example of an excellent book to review is THE MOON-FLOWER VINE by Jetta Carleton. It is beautifully written and has an appealing nostalgic quality. There are a number of very quotable episodes, such as the following, which stand by themselves almost as short stories. But in this moment, when the moonflowers bloom, the great strengths of the book, its wit, grace, and ability to recapture the totality of living, converge.

The girls are grown. They have returned to the Missouri farm, as they do each summer, to spend a few days with their parents, and this day had been looked forward to as the culmination of the visit, the cutting of the bee tree and the watching of the moonflowers opening, "a kind of miracle." Listen as Mary Jo, the girl from New York, the one in television, tells what happened:

THE FAMILY
From THE MOONFLOWER VINE[4]

Jetta Carleton

(*Cut for public performance by Baxter Geeting*)

"Girls?" Our father's schoolbell voice clanged at the bottom of the stairs. "It's late — better get up!"

"The gospel according to Matthew," said Jessica, rolling out of bed. We ran to the stairway to say good morning.

"I'm loaded for bees — got the ax and washtub in the car. If you're going to cut a bee tree with me, you'd better come on!"

"We'll hurry."

"It's a beautiful morning," he called as a parting shot.

I ran to the window and looked out. It was the prettiest morning I ever saw, and I've seen a lot of pretty ones in my day. I get up looking for them. We threw on our clothes, shivering in the delicious chill, and hurried downstairs. The kitchen was empty, but a fire mumbled in the woodstove and the room smelled of fresh biscuits. Sunlight bounced off the silverware and danced on the ceiling. Mama was outside, tidying up the moonflower vine. With a brisk unsentimental hand she stripped off the old yellowed blossoms.

"Have to get these out of the way, to make room for the new ones tonight. Gracious, baby, you'd ought to have a dress on. Aren't your legs cold in them little short pants?"

"Yes!" I said. "I like it." I stuck a marigold in her hair and ran down the path to the john.

While we were eating breakfast, Mama dug out some old lace curtains for us to wrap around our heads. Protection from the bees, she said. . . .

---

[4]New York: Simon and Schuster, Inc., 1962, Chapter 3, pages 38-48, excerpted.

"I think I'll make cookies!" said Leonie.

Mama, Jessica, . . . and I turned on her of one accord. "*Now?*"

. . . .

"Some of those little ginger cookies you're so crazy about."

"Ain't it a little late?" said Mama.

"It won't take but a minute."

Mama looked at her and glanced over at us and kind of smiled. "Well, go ahead. We're not in that much of a hurry, I guess."

"Oh, good! I'll have 'em done in two shakes."

Jessica looked at me and winked. "Let's paper the kitchen before we go."

"And piece a quilt!" I said.

"It won't take but a minute."

Leonie looked around with a hurt innocent face.

"We're teasing you, hon." Jessica gave her a little hug. "You go ahead with your cookies. We'll help you."

We banged around the kitchen with rolling pins and pans, and Jessica put on a lace curtain and sang "Here comes the bride." We were making so much noise we hardly noticed that the dog was barking his head off.

"Now what's the matter with him?" Jessica said, glancing out the window. "Oh, shit!"

"Jessica!" said Mama.

"Here comes the preacher!"

"Oh my goodness, he'll stay all morning!"

"Run and hide — he'll think we're gone!"

We ran for the front room, pulling Mama with us. "We hadn't ought to do this," she protested.

"Sh!"

"It ain't right."

But she stood there as the dog barked himself into a frenzy and the preacher came up, paying him compliments in a bold voice. He knocked at the back door, waited a moment, and knocked again. "Good dog," he said. The barking tapered off and the dog's tail beat a tattoo against the house.

"Brother Soames?" called the preacher. There was a long wait. "Anybody home?"

"We ought to let him in," Mama whispered.

There was another knock, a long wait, and a half-hearted tap. The preacher went down the steps. "Git," he said mildly to the dog.

"Poor little thing," Mama said. "It's like Jesus knockin' at the gate and won't nobody answer. I'm going to let him in. And she marched off to the kitchen. "Hoo-hoo?" she called. "Oh, Brother Mosely! I *thought* I heard somebody."

"Good morning, good morning! I didn't think nobody was home."

"We were all in the front," Mama said. It would not be her fault if he thought she meant the front yard. "Can't you come in for a minute?"

"Or an hour or two," Jessica whispered.

"Thank you," the preacher said. "I hope I caught your good husband at home."

"Yes, he's around here somewhere. Come on in here where it's cooler." We made a dash for the front door, but she caught us as we hit the porch. "Oh, come in, girls," she said, as if we had been outside the whole time. "Here's Brother Mosely — you remember Brother Mosely."

We filed back in and shook hands. The preacher, a meager young man, sway-backed in the pride of his calling, blessed each of us in turn. "Glad to see you again, God bless you, mighty pleased to see you." He passed a few witticisms on female charm and, having dispatched that duty, arranged his features in a solemn look.

"Well, I've come on a sorrowful mission," he said, and there was a weighty pause. "Sad news, I'm afraid. Brother Corcoran has gone to his long home."

"Ah!" said Mama, putting her hand to her cheek. . . . "Poor boy. Papa?" she called, seeing my father pass the window. "Mr. Corcoran's dead."

"Is that right!" Dad come in with an ear of corn in his hand. "Good morning, Brother Mosely."

"God bless you, Brother," said the preacher.

.   .   .   .

"Brother Corcoran wasn't much on church."

"I'm afraid not. Don't know what church he rightly belonged to."

"No, but he ought to have a funeral like anybody else, and I'm aimin' to preach him one."

"Yes, we must give the old soul a Christian burial.

.   .   .   .

". . . Won't be many there, I don't reckon."

"Not many."

"Just you folks and a few neighbors. I'm dependin' on you. . . ."

". . . When are you planning to have the funeral?"

"About three-thirty," said the preacher.

There was a dead silence.

"Three-*thirty*," said my father.

"The body's comin' in on the three o'clock train."

"To*day?*"

"There didn't seem no reason to keep him."

My father and mother looked at each other. They had tried so hard to protect this day. Right or wrong, they had held out against neighbors and duty, friendship and pity. But there was no holding out against death. My father turned back to the preacher.

"I'll be there," he said.

"We'll come," said my mother.

"Fine," said the preacher. "I knew I could count on you folks. I must run on now and get somebody for pallbearers. Shall we have a prayer?"

My sisters and . . . I glanced at each other. It would be lovely in the woods today, and twenty buds hung on the moonflower vine, ready to bloom.

. . . .

So there went the picnic. We put away the basket and pinned up our hair and rushed about pressing dresses. Somewhere along in there, Leonie finished her cookies.

. . . .

The church was crowded by the time we got in. My father went up to the choirloft, Leonie to the piano. The rest of us had to sit in the front pew, staring into the casket. Old Mr. Corcoran lay a few feet away, stern and disapproving against the cheap satin, his long bristly nose pointed upward in contempt.

. . . .

"Brothers and Sisters —" The preacher stood at the pulpit surveying with solemn pleasure a crowd such as he'd never drawn in a month of Sundays. "Brothers and Sisters, rise with me as we pray."

The congregation creaked to its feet. From the back row, a child's voice piped up. "I want to see the man!" She was nosily shushed, and the prayer began.

I counted backwards from a hundred, all the way to zero, and Brother Mosely was still invoking the Lord. Over and over, his earnest voice soared in thunderous tremolo and descended in a minor key. I shifted my weight. My sunburn itched, and one ear hurt where Mama's hat rubbed against it. I sighed discreetly, longing for the golden weather outside. . . .

. . . .

The service went on for more than an hour. But at last it was over. The undertaker wheeled the casket into the vestibule, and the old man lay there in state, waiting the long file of the curious, who had come to gaze pop-eyed. . . .

We were the last ones out. Like relatives we filed out slowly and stood in an indecisive huddle as the undertaker, with a brisk "Okay?" to my father, snapped the lid shut and packed the last of Mr. Corcoran off to eternity.

The worn stones of the church lay in shadow now. It was after five. Around the square and up and down the streets, engines sputtered.

I turned to my father. "Do we *have* to go to the cemetery?"

He hesitated. . . . "I just can't think of the old soul lowered into his grave without somebody there."

As he spoke, the hearse crawled forward, followed by the preacher's Ford. Another car fell into line, followed by another and another. As the hearse turned onto the highway, it was followed by a train reaching half around the square.

"Well," said my father, "if all of them are going —"

My mother looked at him thoughtfully. "If you think it would be all right, if we hurried, we could still get home in time —"

We heard no more. Our solemnity near the breaking point, we started down the steps. By the time we reached the cars, we were what you might call running. . . .

Over the hills we went, hellbent for leather . . across the bridge, past Bitter-water, through Barrow's farm, and down the hill, around the corner, up our lane, into our barn-lot — dust flying, hens squawking, all of us shouting, and the first moonflower just beginning to bloom.

"We made it!" my mother cried.

I'll remember it the rest of my life.

> Wallace Stegner, head of the Creative Writing Center at Stanford University, novelist, essayist, lecturer and recipient of numerous literary awards, gave us in WOLF WILLOW a book combining "childhood rememberance and adult reflec-tion." His total recall of a once familiar smell is done in a creative and poetic way. At this point in the book, Stegner has returned to the Saskatchewan plains where he had grown up and where his family were homesteaders from 1914 to 1920.

THE QUESTION MARK IN THE CIRCLE
From WOLF WILLOW[5]

Wallace Stegner
(1909-   )

My town used to be as bare as a picked bone, with no tree anywhere around it larger than a ten-foot willow or alder. Now it is a grove. My memory gropes uneasily, trying to establish itself among fifty-foot cottonwoods, lilac and honey-suckle hedges, and flower gardens. . . . In the old days we all used to try to grow trees, transplanting them from the Hills or getting them free with any two-dollar purchase from one of the stores, but they always dried up and died. To me, who came expecting a dusty hamlet, the change is charming, but memory has been fixed by time as photographs fix the faces of the dead, and this reality is dreamlike. I cannot find myself or my family or my companions in it.

.   .   .   .

A muddy little stream, a village grown unfamiliar with time and trees. I turn around and retrace my way up Main Street and park and have a Coke in the confectionery store. It is run by a Greek, as it used to be, but whether the same Greek or another I would not know. He does not recognize me, nor I him. Only

---

[5]New York: The Viking Press, 1962, Part 1, Chapter 1, pages 13-19 excerpted.

the smell of his place is familiar, syrupy with old delights, as if the ghost of my first banana split had come close to breathe on me. . . . .

. . . .

Sitting in the sticky-smelling, nostalgic air of the Greek's confectionery store, I am afflicted with the sense of how many whom I have known are dead, and how little evidence I have that I myself have lived what I remember. . . . There is enough left to disturb me, but not to satisfy me. So I will go a little closer. I will walk on down into the west bend and take a look at our house.

. . . .

. . . walking all around the house trying to pump up recollection, I notice principally that the old barn is gone. What I see, though less changed than the town in general, still has power to disturb me; it is all dreamlike, less real than memory, less convincing than the recollected odors.

Whoever lives in the house now is a tidy housekeeper; the yard is neat, the porch swept. The corner where I used to pasture my broken-legged colt is a bed of flowers, the yard where we hopefully watered our baby spruces is a lawn enclosed by a green hedge. The old well with the hand pump is still in the side yard. For an instant my teeth are on edge with the memory of the dry screech of that pump before a dipperful of priming water took hold, and an instant later I feel the old stitch in my side from an even earlier time, the time when we still carried water from the river, and I dipped a bucket down into the hole in the ice and toted it, staggering and with the other arm stuck stiffly out, up the dugway to the kitchen door.

. . . .

. . . I find that I am as unwilling to go inside that house as I was to try to find the old homestead in its ocean of grass. All the people who once shared the house with me are dead; strangers would have effaced or made doubtful the things that might restore them in my mind.

Behind our house there used to be a footbridge across the river, used by the Carpenters and others who lived in the bottoms, and by summer swimmers from town. I pass by the opaque and troubling house to the cutbank. The twin shanties that through all the town's life have served as men's and women's bath houses are still there. In winter we used to hang our frozen beef in one of them. I remember iron evenings when I went out with a lantern and sawed and haggled steaks from a rocklike hind quarter. But it is still an academic exercise; I only remember it, I do not feel the numb fingers and the fear that used to move just beyond the lantern's glow.

Then I walk to the cutbank edge and look down, and in one step the past comes closer than it has yet been. There is the gray curving cutbank, not much lower than I remember it when we dug cave holes in it or tunneled down its drifted cliff on our sleds. The bar is there at the inner curve of the bend, and kids are wallowing in a quicksandy mudhole and shrieking on an otter slide. They chase each other into the river and change magically from black to white. The water has its old quiet, its whirlpools spin lazily into deep water. On the footbridge, nearly exactly where it used to be, two little girls lie staring down into the water a foot below their noses. Probably they are watching suckers that lie just as quietly against the bottom. In my time we used to snare them from the bridge with nooses of copper wire.

It is with me all at once, what I came hoping to reestablish, an ancient, unbearable recognition, and it comes partly from the children and the footbridge and the river's quiet curve, but much more from the smell. For here, pungent and pervasive, is the smell that has always meant my childhood. I have never smelled it anywhere else, and it is as evocative as Proust's madeleine and tea.

. . . .

I pick up a handful of mud and sniff it. I step over the little girls and bend my nose to the wet rail of the bridge. I stand above the water and sniff. On the other side I strip leaves off wild rose and dogwood. Nothing doing. And yet all around me is that odor that I have not smelled since I was eleven, but have never forgotten — have *dreamed,* more than once. Then I pull myself up the bank by a gray-leafed bush, and I have it. The tantalizing and ambiguous and wholly native smell is no more than the shrub we called wolf willow, now blooming with small yellow flowers.

It is wolf willow, and not the town or anyone in it, that brings me home. For a few minutes, with a handful of leaves to my nose, I look across at the clay bank and the hills beyond where the river loops back on itself, enclosing the old sports and picnic ground, and the present and all the years between are shed like a boy's clothes dumped on the bath-house bench. The perspective is what it used to be, the dimensions are restored, the senses are as clear as if they had not been battered with sensation for forty alien years. And the queer adult compulsion to return to one's beginnings is assuaged. A contact has been made, a mystery touched. For the moment, reality is made exactly equivalent with memory, and a hunger is satisfied. The sensuous little savage that I once was is still intact inside me.

group performance

(Choral Speaking and Experimental Group Reading)

> *If you want to lead people or cause them to listen to you,*
> *first discover their needs. . . . The influence of any idea,*
> *says Erich Fromm, depends on the extent to which it ap-*
> *peals to psychic needs of those to whom it is addressed.*
>
> Stuart Chase in "Dynamics of Groups," *Power of Words*

There are many social, artistic, and educational values to be realized through group interpretation which are not possible in individual performance. The two basic types of group performance are choral speaking and experimental group reading, the latter covering a number of approaches to group interpretation of literature.

Various types of group interpretation are in, and then out of, vogue, at times praised and again damned, by teachers of interpretation. Most teachers who have been identified with the study of interpretation for a number of years, however, have come to recognize the special values to be obtained only in various types of group experience. It becomes rather clear also that criticism of such experience arises from a lack of understanding of how to *deal with groups in any artistic endeavor* rather than from basic faults in the concept of group interpretation.

For this reason, we will consider first the knowledges we have concerning group communication, for results do depend upon knowing how to handle groups. You can't have a group work together on anything, particularly in the area of the arts, unless you know how to have it function as a unit, unless you understand how to secure and maintain cooperation of all its members.

basic principles of group cooperation

Stuart Chase, in *Power of Words,* has discussed six principles which can be applied to groups working for significant results no matter what the field of endeavor. We list these following, giving our comments as to their application to our field of study, group interpretation.

1. *Identifying with others.* Leaders of group efforts at interpretation need to discover the desires of members within the group. Members within the group must be placed on friendly terms, but rapport with the leader must be established first. Assumptions by the leader as to a group's needs, interests, abilities, and standards of literary taste are dangerous. Successful cooperation depends on discussing all of these with the group, on obtaining a consensus of judgment.
2. *Participation.* There always are leaders who ignore the law of participation which says that everyone must take an *active* part. Successful groups depend on having active participation by each of the members. The person with the weakest voice is no less important to the group effort than is the one with the golden tone.
3. *Democratic leadership.* Productivity in any group depends on allowing everyone equal voice. A group in which one or two persons constantly dominate group decisions will fall apart. In a choral speaking or play reading group, however, it is necessary of course that some *one* person be able to gain and keep control. This must be managed without an autocratic attitude, however.
4. *Security.* "People perform better in groups when they are emotionally secure," says Chase. In artistic efforts this is even more true. Every effort should be made to have individuals at ease, free of tension, free of stage fright, free of anger and frustration — in other words, receptive to the fullest realization of an artistic experience. An attitude of *joy* and *enthusiasm* in the group project is vastly important.
5. *Open communication lines.* Leaders of group interpretation projects need to be sure they themselves are understood by members of the group. When directions are given, each member must understand the message. Opportunities must be kept open for members of the group to share in experiences relating to study, preparation, and practice.

6. *Better listening.*   Each member of the group should be trained not only to listen to the leader but to listen with that "inner ear" to the total performance. It is important to have each member hear his own voice as a part of the group; this awareness of the total performance will help to eliminate some of the "prima donna" problem in any group.

choral speaking

Choral speaking is a very old form of interpretation. The Greeks were using it effectively hundreds of years ago, when choruses were an integral part of Greek drama. The Roman Catholic high mass has long employed the antiphonal chant between the priest and the choir. Many churches have responsive reading in which the group reads together in response to the minister. In addition we all pledge allegiance to the flag or repeat the Lord's Prayer in unison, although *how* we do it is often a disgrace to humankind!

More recently we have heard commercials on television or radio in which groups of voices (choral speaking groups) present a message much more effectively than could a single voice. In concert the human speaking voice may blend with others to produce a sound effect which is not possible with one voice, no matter how beautiful it may be.

In the 1930's there was a tremendous upsurge in our country in the choral speaking group (or the verse choir as it is sometimes called). Marjorie Gullan, a dynamic British woman who had been experimenting abroad in training groups in classic Greek chorus, old Scottish ballads, and in the reading of the Bible, came to the United States briefly to teach and lecture. Her influence was such that she inspired a number of disciples to go out and organize "verse choirs" in their own areas. Naturally, their zeal for what amounted to a *movement* succeeded in alienating others who hadn't come under Miss Gullan's spell, so the whole idea of choral speaking was discredited by some. Miss Gullan may not be blamed for the misuses to which her excellent training was put. Suffice it to say that there are many good reasons for becoming skilled in the art of choral speaking and for being able to use it as a teaching technique.

Values of Choral Speaking

The group sharing of experience in the interpretation of prose or poetry often brings about literary understandings which an individual might never have alone. Psychologically, as has been pointed out by many, choral speaking may be a very satisfying experience, especially to the person inclined toward shyness. Individuals in a group may realize the thrill of successful performance which they could never know alone.

The Teacher or Student as Conductor

A successful group experience depends on the competent direction of a conductor who understands how to work with groups (as explained earlier in this chapter). In addition to a knowledge of group psychology, the conductor must be deeply appreciative of literary selections chosen for performance, must be thoroughly familiar with them, and should possess tremendous personal enthusiasm and spontaneity.

In mature groups it is very important that selection of material be cooperative. The group should be consulted as to its tastes insofar as possible. The analysis and preparation of a selection also should be a group project. The group should be encouraged to contribute to a total understanding of meaning, mood, and nature of the content.

When it comes to actual performance, however, it is almost entirely up to the conductor to keep the group together, to keep it alive, to maintain spontaneity, and to avoid a mechanical presentation. At times a conductor must resort to imitation to get unity (he may have to say, "Do it this way"), but the performance need not be the result of imitating the director. It should be based on unity of thinking and understanding. (A good conductor strives to remain as unobtrusive as possible.)

In a classroom particularly, the end of performance should not be magnified to the point of destroying the benefits to be obtained from the practice itself. Improvements in posture, breathing, enunciation, vocal quality, sense of timing, and understanding and appreciation of literature are major goals of group interpretation. They should be sought over and above the preparation of a display for public entertainment. The conductor is the one who must keep the educational and esthetic goals in mind and work at all times for their achievement.

Types of Choral Speaking Patterns

The size of the group is a consideration which can not be ignored. Although it is possible to achieve really professional results with a large chorus of trained voices, this is seldom our goal in classroom teaching or even in the ordinary uses to which we may put choral speaking in club, church, or other groups. Fewer than ten persons make choral speaking thin-sounding. More than twenty voices present a problem in coordination in an untrained group. Usually between fifteen and twenty is a workable number for beginners. There are at least four basic patterns used in choral speaking:

1. *Unison.* This may be the best method to start on with a mature group, although difficult with children. Select something simple, rhythmic, and easily understood and loved by all. Lyrics and simple ballads lend themselves to introductory efforts. One charming old traditional ballad whose melody, rhythm, and lilting quality are appealing to most beginning groups of adults is:

Hush-a-ba, Birdie[1]

Hush-a-ba, Birdie, Croon, Croon,
Hush-a-ba, Birdie, Croon.
The sheep are gone to the siller wood
And the cows are gone to the broom, broom.
And it"s braw milking the kye, kye,
And it's braw milking the kye.
The birds are singing, the bells are ringing,
The deer come galloping by, by.
The deer come galloping by.

2. *Choral refrain (or background) and solo.* Another pattern of choral speaking, and probably a good one to experiment with after unison practice, is the solo voice against a background of unison chorus or in opposition to a choral refrain. In the following Negro spiritual, for example, the chorus could continue repeating in the background, very lightly, the "steal away" phrase as the solo voice picks up its part, or the chorus could remain silent throughout the solo part and just voice the refrain.

(Chorus)   Steal away, steal away, steal away to Jesus
Steal away, steal away home,
I ain't got long to stay here.

(Solo)   My Lord, He calls me,

(Chorus   He calls me by the thunder,
quiet or
repeat   The trumpet sounds within-a my soul;
"steal away"
lightly)   I ain't got long to stay here.

---

[1]From "Choral Speaking," Marjorie Gullan, Methuen & Co. Ltd. London, 1931, p. 34.

(Chorus)	Steal away, steal away, steal away to Jesus
	Steal away, steal away home,
	I ain't got long to stay here.

(Solo)	Green trees a-bending,
	Po' sinner stands a-trembling
	The trumpet sounds within-a my soul;
	I ain't got long to stay here.

(Chorus)	Steal away, steal away, steal away to Jesus
	Steal away, steal away home,
	I ain't got long to stay here.

3. *Part work* (*antiphonal pattern*).   A third step might be to divide the group into what have been labeled "light" and "dark" voices. This may be poor terminology, but some voices (in adult groups, usually the male) are heavier in quality while others (usually the female) are lighter. (In children's groups, sex makes little difference; antiphonal work is a bit difficult in any case with the younger child.)

A very simple two-part selection to start on in antiphonal work is the following:

(Light)	If all the seas were one sea
(Dark)	What a *great* sea that would be!
(Light)	If all the trees were one tree,
(Dark)	What a *great* tree that would be!
(Light)	If all the axes were one axe,
(Dark)	What a *great* axe that would be!
(Light)	If all the men were one man,
(Dark)	What a *great* man that would be!
(Light)	And if the *great* man took the *great* axe
	And cut down the *great* tree,
	And let it fall into the *great* sea,
(Dark)	*What a splish-splash that would be!*

As the conductor proceeds with antiphonal work, of course it is wise to divide the voices more carefully as to tone quality, making two, three, or four divisions, and to find material of a more challenging nature to interpret antiphonally.

4. *Combination pattern.*   Finally, as a culmination to the study of various approaches, the conductor and group may try combining all types in

elaborating an arrangement of a selection. Thus we would hear the solo voice, antiphonal responses, unison chorus, and perhaps even duets, trios, and quartets of voices within the total pattern. It becomes a creative challenge to plot and perfect a beautiful performance of a verse drama, for example, or a Biblical selection. A beautiful performance, as Miss Gullan was known to describe it, was one which had "strength and vitality as well as lightness and flexibility."

A simple and effective arrangement of several types of choral speech in one presentation was made a number of years ago by Argus Tressider. It follows:

Dream Pedlary

by Thomas Lovell Beddoes

(Light)	If there were dreams to sell,
(Dark)	What would you buy?
(Light I)	Some cost a passing bell;
(Dark I)	Some a light sigh
(Light)	That shakes from life's fresh crown
	Only a rose-leaf down.
(Group of 4)	If there were dreams to sell,
(Group of 8)	Merry and sad to tell,
(Group of 12)	And the crier rang the bell,
(Light I)	What would you buy?
(Light)	A cottage lone and still
	With bowers nigh,
(Dark)	Shadowy, my woes to still,
	Until I die.
(All)	Such pearl from Life's fresh crown
	Fain would I shake me down.
(Light)	Were dreams to have at will,
(Dark)	This would best heal my ill,
(All)	This would I buy.

Choral Speaking for Children

There are many opportunities to work with children in choral speaking — at Sunday schools; in primary, elementary, and secondary classrooms; in library reading groups. The appreciation of literature, especially poetry, can be effectively taught in this way because children participate enthusiastically in choral reading if it is sympathetically handled by a well trained conductor or teacher. All that has been said with reference to choral reading heretofore may be applied to children. That is, one must have a knowledge of how children function in groups, have respect for each individual, be able to put each one at ease, seek cooperation through agreement rather than by means of autocratic controls.

Arrangements for children's voices may be made with patterns similar to those suggested before, but antiphonal speaking is considered difficult with younger ages. One other approach which has been found particularly adaptable and suitable for children is the "line-a-child" approach discussed in *Oral Interpretation of Children's Literature* by Bamman, Dawson, and Whitehead.[2] One child (or a group of two to four children) speaks a line, followed by another child (or group), then a third, and so on. An eight-line poem with seven participants might be voiced like this (P = participant):

(P1)	The year's at the spring,
(P2)	The day's at the morn;
(P3)	Morning's at seven;
(P4)	The hillside's dew-pearled;
(P5)	The lark's on the wing;
(P6)	The snail's on the thorn;
(P7)	God's in His Heaven —
(All)	All's right with the world.

Robert Browning[3]

In doing choric speech with children it is important to select material of genuine literary merit. Teachers may be tempted to err on the side of inferior selections. As children work with a reading in choral speaking, they will become aware of meanings not at first evident to them. The thrill of discovery will come with repetition, and if a selection is so simple that a child can understand it the first time he hears it, he will have missed an important opportunity for growth in literary appreciation.

Among respected poets who have written highly usable material are Edgar Allen Poe, John Keats, Alfred Tennyson, A. A. Milne, Walter de la Mare, Christina Rossetti, Robert Louis Stevenson, Eugene Field, Phillips Brooks, William Wordsworth, Edna St. Vincent Millay, Sara Teasdale, Edward Roland Sill, Elinor Wylie, and many others. Excellent suggestions for readings for children's groups can also be found in the Bible, especially the Psalms.

---

[2]Henry A. Bamman, Mildred A. Dawson, and Robert J. Whitehead, *Oral Interpretation of Children's Literature,* Dubuque, Iowa. Wm. C. Brown Company Publishers, 1964, pages 46-47.
[3]*Ibid.,* p. 47.

experimental group reading

There are several approaches to group reading, most of which are still in experimental stages and known by a number of terms. Of course groups have been gathering in homes and clubs informally for many years to read aloud plays or stories which are of mutual interest.

Now, however, there is an effort to expand and experiment with group reading, perhaps to formalize it into different styles of performance. Some of the labels which have been applied to these efforts are interesting. STAGED READING or THEATER READING are terms which have been applied to groups on stage, reading a drama. CHAMBER THEATRE has come in some circles to mean the presentation of "undramatized fiction" by a group on stage. READER'S THEATRE covers a broad area of presentations ranging from adaptations of comic strips to the absurdist plays.

The material and the methods for group experimentation in interpretation are still open to a wide range of possibilities. It is quite possible that many types of material and methods, still untried, are adaptable to group readings. It is a challenge to an experienced group of interpreters to discover new materials and new ways of presenting them.

So far, in performance, group interpreters have been borrowing some theater techniques. They have appeared on stage, have used theatrical lighting, have at times arranged participants on different stage levels. For the most part, however, they have rejected scenery, costumes, and stage make-up. Readers may be seated on stools or chairs, or may stand before lecterns. They may simply be seated in a row behind a table. There may be individuals or groups on stage, with a narrator off to the side who fills in necessary running comment to keep the audience informed of what is taking place.

Entrance of a character may be suggested by having the reader turn to the audience; an exit may be suggested by having him turn away or lower his head. Blackouts may be used effectively. Several groups may remain on stage, temporarily blacked out while the active speaker or group is spotlighted.

While properties and make-up are used sparingly if at all, it may be that a group will wish to experiment with using stylized properties and make-up, accenting what heretofore has been subdued.

Selections of all types are open-sesame to success in group interpretation. Some of the most successful performances have been given of plays which ordinarily are the most difficult to produce — plays that call for huge casts, elaborate settings, and expensive costumes. Plays which lack plot and may be slow when acted often lend themselves beautifully to group interpretation if the emphasis is on elegant or beautiful lines and character development.

Some short stories and even novels have been adapted to group interpretation in experimental theatre. A narrator may maintain the thread of the story while dramatic episodes are read by members of the group. It is possible for one reader to assume several roles.

Finally, long poems, often rich in characterization, such as Edgar Lee Masters' *Spoon River Anthology* and Stephen Vincent Benét's *John Brown's Body*, are almost made to order for group interpretation.[4]

summary

Group performance in the area of interpretation depends on understanding certain basic principles of effective group communication: identification, participation, democratic leadership, security, open communication lines, and good listening. These principles may be applied to the two main types of group interpretation, namely choral speaking and experimental group reading.

Goals in choral speaking should emphasize improved posture, breathing, enunciation, vocal quality, sense of timing, and understanding and appreciation of literature. Performance is a secondary goal but, even so, a valid one.

Types of choral speaking fall into four basic patterns: unison, choral refrain and solo, part or antiphonal work, and combinations of these. All except antiphonal may be used with younger children, but "line-a-child" arrangements are highly recommended for them.

Group reading is constantly expanding and undergoing experimentation. Some of the terms which have been applied to different approaches are STAGED READING, THEATRE READING, CHAMBER THEATRE, and READER'S THEATRE.

The current emphasis is on the preparation of any type of poetic, dramatic, or fictionalized material which can be adapted to group reading on a stage with limited use of technical theatre accouterments. The total movement presents an exciting challenge to experienced and creative interpreters.

---

[4]Excellent list of material is given in Chloe Armstrong and Paul D. Brandes, *The Oral Interpretation of Literature,* New York: McGraw-Hill Book Company, Inc., 1963, page 292.

applications: _____

1. Search out at least three selections of poetry which you would enjoy using as choral speaking selections with children ages 6 to 8. Plan how you would arrange the voices of a group with about 12, half boys, half girls. Indicate on your copies how you would present the selections to the group in order to awaken interest, get cooperation, and keep control without becoming a dictator.
2. Find an outstanding selection for a group of children ages 9 to 12, and mark it for choral speaking. Outline steps in presenting the selection to the group.
3. Find a ballad you would enjoy conducting with a more mature group, young adults. Mark it for choral speaking and outline how you would present it to the group.
4. Find an outstanding prose selection for use in any age group. Decide what you would do with it in arranging it for choral speaking. Before what audience would this selection be appropriate?
5. List at least five selections which you can imagine being done in some type of group experimental reading.
6. Take one of these five foregoing suggestions and rough out the manner in which you would direct a group in preparing it for performance. Describe methods of staging, costuming (if any), and lighting; and outline special effects you would seek in the performance.

preview of chapter 14:
PERFORMANCE ON RADIO AND TELEVISION

The tremendous growth of radio, and particularly of television, is demanding persons who can perform as announcers, actors, panelists, teachers, speakers, commentators, and readers. All of these require a knowledge of, and skill in, oral interpretation. In all, the key to outstanding performance is the ability to communicate within the special demands of the media. General skills of interpretation are useful in mass media, but some special types of knowledge are necessary: how to prepare copy for radio and television; how to prepare yourself with proper dress and make-up; how to identify and handle microphones; how to follow directions; how to conduct yourself before television cameras; how to read from script and cue cards. We will be discussing all of these and also consider the problems inherent in tape recording.

selections for study and interpretation

The following selections can be used for adult verse choir. They are arranged in order of simplicity, the easier, more appealing selections for younger audiences being given first.

THREE MICE
Charlotte Druitt Cole

Three little mice walked into town,
Their coats were gray, and their eyes were brown.

Three little mice went down the street,
With woolwork slippers on their feet.

Three little mice sat down to dine
On curranty bread and gooseberry wine.

Three little mice ate on and on,
Till every crumb of bread was gone.

Three little mice, when the feast was done,
Crept home quietly one by one.

Three little mice went straight to bed
And dreamt of crumbly, curranty bread.

JONATHAN BING
Beatrice Curtis Brown

Poor old Jonathan Bing
Went out in his carriage to visit the King,
But everyone pointed and said, "Look at that!
Jonathan Bing has forgotten his hat!"
(He'd forgotten his hat!)

Poor old Jonathan Bing
Went home and put on a new hat for the King,
But up by the palace a soldier said, "Hi!
You can't see the King; you've forgotten your tie!"
(He'd forgotten his tie!)

Poor old Jonathan Bing,
He put on a beautiful tie for the King,
But when he arrived an Archbishop said, "Ho!
You can't come to court in pajamas, you know!"

Poor old Jonathan Bing
Went home and addressed a short note to the King;
"If you please will excuse me, I won't come to tea,
For home's the best place for all people like me!"

THE OWL AND THE PUSSY-CAT

Edward Lear
(1812-1888)

The Owl and the Pussy-cat went to sea
    In a beautiful pea-green boat:
They took some honey, and plenty of money
    Wrapped up in a five-pound note.

The Owl looked up to the stars above,
    And sang to a small guitar,
"O lovely Pussy, O Pussy, my love,
    What a beautiful Pussy you are,
            You are,
            You are!
    What a beautiful Pussy you are!"

Pussy said to the Owl, "You elegant fowl,
    How charmingly sweet you sing!
Oh, let us be married; too long we have tarried:
    But what shall we do for a ring?"
They sailed away, for a year and a day,
    To the land where the bong-tree grows;
And there in a wood a Piggy-wig stood,
    With a ring at the end of his nose,
            His nose,
            His nose,
    With a ring at the end of his nose.

"Dear Pig, are you willing to sell for one shilling
    Your ring?" Said the Piggy, "I will."
So they took it away, and were married next day
    By the turkey who lives on the hill.
They dined on mince and slices of quince,
    Which they ate with a runcible spoon;

And hand in hand, on the edge of the sand,
They danced by the light of the moon,
The moon,
The moon,
They danced by the light of the moon.

You Are Old, Father William
ALICE'S ADVENTURES IN WONDERLAND

Lewis Carroll (Charles Lutwidge Dodgson)
(1832-1898)

"You are old, Father William," the young man said,
"And your hair has become very white;
And yet you incessantly stand on your head —
Do you think, at your age, it is right?"

"In my youth," Father William replied to his son,
"I feared it might injure the brain;
But now that I'm perfectly sure I have none,
Why, I do it again and again."

"You are old," said the youth, "as I mentioned before,
And have grown most uncommonly fat;
Yet you turned a back-somersault in at the door —
Pray what is the reason of that?"

"In my youth," said the sage, as he shook his gray locks,
"I kept all my limbs very supple
By the use of this ointment — one shilling the box —
Allow me to sell you a couple."

"You are old," said the youth, "and your jaws are too weak
For anything tougher than suet;
Yet you finished the goose, with the bones and the beak;
Pray, how did you manage to do it?"

"In my youth," said his father, "I took to the law,
And argued each case with my wife;
And the muscular strength which it gave to my jaw,
Has lasted the rest of my life."

"You are old," said the youth; "one would hardly suppose
That your eye was as steady as ever:
Yet you balanced an eel on the end of your nose —
What made you so awfully clever?"

"I have answered three questions, and that is enough,"
　　Said his father; "don't give yourself airs!
Do you think I can listen all day to such stuff?
　　Be off, or I'll kick you down-stairs!"

WHERE DO THE GYPSIES COME FROM?

Henry Howarth Bashford

Where do the gypsies come from?
The gypsies come from Egypt.
The fiery sun begot them;
Their mother was the desert dry.
And while she lay there basking,
She gave them food for the asking
And an emperor's bone to play with
Whenever they tried to cry.

What did the gypsies do there?
They built a tomb for Pharaoh,
They built a tomb for Pharaoh
So tall it touched the sky.
They buried him deep inside it
And let what would betide it;
Then saddled their lean-ribbed ponies
And left him there to die.

What do the gypsies do now?
They follow the sun, their father;
They follow the sun, their father,
They know not whither or why.
Whatever they see they take it,
And if there's a law they break it.
So never you talk with a gypsy,
Or look in a gypsy's eye!

SPIN, LASSIE, SPIN

Lady Strachey

Spin, lassie, spin
An even thread and thin,
From this fleecy wool of thine
I would have a plaidie fine,
Spin, lassie, spin.

Spin, lassie, spin
An even thread and thin,
Blue and green my plaid shall be
And all the lads will envy me,
Spin, lassie, spin.

Spin, lassie, spin
An even thread and thin,
When I'm in my plaidie drest
I'll kiss the lass that I love best
Spin, lassie, spin.

ST. CATHERINE, ST. CATHERINE!

Traditional Ballad

St. Catherine, St. Catherine, O lend me thine aid
And grant that I never may die an old maid.
A husband, St. Catherine —
A good one, St. Catherine —
But any one better than no one, St. Catherine.
A husband, St. Catherine —
Rich, St. Catherine —
Young, St. Catherine —
Handsome, St. Catherine —
Soon, St. Catherine!!

WHISTLE, WHISTLE, OLD WIFE

Traditional Ballad

Whistle, whistle, old wife and you will get a hen.
"I wouldn't whistle," said the wife, "if you could give me ten!"

Whistle, whistle, old wife and you will get a coo.
"I wouldn't whistle," said the wife, "if you could give me two."

Whistle, whistle, old wife and you will get a gown.
"I wouldn't whistle," said the wife, "for the best one in town."

Whistle, whistle, old wife and you will get a man.
"Wheeple, whopple," said the wife, "I'll whistle if I can!"

INTRODUCTION TO SONGS OF INNOCENCE
William Blake
(1757-1827)

Piping down the valleys wild,
 Piping songs of pleasant glee,
On a cloud I saw a child,
 And he, laughing, said to me:

"Pipe a song about a Lamb!"
 So I piped with merry cheer.
"Piper, pipe that song again;"
 So I piped: he wept to hear.

"Drop thy pipe, thy happy pipe;
 Sing thy songs of happy cheer!"
So I sang the same again,
 While he wept with joy to hear.

"Piper, sit thee down, and write
 In a book, that all may read."
So he vanished from my sight;
 And I plucked a hollow reed,

And I made a rural pen,
 And I stained the water clear,
And I wrote my happy songs
 Every child may joy to hear.

THE BANKS O' DOON
Robert Burns
(1759-1796)

Ye banks and braes o' bonnie Doon
 How can ye blume sae fair!
How can ye chant, ye little birds,
 And I sae fu' o' care!

Thou'lt break my heart, thou bonnie bird
 That sings upon the bough;
Thou minds me o' the happy days.
 When my fause luve was true.

Thou'lt break my heart, thou bonnie bird
 That sings beside thy mate;
For sae I sat, and sae I sang,
 And wist na o' my fate.

Aft hae I roved by bonnie Doon
  To see the woodbine twine,
And ilka bird sang o' its luve;
  And sae did I o' mine.

Wi' lightsome heart I pu'd a rose,
  Frae off its thorny tree;
And my fause luver staw the rose,
  But left the thorn wi' me.

BREAK, BREAK, BREAK

Alfred, Lord Tennyson
(1809-1892)

Break, break, break,
  On thy cold gray stones, O Sea!
And I would that my tongue could utter
  The thoughts that arise in me.

O well for the fisherman's boy,
  That he shouts with his sister at play!
O well for the sailor lad,
  That he sings in his boat on the bay!

And the stately ships go on
  To their haven under the hill;
But O for the touch of a vanished hand,
  And the sound of a voice that is still!

Break, break, break
  At the foot of thy crags, O Sea!
But the tender grace of a day that is dead
  Will never come back to me.

WAITING

John Burroughs
(1837-1921)

Serene, I fold my hands and wait
    Nor care for wind, nor tide, nor sea.
I rave no more 'gainst Time or Fate
    For lo! my own shall come to me.

I stay my haste, I make delays,
    For what avails this eager pace?
I stand amid eternal ways,
    And what is mine shall know my face.

Asleep, awake, by night or day,
    The friends I seek are seeking me;
No wind can drive my bark astray
    Nor change the tide of destiny.

What matter if I stand alone?
    I wait with joy the coming years;
My heart shall reap where it hath sown
    And garner up its fruits of tears.

The waters know their own and draw
    The brook that springs in yonder heights;
So flows the good with equal law
    Unto the soul of pure delights.

The stars come nightly to the sky
    The tidal wave unto the sea;
Nor time, nor space, nor deep, nor high,
    Can keep my own away from me.

THE SPIRES OF OXFORD

Winifred M. Letts
(1882-   )

I saw the spires of Oxford
  As I was passing by,
The gray spires of Oxford
  Against the pearl-gray sky.
My heart was with the Oxford men
  Who went abroad to die.

The years go fast in Oxford,
  The golden years and gay,
The hoary Colleges look down
  On careless boys at play.
But when the bugles sounded war
  They put their games away.

They left the peaceful river,
  The cricket-field, the quad,
The shaven lawns of Oxford,
  To seek a bloody sod —

They gave their merry youth away
  For country and for God.

God rest you happy gentlemen,
  Who laid your good lives down,
Who took the khaki and the gun
  Instead of cap and gown.
God bring you to a fairer place
  Than even Oxford town.

SEA-FEVER

John Masefield
(1878-   )

I must go down to the seas again, to the lonely sea and the sky,
And all I ask is a tall ship, and a star to steer her by,
And the wheel's kick and the wind's song and the white sail's
      shaking,
And a gray mist on the sea's face and a gray dawn breaking.

I must go down to the seas again, for the call of the running
      tide
Is a wild call and a clear call that may not be denied;
And all I ask is a windy day with the white clouds flying,
And the flung spray and the blown spume, and the sea-gulls
      crying.

I must go down to the seas again to the vagrant gypsy life,
To the gull's way and the whale's way where the wind's like
      a whetted knife;
And all I ask is a merry yarn from a laughing fellow-rover,
And quiet sleep and a sweet dream when the long trick's over.

from
THE BARREL-ORGAN

Alfred Noyes
(1880-1958)

There's a barrel-organ caroling across a golden street
  In the City as the sun sinks low;
And the music's not immortal; but the world has made it sweet
  And fulfilled it with the sunset glow;

And it pulses through the pleasures of the City and the pain
    That surround the singing organ like a large eternal light;
And they've given it a glory and a part to play again
    In the Symphony that rules the day and night.

  . . . .

Go down to Kew in lilac-time, in lilac-time, in lilac-time;
    Go down to Kew in lilac-time (it isn't far from London!)
And you shall wander hand in hand with love in summer's
        wonderland;
    Go down to Kew in lilac-time (it isn't far from London!)

The cherry-trees are seas of bloom and soft perfume and sweet
        perfume,
    The cherry-trees are seas of bloom (and oh, so near to
        London!)
And there they say, when dawn is high and all the world's a
        blaze of sky
    The cuckoo, though he's very shy, will sing a song for London.

JESSE JAMES

William Rose Benét
(1886-1950)

A DESIGN IN RED AND YELLOW FOR A NICKEL LIBRARY

        Jesse James was a two-gun man,
            (Roll on, Missouri!)
        Strong-arm chief of an outlaw clan,
            (From Kansas to Illinois!)
        He twirled an old Colt forty-five;
            (Roll on, Missouri!)
        They never took Jesse James alive.
            (Roll, Missouri, roll!)

        Jesse James was King of the Wes';
            (Cataracts in the Missouri!)
        He'd a di'mon' heart in his lef' breas';
            (Brown Missouri rolls!)
        He'd a fire in his heart no hurt could stifle;
            (Thunder, Missouri!)
        Lion eyes an' a Winchester rifle.
            (Missouri, roll down!)

Jesse James rode a pinto hawse;
Come at night to a water-cawse;
Tetched with a rowel that pinto's flank;
She sprung the torrent from bank to bank.

Jesse rode through a sleepin' town;
Looked the moonlit street both up an' down;
Crack-crack-crack, the street ran flames
An' a great voice cried, "I'm Jesse James!"

Hawse an' afoot they're after Jess!
        (*Roll on, Missouri!*)
Spurrin' an' spurrin' — but he's gone Wes'.
        (*Brown Missouri rolls!*)
He was ten foot tall when he stood in his boots;
        (*Lightnin' like the Missouri!*)
More'n a match fer sich galoots.
        (*Roll, Missouri, roll!*)

Jesse James rode outa the sage;
Roun' the rocks come the swayin' stage;
Straddlin' the road a giant stan's
An' a great voice bellers, "Throw up yer han's!"

Jesse raked in the di'mon' rings,
The big gold watches an' the yuther things;
Jesse divvied 'em then an' thar
With a cryin' child had lost her mar.

.   .   .   .

They're creepin'; they're crawlin'; they're stalkin' Jess;
        (*Roll on, Missouri!*)
They's a rumor he's gone much further Wes';
        (*Roll, Missouri, roll!*)
They's word of a cayuse hitched to the bars
        (*Ruddy clouds on Missouri!*)
Of a golden sunset that busts into stars.
        (*Missouri, roll down!*)

Jesse James rode hell fer leather;
He was a hawse an' a man together;
In a cave in a mountain high up in air
He lived with a rattlesnake, a wolf, an' a bear.

Jesse's heart was as sof' as a woman;
Fer guts an' stren'th he was sooper-human;
He could put six shots through a woodpecker's eye
And take in one swaller a gallon o' rye.

They sought him here an' they sought him there,
  (*Roll on, Missouri!*)
But he strides by night through the ways of the air;
  (*Brown Missouri rolls!*)
They say he was took an' they say he is dead.
  (*Thunder, Missouri!*)
But he ain't — he's a sunset overhead!
  (*Missouri down to the sea!*)

Jesse James was a Hercules.
When he went through the woods he tore up the trees.
When he went on the plains he smoked the groun'
An' the hull lan' shuddered fer miles aroun'!

Jesse James wore a red bandanner
That waved on the breeze like the Star Spangled Banner;
In seven states he cut up dadoes.
He's gone with the buffler an' the desperadoes.

Yes, Jesse James was a two-gun man
  (*Roll on, Missouri!*)
The same as when this song began;
  (*From Kansas to Illinois!*)
An' when you see a sunset bust into flames
  (*Lightnin' light the Missouri!*)
Or a thunderstorm blaze — that's Jesse James!
  (*Hear that Missouri roll!*)

performance on radio and television

*We are concerned [in television] with a precocious, modern
prodigy whose vital statistics are out of date even as they
are recorded. Television's present is already past; it has
only a future.*
    Charles A. Siepmann

*Only a fool or an ostrich could deny the impact of the . . .
medium [television]. If it is agreed that all education depends on effective communication, then television is a new
dimension of education.*
    Grace and Fred M. Hechinger

Many of you who are studying interpretation have been, or
will be, confronted with practical situations demanding performance on
radio or television as announcer, actor, panelist, teacher, speaker, commentator, or reader.

Ashley Montague has summed up the growth of television by saying that
"in less than a single generation television has become the most important
means of communication in the country." We know that a large share of
what is being communicated both on radio and television is being interpreted from manuscript. This tremendous increase in the mass media demands performers who can read and interpret effectively.

Several professions will make even greater demands in the future on
persons who enter them to be able performers on radio and television. One
of these will be the teaching profession. Even now the demand far exceeds

the supply of teachers who can perform in television. The vast numbers of students to be educated, the great amount of knowledge to be digested and transmitted, and the diminishing supply of good teachers and classroom space and equipment are already placing a real premium on the master-teacher who is able to interpret his subject on television and who knows how to communicate within the unique demands and limitations of this medium.

All types of government service, politics, and public life will be increasingly in need of radio and television performers. Political conventions and presidential elections of recent years have convinced us that in our time no one can ignore the importance of being able to truly communicate on the air.

Then, too, the area of entertainment, which eats up talent so rapidly, will always be searching for new and better performers.

There is no end to the opportunity in sight for the personable interpreter who is willing to master the special techniques required by the media that have "only a future."

communication and the mass media

The meaning of communication in relation to radio and television takes on added significance because of the tremendous numbers of people involved on the listening (and viewing) end. Thousands, instead of one, two, or an audience, will be influenced by a performer's efforts at communication. We have already emphasized that words mean what they mean to listeners because of the listeners' backgrounds of understanding (frames of reference); but words also mean something because of the interpreter's understanding of the words he is speaking. The listener may have a reaction of fear, dislike, and distrust upon reading in print the word *liberal,* but a television announcer whom he trusts and likes may make of this word a very different thing. He may, by tone quality, inflection, and gesture indicate that this word *liberal* means being open-minded, intelligent, and fair. He may influence thousands of people to re-think their attitudes toward *liberal.*

Most performers on radio and television are aware that a mere reading of their manuscript or copy without mistake is just the beginning of their task. Announcers, panelists, and teachers to whom we listen with respect are persons with genuine integrity who read with meaning, and who project words from the copy to the listener (or viewer) in such a way as to capture, keep, and often (yes, let's face it) influence his points of view. The effective performer, again, is the one who communicates best.

It is difficult to explain just why certain performers are more appealing than others. The intangible qualities that create rapport, that establish the communication link between performer and listener (viewer), are not easily determined. Generally, however, persons who have real rapport with their listeners are individuals who are in themselves interesting, enthusiastic, intelligent people. They are people who have developed a speech personality in keeping with their basic type of person. Eric Sevareid is sophisticated, but honestly so. We accept and appreciate him as an intellectual. Danny Kaye is warm and friendly, a wondrously talented person with many facets of personality, but he communicates always a basically stable character. The performers whose appearances are demanded year after year, and who seem never to wear thin their relationships with listeners and viewers, are those people who give us the impression of being able to be themselves successfully. As Stuart H. Hyde has said, "Nothing is more annoying to the listener or viewer (although the layman will not analyze his feelings) than an announcer whose vocal tones, whose manner of articulation, and whose patterns of inflection and physical expression are at odds with his basic personality."[1] To be able to communicate successfully on radio or television is the supreme test of having mastered an art which does not call attention to itself.

general skills demanded in radio and television

Interpretative skills discussed in this book, skills relating to voice, diction, and bodily control, are basically the same as those demanded in mass media. Good breathing habits, clear enunciation, correct pronunciation, communicative voice and expression, and poise are all imperative.

Bodily movement must be modified to meet special requirements of a medium dependent on microphones of limited range and upon cameras of limited maneuverability. But this does not mean the body should ever appear stiff and immobile. Movement is possible within prescribed areas and under well defined conditions.

In the case of television, because of its emphasis on the visual aspects, how one uses his eyes, mouth, and hands has considerable bearing on interpretation. But, on both radio and television, no amount of skill will substi-

---

[1]Stuart H. Hyde, *Television and Radio Announcing*, Boston: Houghton Mifflin Company, 1959, page 38.

tute for adequate preparation of copy. Few indeed are the performers who can take copy "cold." Preparation of the manuscript is the most important requirement for being a successful radio or television performer.

preparation of copy for performance

Copy may be a news story, a sportscast, a lesson to be taught a certain group of television students, a reading to be presented as part of a variety entertainment, a theatrical review, a book commentary, an inspirational message, or any number of other written assignments to be interpreted. The procedure of preparation is basically the same; again, the approach is similar to preparation for typical audience situations.

We should perhaps approach the preparation as follows:

1. Read the copy over at least twice, getting the general approach, meaning, and mood.
2. Underline and look up any words or quotations you do not fully understand. Not only know dictionary definitions, but decide in what way the author is using a word in his copy.
3. Read the copy aloud, noting as you read any problems in pronunciation, punctuation or structure. Clear up these matters before proceeding.
4. If the copy is such that you cannot fully appreciate subtler meanings, abstract terms, and the author's intentions without more study, research the background of the material and the writer. Get other points of view to compare with your own.
5. Now, read aloud once more, visualizing about three listeners at a distance of five to ten feet in a comfortable living room. This is most likely all the audience you will have. (Compounded hundreds of times, of course.) Talk to these people in a friendly, natural voice.
6. Practice reading to your little family group (of imagined listeners) until you are sure of every word, every sentence, every paragraph, and every idea. If the copy should be removed, you could ad lib a reasonable facsimile! Be sure of your preparation before you go to the studio to perform on radio or television!

preparation of yourself for performance

Nothing equals mental composure for any performance task you face. But mental composure (in television especially) is based considerably on knowing you look well and are dressed appropriately. The discerning and cold-blooded eye of the camera is unrelenting in its judgment of your appearance, recording every mistake in make-up, every wrinkle in your suit. A good performance is based on careful preparation, both mental and physical. Ease before the camera is based on the assurance that you are creating a favorable picture.

We can not undertake to detail all the items of makeup and dress which influence the camera's judgment of your appearance. We will suggest a few of the most important.

Make-up

Television make-up is influenced by the peculiarities of a camera picture tube, by lighting, and by surrounding colors. In color television, attention to pleasing color harmony is important, whereas in black-and-white television one need be concerned only with the registration in shades of gray.

It is important to study your face to see how make-up may improve or correct features if they need to be corrected. Mouths can be made smaller or larger; the distance between eyes can be made to appear smaller or wider; and prominent noses can be made to appear smaller by means of skillful make-up. Always, make-up must be applied smoothly. Unlike make-up for theatricals, it should not be used to excess; the camera is looking at you closely, not from a distance. Most performances require a completely natural appearance; this will mean little make-up for some, a great deal for others. Sometimes men will require make-up to appear cleanly shaved because the camera tends to exaggerate any tendency to shadow or darker tones in the complexion.

In selecting make-up, remember that light make-up complements light colors, dark make-up is better with darker colors. Special make-up is not required on most local shows. On larger shows, professional make-up artists are in charge.

Hair Styling

Since in television the camera is focussing on the face so much of the time, hair styling is very important. The face is framed by the hair, and it is a good idea to think of it as a frame. Beehives, flattops, tricky points, and such may be quite acceptable when the head is seen in relation to the entire body (as on a stage) but may make the face appear ridiculously small or large in a close-up. A modification of current high style is almost always desirable if one wishes to appear to be groomed in good taste.

Dress

Audiences are quick to note major faults in clothing. You need to be dressed in attractive, but not showy, fashion and always in keeping with the type of program on which you are to appear. If you are participating in an evening show for entertainment, your dress or suit will be quite different from that you would wear as a television teacher presenting a lesson in Spanish for junior high school students.

In all cases, think of your appearance in terms of the long-shot and the close-up. Cut and fit (and skirt length) will be noted in long-shots. Close-ups will reveal texture of material and jewelry. Lightweight fabric generally photographs better; some gloss is permissible in women's clothes, but a man needs to be careful of glossy suits, which may give the wrong impression if they are too shiny! Things which do not appear well on camera include stripes and polka dots, very busy patterns, black and white — and particularly black and white used together. These tend to vibrate or "bleed" onto the set. Jewelry must be used carefully; anything flashy, dangly, or noisy is best eliminated. Handsome jewelry may greatly improve a costume, however. Pearls, fur, soft wool, modest plaids — all of these look well on camera. Pastel colors photograph well. Warm colors (reds, orange, tan, and brown) photograph lighter than they are; cool colors (blues, greens, and purples) tend to photograph darker.

performance techniques

Let us assume that you have properly prepared for performance, your copy is thoroughly mastered, and you are impeccably dressed and made up for your appearance (if you are going on television). Your mind is at ease as you drive to the station because you *know* you are ready to do your best.

The actual physical problems you will encounter at the station are not confusing or difficult. You will have the help of experts on every side. A good performer is much like a good driver, who knows that in a car with automatic gearshift he should leave the shifting up to the car. What you need to know will be given to you in the way of clear, explicit directions. Your job is to follow those directions; to avoid experimenting with ideas of your own; to keep "hands off" the shifting of the gears, which run well when allowed to function as planned.

Conference with the Director and Floor Manager

Usually you are told what is expected of you by the director (or floor manager sometimes), who has plotted out the course of the entire program. When the performance starts, the director may vanish to the control room, but the floor manager is always there to remind you of what to do, to point to the right camera, to slow you down or speed you up to fulfill time limits, to assist you in any moving about which has been planned in advance. If, in receiving instructions before a program, you do not fully understand, do not hesitate to ask questions. Make sure you know where to sit or stand, when and how to move, and how to handle any objects you may have to touch. Obey directions completely from there on, and do not endeavor to innovate any ideas of your own. Nothing can confuse and upset a program more completely than having ideas sprung on directors, technicians, and camera men on the spur of the moment!

Using the Microphone

You will have your voice picked up by any one of a number of types of microphone; at times you may be using different types within the same program. In any case, however, certain rules are basic.

1. Never touch a microphone which has been put in adjustment for performance. Keep your hands off of the microphone and the microphone stand if there is one. They should be handled only by trained personnel. Even if you think a microphone is poorly placed, do not question the judgment of the sound man, who is an expert.
2. Talk in a normal tone of voice, pitching your voice to its comfortable "low," unless you are directed to do otherwise. A "level" or test of your voice may be taken before the program, and you may be requested to pitch your voice in a certain way. In this case, try to follow instructions.
3. Ignore the microphone during performance. Talk as if it were not there. Never lean toward it, turn toward it, or shout into it. To show your listeners or viewers that you are even conscious of its presence is the mark of the amateur.

There are certain types of microphone which you may encounter. They include:

1. The lavaliere or collar or necktie microphone, as it is variously called, which is increasingly used and which is excellent for the interpreter because it frees the hands for gesture and handling of script and objects. If you do not know how to fasten it on, ask. Your main job is to see that it is free of clothing, jewelry, and tie clasps. Also, keep your hands off of it. All of these are apt to cause noises or muffle your voice.
2. The desk microphone is used most frequently in panels. You have few worries here. It is placed and adjusted properly by the audio man. You do well to ignore it thereafter.
3. The stand microphone may be set up for you to use if you are reading before an audience. It, too, will be adjusted to your height and voice.

You will be shown where to stand to speak into it properly. Do not touch the stand or attempt a readjustment unless it should fall down, which it hardly ever will do once it has been adjusted for performance.

4. The hand microphone is a bit tricky for amateurs. If you need to use one, remember it must be kept close to the source of the sound you want heard. It is nondirectional and will pick up distracting noises. If it is on a cable and you must walk a distance with it in hand, be sure you do not tangle the cable around something on the way.

5. The boom microphone is placed on a movable mechanism which can be raised or lowered or slanted to suit needs. You have no real problems in dealing with it. Just don't stand up and hit your head on it!

Behaving Before the Camera

The first thing to do in confronting a television camera is to have the proper attitude toward it. Know that it will record everything it sees you do. It has perfect eyesight and no charity. If you scratch, twitch, or look frightened, it will reveal your faults to your viewers. All television cameras are candid. Therefore, it is important to make up your mind that you *will* appear relaxed, attractive, and well prepared *because you are.*

The camera is quite stupid, too. If you move out of focus, it won't follow you. If you move too rapidly, it will be at some loss as to what to do. All movements must be made carefully and smoothly, especially in close-up. Don't shuffle papers, move objects about, clasp and unclasp your hands, drum the table, or indulge in any unnecessary gestures. Every movement must be deliberate, smooth, and purposeful.

All major movements are agreed upon with your director before your program goes on the air. Should you take a sudden notion to change plans, everyone will be upset. If it is absolutely imperative that you *do* change plans, however, you will be able to suggest this in a few ad lib remarks which may be heard by your viewers and quickly interpreted by your director. Directors are not at all stupid. They are very quick to get an idea if you prepare them a bit. "I had planned to read a selection from the book at this point, but our time is running short, so I think we will go directly to the pictures we have selected to show you." Ad lib for another few seconds and the director will have the second camera focused on the pictures, ready to follow you in your script.

Even though a camera is uncharitable and stupid, you should have no fear of it. It merely puts you into a room in which there are one to three friendly people. Most experienced performers visualize an average family placed about five to ten feet from them. You practically *never* face an audience on television. Your performance therefore should be directed to a few. Your approach should be friendly, intimate, natural. To shout or be theatrical will frighten that family away. They'll turn you off.

Most cameras have four lenses. One of these is on-the-air while that camera is "live." The floor manager (or the camera man) will signal you where to look, which lens to peer into if you want to look into the very eyes of your viewers. When there are two or more cameras, you need also to know which camera is taking the picture. Again, the floor manager will cue you in. Watch for his directions. He will tell you how he does it before you go on the air. His directions are so clear, however, you won't have trouble following him if you know your copy well enough to be alert for directions. If you should be reading and glance up and into the wrong camera, show no distress. Simply glance down again at your copy, and this time look up at the camera which is "live." If you are participating in a group, think of the camera as a listener only, glancing in its direction from time to time.

Reading from Script, Cue Cards, and Other Devices

In radio, the problem of script is simpler than on television. No effort need be made to hide copy. The chief concern is to be sure it creates no noise. Pages of script may be dropped on the floor as you finish with them; or cards, which make less noise, may be used.

In television, a script may be placed out of sight behind a display, laid out on a table toward which you may glance, or put up on a lectern if you are giving a lecture or recital where everyone knows you are using copy.

There are other types of memory aids in use. Cue cards or "idiot sheets" may be held for you by someone close to the camera. There are cardboard rolls fastened below the lens sometimes. Your script may roll out before your eyes as you read it, your eyes *almost* in focus for the viewer.

The best device, however, is the TelePrompTer, an arrangement which places your script directly in front of the camera lens. You can see it clearly, and your eyes are in perfect focus for the viewer. But the viewer can't see the script. It is capable of holding enough copy to last an hour and a half.

tape recording

A final word about tape recording. The widespread use of this device in both radio and television, has influenced the production of shows (documentary, dramatic, and others) in piecemeal fashion. Episodes done out of sequence are put together for a finished performance. The announcer, narrator, actor, or interpreter on such programs is at times ignorant of the total show. A commentator may be reading material he cannot fully understand because he does not know what it means out of context. While this is lamentable in view of the fact that a total picture is preferable to a fragmented view for complete understanding, it is a practical situation you may sometime have to face. If so, remember the professional performer always works within his limitations. Your primary task in this, as in any interpretative assignment, is to communicate meaning and emotions as best you can, rather than merely to read words that appear in a script or on a cue card.

summary

We have surveyed the special types of knowledge and skill we should have (in addition to those we have already studied) if we expect to perform on radio or television. The opportunities for performance are unlimited. The field is open to a variety of professions, ranging from teaching and politics to acting and entertainment. All performers in mass media need to know how to interpret effectively from manuscript.

Communication is paramount in radio and television. No one can be coerced into listening to or watching a performer who is not communicating. But it is difficult to establish the bases for rapport with listeners and viewers. It is generally agreed that persons who are basically sincere, interesting, and intelligent will maintain good audience rapport and be in demand as performers.

In preparation for performance, three things are essential: knowing one's copy well, being attractively groomed, and being mentally and physically poised. In addition, one must know how to use microphones (keep hands off, and trust the audio expert); perform before cameras (follow directions alertly); read accurately and with proper interpretation from script or cue card; and always, *always* cooperate completely with a director's plans and wishes.

Although tape recording presents problems because it is often done in fragments, basically the narrator's task always is to communicate meaning and emotions from the script, thinking of words as symbols for understanding.

applications: ─────────────────────

1. Visit your school's audio-visual department (if there is one) and become familiar with all equipment there which you might encounter in a radio or television station.

2. Better yet, visit a radio station and a television station in your area and arrange, if possible, to be on a program. If you have an educational television station in your area, you may be able to prepare a program with a group which will be very acceptable to the program director. At least talk with him and find out how you can have practical experience.

3. Prepare a script for possible presentation on anything which interests you particularly: a Sunday school lesson for a class of small children; a book review for an adult group; a poetry reading of avant-garde poetry for your friends. Think in terms of a 15-minute (14:50) show. Time it accurately, and practice it until you can get off the air *exactly* on time. Give it — somewhere! Good luck and best wishes for the future as a skilled interpreter and joyful person.

index of topics

index of selections

321